I0213108

Patrick Street around 1880

# Introduction

This book could not have been written without the immense help and cooperation I received from the following people Anne-Marie Brennan, Gabriel Arthur and Nick Arthur. I also received a lot of help from other people who are not family members people like George Quain and many others too numerous to record here but to them I am forever grateful for all the help they gave me. My great uncle Brother Charles "Firmin" Arthur did a lot of family research in his lifetime and I was fortunate to be given a copy of his research by Gabriel Arthur his nephew which was of immense help to me.

I do not have a separate page for references however I did include them in the text where I had the original source but sometimes my notes did not contain the original source. Much came from old family records so no specific reference for them. Most of the photos are family ones but a small number are not so where possible I got permission to reproduce them but in some cases I could not trace any copyright owner. No infringement of copyright is intended and should omissions be identified they will be rectified in subsequent edition.

The crest on the cover is the crest of the Arthur family of Limerick city.

978-1-9162086-1-2

Second Edition 2019

All rights reserved. No part of this publication may be reproduced, stored in a retrieval system or transmitted in any form or by any means without prior permission in writing from the author.

Should you wish to contact me you can do so at the email address below.

mick@thearthurfamilyoflimerickandclare.com

**© Michael Kelly 2019**

# Forward

I have been researching the Arthur family history for over fifteen years and I am delighted to finally be gathering all my notes into one place. I hope this book will be of interest to family members and to others who are interested in the history of Limerick as the history of the family and the city were intertwined down the decades.

This is about the Arthur family of Limerick and their descendants who are spread all over Ireland and abroad but I hope it also gives a little insight into the world the Arthur family was living in at different times in Irish history.

Finding records of the family was difficult as not many records from before the mid 1800's exist in Ireland. However the fact that the Arthur family was so prominent means that there are some records for the family unlike for the vast majority of families in Ireland. Some of these records are directly about the Arthur family and others are ones in which the Arthur's are mentioned. Indeed even while writing new records are being found and if anyone who reads this book has records that are not in the public domain I would be very grateful if they would share them with me perhaps for inclusion if any further edition of this book.

Presenting their story without having breaks in the narrative was impossible as the records simply do not exist or have not yet turned up but it is clear from the records that do exist that the Arthur family was in Limerick city down the ages, remained there and they were all related to each other.

All descendants of this family should be proud of their roots as very few Irish families can claim a history like the Arthur family of Limerick city can.

While this book is about the Arthur Family of Limerick I have as of yet found no descendants who still live in Limerick city although there may be some of whom I am not aware. There are only two descendants of this branch of the Arthur family still living in Clare which was the second home for the family. Now there are Arthur's who are living in Limerick and Clare but they seem to be descended from the Arthur families who came over with the Normans and they are not directly related to the Arthur family of Limerick.

If anyone who reads this book has information about descendants whom I have not included please get in contact with me using the e-mail address at the bottom of the introduction page as I am sure that there are still many family members out there of whom I have as yet no knowledge.

# Index of images.

# CONTENTS

## *More Photos*

# Chapter 1

*The History of the Arthur surname*

Surnames became necessary when governments introduced personal taxation. In England this was first known as Poll Tax. It should be noted that surnames begun to develop in Ireland long before they begun to arise in England. Throughout the centuries, surnames in every country have continued to "develop" often leading to astonishing variants of the original spelling.

There are a number of theories that I have come across as to how the surname ***ARTHUR*** originated. I am including the most interesting versions that I have come across in this chapter.

This unusual and interesting name is the subject of some controversy regarding its origins. One version is that it derives from the Celtic personal name "Arthur", but there is some doubt as to the etymology of the name. It is thought to be composed of "art", in Old Welsh "arth", meaning "bear", with the Old Welsh "gwr", meaning "hero". The name development includes: Robertus Arcturi (1197, Herefordshire); Adam Arthur (1246, Lancashire); and Henry Artur (1327) Somersetshire. The Celtic name "Arthur", for centuries now associated with the legendary Celtic British leader who is supposed to have fought ten victorious battles against the Saxon invaders but while the names of the supposed battles are known (recorded hundreds of years later). Where they occurred is not known for certain indeed there have been many places proposed as the sites of each of his battles. The modern

forms of the name are Arthur, Arter, Artharg, and Arthars, the last two being the patronymic forms, meaning "son of Arthur. The first recorded spelling of the family name is shown to be that of Geoffrey Arthur, which was dated 1135, in "Records of Oseney Abbey", Oxfordshire, during the reign of King Henry I who was known as "The Lion of Justice", 1100 – 1135. It is believed by traditional historians that most of those who carry the ARTHUR surname in the south of Ireland are descended from Arthur families who arrived here with Strongbow when he invaded Ireland and settled as farmers around the village of Emily on the Tipperary, Limerick border. My research indicates that this is true but not for all in the south who carry the surname.
While origin of the name Arthur remains a matter of debate. Some suggest it is derived from the Roman nomen gentile (family name) Artōrius, of obscure and contested

etymology (but possibly of Messapic or Etruscan origin). Some scholars have suggested that is relevant to this debate that the legendary King Arthur's name only appears as *Arthur*, or *Arturus*, in early Latin Arthurian texts, never as *Artōrius* (although Classical Latin Artōrius became Arturius in some Vulgar Latin dialects). However, this may not say anything about the origin of the name *Arthur*, as *Artōrius* would regularly become *Art (h) ur* when borrowed into Welsh. I think this is interesting but if correct could only apply to those carrying the Arthur surname whose ancestors originated in England.

Don't know about this theory but I must say that I find it interesting as it could tie into the theory of the name having its origins in the region of Dal Riada in ancient

Scotland which was formed when the Irish from the North Antrim Kingdom of Dal Riada in the North of Ireland invaded the west of Scotland in the late 400's to early 500's. This therefore could back up the theory that the name has Celtic origins. Indeed Áedán Mac Gabrán (c 532- 609) one of the of the kings of Dal Riada in Scotland had a son who was called Arthur and he was what was called a Dux Bellorum i.e. a war leader not a king and he fought in many battles. He was a younger son of the King of Dal Riada and as such he was unlikely to become king. In my opinion this Arthur could well be the origin of the Arthur legend as he fought in many battles. Eventually he was killed in battle however it should be noted that most of his battles seem to have been fought against the North Britons and the Picts. He does not seem to have fought the Saxons very often. The tales of his prowess in battle may have been brought to Wales by the North Britons when they migrated there. There they grew into the tales which were written down hundreds of years later and became the story as we know it of King Arthur. The information about this war leader in Dal Riada is to be found in an Irish book called "Life of Saint Columba" which was written much earlier than any records from Britain.

Here is another possibility for the evolution of the surname Arthur. It could be a strong man from Ar (Latin *vir*) which means a man and Thor strong. In the Gaelic Air is the same as Fear which means *a man* and the ancient Scythians called a man *Aior*. Thor was the Jupiter of the Teutonic races, their god of thunder. In Welsh Arth is a bear which is an emblem of strength and courage and ur a noun termination which means a man. So Arthur could be a bear-man, a hero, a man of strength or even the name of a British prince. Interesting isn't it. The name did occur in

Wales so it is possible that some of the above may have been responsible for the origin of the name in that country.

Another possible origin for the Arthur surname peculiar to the Limerick / Clare area is that the name is derived from "Artureigh" who were a clan based in Clare and were loyal to who were to become known as the O'Brien family who were kings of Dal Cais. They were said to derive their name from a common ancestor they had with the O'Brien's of Clare. This common ancestor was a man called Cormac Cas who was King of Munster in the mid 200's A.D and it is likely that he was the origin of the Dál gCais from whom Brian Ború and the O'Brien family came. The Artureigh who were a Clare clan fought with Brian Ború as well as being allies of the O'Brien. When the wars were over they moved into what was then Viking Limerick although the Limerick Vikings by then owed allegiance to the O'Brien kings. In Limerick there was a Viking surname "Arnthorr" which seems to have been derived from "Arn", eagle, and "Thor", the name of the god of thunder. Now the Artureigh who came in from Clare wanting to fit in with the Vikings in Limerick (Limerick at this time was under the protection of the O'Brien and was no longer an independent Viking city) being sensible decided to take on the nearest name to their own in the city which was Arnthorr so they changed their surname to Arnthorr. So the family name in the city of Limerick while not yet Arthur is pre Norman. The Normans then arrived and with them they brought people from the South West of England and Wales whose surname was Arthur. These Arthur's who were farmers were given farm land on the Limerick/ Tipperary border in the Emily area. Now once again the Arthur's being aware

of their need to fit in with their new overlords they changed their name once more to the nearest one among the new comers which was Arthur. The following quote from the eminent Edward MacLysaght gives weight to the claim that the Limerick Arthur family were the only one to originate in Ireland. "This pre-Norman family has been prominent in Limerick since the twelfth century. **A Guide to Irish Names** (1964) by Edward MacLysaght".
I believe this is the likely origin of the Arthur family of Limerick city.

I believe this is the likely origin of the surname, remember the Arthur's who came over with the Normans settled as farmers on what is now the Limerick Tipperary border near Emily. Do not forget that they were farmers not merchants so how did they become important merchants and provide so many Mayors to Limerick when before the Black Death between 1348 and 1350 all the areas of Ireland that were under Norman domination including Limerick were subject to what we call the feudal system of organizing society (the areas of the country not under Norman domination were not party to this system and still adhered to the old Irish ways). This social system did not allow for movement between the social classes or for movement from country to town. It was a very rigid form of society so therefore it seems to me that it would have been very unlikely that farmers could have moved to the city and become wealthy merchants within such a short time of arriving in the Limerick area as farmers with the Normans. Only a freeman could have moved from his lord's domain and virtually all farmers were not freemen so they were tied to their overlord and his lands as serfs etc.

However if the Arthur family were already there when it was a Viking city and had changed their family name and adopted their customs in order to fit in, it would make sense that they had become merchants just as many Vikings were. I concede that the evidence for this theory is scant as there is little or no documentary evidence from that time for it but remember that there is little documentary evidence for anything at this time. If the Arthur family were already there then it would explain how they could rise to become Mayor's so early in the City's history. Well before the advent of the Black Death the Arthur family were a senior family in the city. It should be noted that the aforementioned Black Death was instrumental in speeding the end of the feudal system.

So in conclusion there are in fact three different origins for the Arthur surname in Ireland, the first one is that they are descended from the Arthurs who came over with the Normans, the second one is that the Arthur's particularly in the North of Ireland are descended from Scots settlers who were brought over during the Plantation of Ulster under King James I and finally there are the Arthurs of Limerick who are the only branch of the Arthur family who originated in Ireland. DNA may in time prove this in my case the vast majority of my DNA is Irish but I do have Norman and Viking DNA as well. I have much more Viking than Norman DNA. My DNA profile indicates to me that my background including my Arthur family background derives from native Irish roots with some help from the Vikings with only a little help from our Norman invaders.

# Chapter 2

*Here are some of the earliest references to the Arthur family in Limerick along with the story of Nicolas Arthur.*

It is difficult to trace the name back much before 1300 A.D. as the documentary evidence before the late 1700's is scant and before 1300 A.D. is almost non-existent. Most of what little evidence there is in existence is in documents from elsewhere that mention Limerick in that time. However it is certain that there were people called Arthur or if you prefer people, who changed their surname to Arthur in the city before that time,

The first person with the Arthur name that I have come across is a Thomas Arthur who died about 1204 aged 76 years. Henry the Second of England conferred high honours upon him as well as great quantities of land in 1178. (Source The Old Limerick Journal, Arthur's Quay by the late Jim Kemmy).

The following are all from Brother Charles (Firmin) Arthur's research although I believe he may have got them from the work of Doctor Thomas Fitz William Arthur 1593 – 1666 (More about him later in this book) who traced the family to remote antiquity and whose original manuscript is now held in the British Library Manuscript collections.

There was a Robert Arthur in 1216 who was a benefactor to the great Abbey of St. Thomas in Dublin.

Nicolas Arthur who died in 1246 aged 72.

William Arthur who married Ann Basset and died in 1315.

John Arthur who died in 1326.

Martin Arthur who was wealthy and powerful built a magnificent peristyle of marble in the Dominican Church of St. Saviour. He died in 1326 at the age of 66.

John Arthur a remarkable and distinguished mayor who died in 1352. I think he died in office but I am not certain.

Richard Arthur who married Elizabeth, heir of Roger Twitt of Bristol and he died during the reign of the black prince.

Edmond Arthur who married Lucy Clarke of Somerset and he died in the eleventh year of the reign of Henry IV.

Thomas Arthur who married the daughter of Thomas Fitz Edmond Cummings. I don't have any date for him except that he was involved with a Desmond Carew.

Thomas Arthur who married Joan daughter of M. Power of Limerick. He died on 14th February 1360 and is interred at St. Mary's.

John Arthur who married Julia daughter of Oliver Burke. John died in 1395.

Thomas Arthur was consecrated Bishop of Limerick on the 14th of April 1400.

Nicolas Arthur who married Phyllis daughter of James White. Nicolas died in 1442

James Arthur who married Mary daughter of William Strich was Mayor of Limerick

John who married Elinor daughter of William Buxton of Bristol. John died in 1525 in Limerick.

Nicolas Arthur who married Elinor daughter of Mc Commine. Nicolas was one of Limericks Mayors.

Sir Nicolas Arthur was married to Margaret daughter of Sir William Blake. This Nicolas had no children but he had several favours placed upon him by Henry VIII.

Thomas Arthur who married Margaret daughter of John McNamara from Co Clare.

Nicolas Arthur who married Winifred Moure. Nicolas was lieutenant to the Rt. Hon. Daniel Lord Viscount Clare.

Francis Arthur who married Margaret daughter of McNamara of Co. Clare had three sons and eight daughters, the eldest of whom was the 4th Abbess of the Benedictine convent at Ypres in Belgium. As all of the Abbesses of this convent in its formative years were from Ireland they are referred to as The Irish Dames of Ypres collectively and they had a book written about them. She was born 1673 and died 1743. It should be noted that she and her fellow nuns went to a lot of trouble to found the convent in Ypres and they were so poor in the beginning that the mother house would not help them financially and because of this they would not allow any of the postulants there to be professed. James Stuart III (the Old Pretender) of England agreed to give them some financial help and he gave them £500. This finally helped to get the convent established on a firm financial footing. It might be of interest to note that the nuns from this convent eventually had to flee their convent during the First World War and eventually in1920 they came to a place called Kylemore Abbey in Galway where they founded a new convent. They had a boarding school there until 2010 when the boarding school closed but the nuns are still at Kylemore Abbey where it is now open to the public but they never returned to the abbey in Ypres.

Now for perhaps the most famous and colourful Arthur of that time. Of course I am talking about Nicolas Arthur (1405 – 1465). The story of Nicolas Arthur unfolds like a story from the Arabian Nights and he was mayor of Limerick no less than seven times.

He was a bold and enterprising adventurer exporting pelts of fur bearing animals such as stoat, pine martin, otter, squirrel and hare. He also dealt in tables of polished marble, scarlet and fine mantles. Among his live cargo were hounds, falcons and horses of generous breed.

Using your imagination you can see the intrepid merchant sailing out of the little harbour on which the potato market was to be found in later times with his noisy squawking cargo. In 1428 he was captured by pirates from Brittany and imprisoned for two years in St. Michael's Mount. He was robbed of his cargo, which was worth 700 marks (a very large sum at that time) and his ship, which he had chartered from his friend John Church was sold. Finally he was released when his family paid a ransom of 400 marks. A mark at this time was not necessarily a coin but was

about 8 ounces of gold or silver and but this weight could vary depending on which country was calculating the value to use in marks.
Once he was free he set about recovering everything that had been taken from him. To this end he went to the court of Henry VI where he obtained letters patent dated 29th July 1430 which entitled him and his friend John Church to make reprisals to the value of £5,332.13.4 sterling, from the property of that Duke wherever found within the domains of the King of England. These letters patent endowed Nicolas with the right to rob every Frenchman he met in the king's domains whether on land or sea until the desired sum was accounted for. In effect what the letters meant was that he was a legal pirate until he recovered the value that had been stolen from him from those who had taken it. The letters did not allow him to attack anyone else only those against whom he had a grievance. Elizabeth I gave similar letters to people like Drake to raid the Spanish and because they had Royal approval they were not officially pirates but they were not exactly servants of the crown either and they were called privateers. He was also granted a fishery at Castle Beagh as well as being appointed Constable of Limerick Castle.
On 30th October 1431 he married Katherine Skyddy of Cork. He had to get a dispensation from the Pope as the bride was related to him in the fourth degree. He had six sons four of whom became mayors of Limerick, another was appointed to the important office of bailiff, an office, which took on odious connotations early in the eighteenth century, and Thomas the youngest would become bishop of the diocese of Limerick.

# Chapter 3

*The members of the Arthur family who were Mayors and Sherriffs of Limerick.*

The list below contains the names of many members of the Arthur family who served the city of Limerick with disctinction in the positions of both mayor and sheriff up to about the year 1700. After that time the penal laws in Ireland prevented any Catholic from standing for any public office. As most of the Arthur family of limerick remained Catholic they were no longer allowed to hold any public office or profession except funnily enough that of doctor of which more anon.

Eventually due to the laws that prevented Catholics from holding public office no more were elected to these prestidious public offices. Strangely enough for some reason they were not prevented from becoming a doctor although they had to go to the continent to train as a doctor as they were not allowed to train in Ireland. A number of the Arthur family were doctors in Limerick including the famous Dr. Thomas Arthur and his nephew also called Dr. Thomas Arthur.

It should be noted that there are a number of names like John Fitz-Thomas Arthur; in this list. The Fitz was used in the same way as Mac was in the Irish language and Ben is used in the Arabic language. So John Fitz Thomas Arthur means John the son of Thomas Arthur

| MAYORS OF LIMERICK | YEAR | SHERIFFS OF LIMERICK | YEAR APPOINTED |
|---|---|---|---|
| Nicolas Fitz Thomas Arthur | 1241 | | |
| John Fitz-Thomas Arthur | 1365 | John Arthur, W | 1371 |
| John Arthur | 1403 | Thomas Arthur | 1407 |
| John Arthur | 1404 | Thomas Arthur | 1408 |
| Thomas Arthur | 1426 | Thomas Arthur | 1408 |
| William Arthur | 1431 | Richard Arthur | 1423 |
| William Arthur | 1440 | David Arthur | 1450 |
| William Arthur | 1441 | John Arthur | 1460 |
| Nicholas Arthur | 1442 | Peter Arthur | 1463 |
| Nicholas Arthur | 1444 | John Fitz-William Arthur | 1464 |
| Richard Arthur | 1445 | Daniel Arthur | 1469 |
| Nicholas Arthur | 1446 | Edmond Arthur | 1475 |
| Thomas Arthur | 1450 | Edmond Arthur | 1476 |
| Richard Arthur | 1451 | Edmond Arthur | 1477 |
| Nicholas Arthur | 1452 | David Arthur | 1480 |

| MAYORS OF LIMERICK | YEAR | SHERIFFS OF LIMERICK | YEAR APPOINTE |
|---|---|---|---|
| Nicholas Arthur | 1454 | George Arthur Walter Arthur | 1481 |
| Richard Arthur | 1460 | Myles Arthur, A | 1486 |
| Nicholas. Fitz-Thomas Arthur | 1462 | Myles Arthur, A | 1487 |
| Nicholas Arthur | 1463 | Christopher Arthur | 1489 |
| Nicholas Arthur | 1464 | Christopher Arthur | 1491 |
| Thomas Arthur | 1466 | William Arthur | 1492 |
| Thomas Arthur | 1467 | Nicholas Fitz-John Arthur | 1504 |
| Thomas Arthur | 1469 | James Fitz-Edward Arthur | 1514 |
| John Arthur | 1471 | William Arthur | 1515 |
| Patrick Arthur | 1472 | Richard Milonis (Fitz-Milo) Arthur | 1516 |
| John Arthur | 1474 | Peter Walter Arthur | 1517 |
| Patrick Arthur | 1476 | Daniel Fitz-John Arthur | 1519 |
| MAYORS OF | YEAR | SHERIFFS OF | YEAR |

| LIMERICK | | LIMERICK | APPOINTED |
|---|---|---|---|
| Thomas Arthur | 1479 | John Fitz-Nicholas Arthur; Peter Fitz-Christopher Arthur | 1527 |
| Patrick Arthur | 1480 | Roland Arthur | 1531 |
| David Arthur | 1482 | Oeunepherous Fitz-Christopher Arthur | 1535 |
| John Fitz-Nicholas Arthur | 1483 | Hector Fitz-James Arthur | 1544 |
| John Arthur | 1486 | Thomas Arthur | 1547 |
| John Arthur | 1487 | Edward Fitz-Daniel Arthur | 1550 |
| Thomas Arthur | 1489 | Richard Arthur | 1557 |
| Patrick Arthur | 1490 | Daniel Fitz-David Arthur | 1570 |
| Christopher Arthur | 1501 | George Fitz-Daniel Arthur | 1571 |
| William Arthur | 1506 | Milo Fitz-Eustace Arthur | 1573 |

| MAYORS OF LIMERICK | YEAR | SHERIFFS OF LIMERICK | YEAR APPOINTI |
|---|---|---|---|
| Nicholas. Thos. Fitz-W. Arthur | 1508 | William Fitz-John Arthur | 1576 |
| Christopher Arthur | 1524 | Walter Fitz-Patrick Ryan | 1577 |
| Daniel Fitz-George Arthur | 1532 | Edward Fitz-Hector Arthur | 1580 |
| John Fitz-Nicholas Arthur | 1534 | Dom. Fitz-John Arthur | 1594 |
| John Fitz-Nicholas Arthur | 1547 | Wm. Fitz-Thomas Arthur | 1597 |
| Edward Fitz-Daniel Arthur | 1558 | Robert Arthur | 1600 |
| Thomas Fitz-John Arthur | 1565 | Jas. Fitz-Edward Arthur | 1601 |
| Thomas Fitz-John Arthur | 1573 | Christopher Arthur | 1606 |
| Thomas Fitz-John Arthur | 1577 | John Fitz John Arthur | 1613 |
| Nicholas Fitz-Thomas Arthur | 1592 | Christopher Fitz- D. Arthur | 1614 |
| Nicholas Arthur | 1607 | Walter Arthur | 1615 |

| MAYORS OF LIMERICK | YEAR | SHERIFFS OF LIMERICK | YEAR APPOINTED |
|---|---|---|---|
| Patrick Arthur | 1608 | John Arthur | 1666 |
| Patrick Arthur | 1648 | James Arthur | 1690 |

As can be seen many members of the Arthur family held high positions in Limerick until 1608. Here the Penal Laws intervened and only a few members of the family held any office until 1849 when David Leahy Arthur became High Sheriff (he was from Cork as were his family). This man was not really an Arthur. His father Daniel Leahy was married to Catherine O'Sullivan but after she died he married Margaret Arthur the daughter of Francis Arthur and they had two sons, Daniel and John. Daniel's son David was the main beneficiary of the will of Francis when he died because his mother was a daughter of Francis. Daniel took on the Arthur surname as a mark of respect for the Arthur family. Daniel Leahy Arthur's grandfather was the lawyer for Francis Arthur.

From the time of the Normans until 1608 the Arthur's were along with other families were among those who saw themselves as the aristocracy and prince merchants of Limerick. As can be seen from the table of Mayors and Sheriffs the Arthur family held those high offices an unusually large number of times for one family. Indeed it would seem that the gaps between a member of the Arthur family holding one office or the other were quite short. Indeed while the high offices in Limerick were usually held by members of the wealthy merchant class because of this you will not see nearly as many different surnames on the list of high office holders as you might expect in a city the size of Limerick. Now even though the high office holders were drawn from a restricted number of families it seems that members of the Arthur family held these high offices more often than any other of the great families.

Below is a map of Limerick city as it was in 1587.

# Chapter 4

*Many members of the Arthur family entered the religious life.*

It was the tradition that the Arthur family were buried in the chapel of St. Nicolas better known as the Arthur chapel in St. Mary's Cathedral, Limerick. They also had an ancestral monument on the left hand side of St. Catherine, Virgin and Mary's alter.

Down the years the Arthur Family contributed many of its number to the religious life as priests, nuns and brothers. Along with contributing a large number of clergy, Christian Brothers and Nuns to the Catholic Church the Arthur family also contributed a number of its members as clergy to the Church of Ireland as well as at least one nun in an Anglican order of nuns.

Below you will find a list of many of the members of the wider Arthur family who devoted their lives to the church. Below the list I will look in more detail at the lives of some of these people who devoted their lives to the church whether they were Catholic or Protestant.

| |
|---|
| Most Rev. Thomas Arthur, consecrated 1472 |
| The Very Rev. David Arthur Dean of Limerick. 1583 |
| Rev. Fr. Arthur of 1604. |
| Rev. Robert Arthur O.P. 1613 |
| Most Rev. Richard Arthur, consecrated 1623 |
| The Rev. Geoffrey Arthur 1519 |
| Very Rev. Edmond Arthur 1580 |
| Rev Professor A Arthur O.P. 1587 |
| Very Rev, Prior James Arthur O.P. 1689 |

| |
|---|
| The Right Rev. Abbess Margaret Xaveria Arthur, Received abbatical benediction 1724 |
| Ar. Arthur (Daughter of Francis 1798) Princethorpe. |
| Very Rev. Francis Arthur 1876 |
| The Very Rev. Patrick McDonough p.p. 1903 |
| Most Rev. John McCarthy, consecrated 1917 |
| The Very Rev. Francis Cassidy p.p. 1926 |
| Rev Francis Shaw S.J. 1927 |
| The Very Rev. William Cassidy P.P. 1932 |
| The Rev Br. William Canice Arthur1941 |
| The Very Rev. Cannon Charles Arthur p.p. 1946 |
| The venerable Archdeacon Cassidy 1950 |
| The Rev Br. Charles Firmin Arthur 1950 |
| The Rev. Mother Clare Arthur 1950. |
| Sr. M. Aquin Arthur |
| Sr. M. Augustine Arthur. |
| Sr. M. Bernadine Cassidy |
| Sr. Bernard Marian |
| Sr. M Columbanus Marian |
| Sr. M. Lucy Flatly (Mercy Order). |
| Sr. M. Flatly (Loreto Order) |
| Sr. M. Francis O'Dea (Mercy) |
| Mother M. Xaveria Arthur O.S.B. |
| Mother M. Theresa O.S.B. |
| Sr. M Ignatia Arthur (Loreto) |
| Sr. M. Aloysia Arthur (Loreto) |
| Sr. M. Agnus Warren Darley O.S.B. |
| Mother M. Angela Warren Barley, Sister of Charity. |
| Fr. Frank Arthur. (son of Joseph Arthur) studied at Freiburg Switzerland. While there as a student Fr. Frank met Cardinal Hume Frank also spent time teaching at an American College. |
| Rev. Lucius Arthur, of Glenomera, Co. Clare, Ireland, born |

| 1810 and died Jan 4th, 1887, aged 76 years. He was an Anglican Clergyman. |
|---|
| Rev Henry Arthur cannon of Ferns, diocese of Ossary. He was an Anglican Clergyman b. 12th November 1820. |
| Rev Frederic Brian Ború Arthur b 12th Sept 1822 d. 19th Jan 1870. He was an Anglican Clergyman. |
| SR. Cecily Arthur b.1880 d 22nd June 1962. She was a nun in an Anglican order. |

Above are some of the members of the Arthur family who became, Priests, Nuns, Christian Brothers, Church of Ireland Clergymen or Anglican nuns. If I have omitted anyone please forgive me and let me know about them and I will include them in the list if there is another edition of this book I will put them on the web site.

The family contributed many of its members to the religious and secular ranks of the clergy and several of them became illustrious, reflecting credit not only their family, on Limerick but also on Ireland.

*Let us now look at some individual family members who became illustrious in the religious life.*

<u>THOMAS ARTHUR:</u> *Benefactor of St. Mary's.*

This Thomas Arthur was born in 1378 and while he never joined any religious order I think he deserves to be here because of his actions when alive. Thomas married Johanna daughter of David Murrough of Cork. Now this pious couple at their own expense built the Eastern font and costly wrought window of the choir of the Cathedral

Church of the Blessed Virgin Mary in Limerick. On the Eastern door of the church they had the armorial bearings of the Arthur family and the armorial bearings of the Murrough sculpted. It was said that they did not do these things through a spirit of pride and vain glory but in order that others would imitate the memorial of their piety. This Thomas Arthur served as mayor of Limerick on two occasions and he died in 1427.

## THOMAS ARTHUR: *Bishop of Limerick*

The Most reverend Thomas Arthur was bishop of Limerick in 1472. He was a grandson of Thomas Arthur 1378 – 1427. He was the third son of Nicolas Arthur (mentioned in the last chapter) and Catherine Skyddy of Cork City. His father Nicolas was the most eminent citizen of his time and was a personal friend of the kings of England to whom he used to give many valuable gifts. This bishop had five biographers all of whom rose to distinction in Limerick. During this time Robert Arthur was mayor of Limerick and Bishop Thomas died on the 19th July 1486.

## GEOFFREY ARTHUR:

About the time Bishop Arthur died 1486 Geoffrey Arthur held the post of ninth Treasurer of St. Mary's Cathedral. It was more than likely that he was high ecclesiastic as well as being treasurer. There is an inscription in Latin on his tomb in St. Mary's Cathedral, which translates as follows "here in the bottom of the tomb, removed from the world, Geoffrey Arthur treasurer. He rested in perpetual peace in the year of the crucified lord 1519."

VERY REVEREND EDMOND ARTHUR: *Arch Priest of Limerick*

In the year 1580 during the Elizabethan persecutions the Very Rev. Edmond Arthur, Arch priest of Limerick ministered to the persecuted Catholics. He spoke both Irish and English fluently. This priest had general charge of worship in this archpresbyterate, and the parishioners of the smaller parishes had to attend Sunday Mass and hold baptisms at the principal parish while the subordinate parishes instead held daily mass and homilies

JAMES ARTHUR M.A.

James Arthur of Limerick was a Theologian in Louvain in 1580 and he was a master of arts. At that period no student according to the Penal Laws could study for the priesthood, so young James left his native Limerick to become a priest and then returned to his native country to help minister to the people.

REV. JAMES ARTHUR O.P.: *of the Order of Saint Dominic.*

The Rev. James Arthur O.P. was born in Limerick in 1587. He was the son of William Arthur and Beatrice Creagh. These were the days of religious persecution and as James grew up he begun to realize that he had a vocation for the religious life. At this time all the religious houses in Ireland lay in ruins so in order to pursue his dream of joining the Dominican Order he had to leave Ireland and go to Spain.

He went to Spain where in 1606 he entered the Irish Secular College in Salamanca. Later he joined the Dominicans. He attended the University of Salamanca 1610-16 and began teaching there about 1616. Already in 1626 he was recommended to *Propagande fide* by the Irish Dominican procurator as suitable for episcopal office in Ireland. In the same year he was named lector of theology at Léon and was temporarily lector in theology in Salamanca in 1627-8. He also filled academic posts in other parts of Spain. In 1630 he was named regent of the *collegio de San Tommaso* in Naples and was regent of the *studium generale* in Avila in the 1630s. He was later regent of studies at the theological graduate college of San Gregorio, Valladolid and was nominated to the principal chair of theology at Coimbra University by Philip IV in 1640. It appears that while there he refused to take an oath imposed on all professors to defend the doctrine of the immaculate conception of the Virgin Mary. Although he had been on the continent for so long he was known in Ireland. In 1632, for instance, thc bishop and clergy of Limerick wanted him as coadjutor. In the early 1640s he appears to have retired to the Portuguese Dominican College in Lisbon and in 1649, Dominic O'Daly referred to him as a most discerning man who might be sent to Ireland to assess the situation there. A devoted Thomist, Arthur wrote a series of commentaries on virtually the entire *Summa Theologiae* which survived in manuscript form in Spain and Portugal entitled *Commentaria in totam fere S. Thomas de Aquino Summam*. Soon after his death, his former pupil, John Baptist de Marinis, by then master general of the order, directed Dominic O'Daly to collect and publish Arthur's manuscripts. Only one volume, it would seem, appeared, in 1655. He died at the Portuguese College of St Dominic in Lisbon on 1st February 1654.

THE MOST REV RICHARD ARTHUR: *Bishop of Limerick.*

Richard Arthur was born in the city of Limerick around 1560 (no record of his birth). He went abroad to study for the priesthood as there was no place in Ireland where he would be allowed to study. In 1613 he was appointed vicar general of the diocese of Limerick. At that time there were two sets of bishops in Ireland, there were those who were appointed by the English and those who were appointed by the Pope.

In 1623 he was appointed Bishop of Limerick by Pope Urban VIII and the most Rev. Doctor Roth Bishop of Cork consecrated him with the assistance of the abbot of Holy Cross Abbey. When you consider that he was not recognized by the English authorities working as bishop would be difficult.

He was a great benefactor of the diocese. In 1624 he presented two plate cruets to the diocese and in 1625 he presented a crucifix (pictured below) which was hollowed inside to contain relics. The pedestal of this crucifix was set with semi-precious stones and it was designed to be carried before the bishops. In 1627 he also presented a large gilded chalice (photo below) an enamelled paten as well as an enamelled plate pax. The enamelling represented the crucifixion and a soldier piercing the side of Christ with a lance. In 1534 he presented a monstrance for The Blessed Sacrament which was supported by four pillars and had a cover to the diocese.

The Arthur Chalice

The Arthur Cross

On October 30th 1634 Dr. Richard received the Papal Nuncio Rennuccini at his Cathedral of St. Mary's Limerick. The clergy and all the municipal authorities in solemn procession accompanied Cardinal Rennuccini the Papal Nuncio from St. John's gate to the Cathedral.

On the occasion of the visit of Rennuccini Dr. Arthur wore a glorious mitre and carried a splendid crosier both of which were admired by the nuncio. The mitre was afterwards entrusted to the hands of a wealthy merchant in Limerick to prevent it falling into the hands of the English. This merchant took out some of its precious stones and replaced them with false ones it is said that he had no luck afterwards for doing this and died not long afterwards in 1646. During his visit Nuncio Rennuccini reconsecrated St. Mary's as a Cathedral.

On the 23rd May 1646 Richard died and his funeral was attended by the Nuncio and all the clergy. He was buried in his Cathedral of St. Mary's and he was succeeded by Bishop Edward O'Dwyer.

## ROBERT ARTHUR O.F.M.:

A letter written on Jan. 30th 1630 describes a raid on the Friars Chapel in Cook Street Dublin by the mayor, the Protestant Archbishop of Dublin, the sheriff and soldiers. During the raid two young friars were taken who were later rescued. Along with the two friars a Robert Arthur was captured and committed to the castle it is possible that this was the famous Robert Arthur O.F.M. also called Chamberlain who died in Louvain in 1636. Meehan "Earls" (p 136) says that this Robert Arthur was a native of Limerick. He was a Doctor of Theology at the University of Salamanca as well as being confessor and confident to Hugh O'Neill of Tyrone.

## ABBESS MARGARET ARTHUR 1673 – 1743:

Mother Margaret Xavier Arthur. Portrait I believe is in Kylemore Abbey

Margaret Arthur (mentioned in last chapter) was the eldest of the eight children of Francis Arthur. After the treaty of Limerick 1691 the whole family left Limerick for France where they were part of the court of King James II at St. Germain.

Queen Mary of Modena asked Margaret to go to the Ursuline convent at St Germain. While she was there she decided to enter the religious life. Fr Jeremy O'Donnell who was chaplain to the Irish Abbey at Ypres (Belgium) came to St Germain on a visit and persuaded her to go to

Ypres as Abbess Butler was living alone there with only four lay nuns.

After three months at Ypres she was sent to Ghent on 10th Jan. 1696. In Jan. 1697 she returned to Ypres with the name Sr. Margaret Xaveria Arthur. Because Ypres was so poor the Bishop refused to let her and other postulants profess until Queen Mary of Modena provided a dowry for each of the four postulants and on Dec 19th 1700 she made her profession. She held a number of posts within the abbey until 19th March 1724 when she was elected abbess.

Mr. Daniel Arthur (a cousin of the Abbess) who was a merchant banker in Paris Madrid, and London acted as financial agent to the community at Ypres. Daniel Arthur was from Limerick originally before he went to France to make his fortune.

In 1740 after a bad winter when the community accumulated many debts and had no way of paying them they were given a gift of £500 by James III (The Old Pretender). This gift enabled the community to pay off their debts.

On the 5th Of March 1743 Sr. Margaret Xaveria Arthur died when she was 70 years of age.

<u>CATHERINE HELEN ARTHUR (Mother M Xavier):</u>
*S.B. of the Benedictine Convent Princethorpe England. Born 1780. Died 1860.*

Catherine Helen Arthur was born on the 20th of March 1780 in the city of Limerick the daughter of Francis Arthur who was the son of Patrick Arthur. When she was eighteen years of age her father was sentenced to transportation to Botany Bay. (More about this later)

Catherine Helen was one of the first pupils to attend Bodany Hall, Norfolk where a school had been opened in 1793 (This was one of the first catholic schools to be allowed to operate in England after the reformation). This was only three years after the O.S.B. order had arrived in England from France. It wasn't long before she decided to join the order and when she made her wishes known to her parents her wishes were opposed and they did all they could to change her mind but to no avail. It was not until 1814 when her brother Patrick Edmund and her mother died within a short time of one another that her father's heart softened. Francis believing that God was asking of him yet another sacrifice he finally gave the long desired permission to become a Benedictine nun. Meanwhile the community had left Bodany Hall, which had become too small for the increasing numbers of both nuns and pupils. They went to Heath Hall, Yorkshire. Catherine applied to be received as a postulant and she entered the order on Jan 7th 1814 aged 34.

Francis wished her to be received into the order on the understanding that in time she would make a foundation in Ireland and promised a large fortune for that purpose.

However the Prioress Madame De Mirepoix absolutely refused to receive her under such conditions and in consequence Francis withdrew the dower to which she had a right, however the dowry was restored at a later time. The dowry was very important to a woman entering an order as those who brought a big dowry could aspire to rise in the order but if they had nothing to bring they became what were called kitchen nuns, they did all the manual work and in effect they were servants to the other nuns who had risen in the order. Catherine took her final vows on May 16th 1816 and was immediately appointed first mistress of the school. Later on she became bursar and in 1835 the convent moved to Princethorpe. Not long after the move to Princethorpe her niece Mary Jane Arthur (the daughter of Francis son Patrick Edmund) became a novice there. In 1842 Eliza Arthur who was Mother Xavier's sister generously offered to complete some apartments of which one would be for her own use in return for being allowed to live at the monastery. She had married a Mr. Scully who sadly had died. She also built the village school and gave to various other charities. Ultimately Mrs. Scully left to become a Carmelite Nun in Darlington.

In 1866 Mother Xavier celebrated her Golden Jubilee together with the Mother Prioress Sr. Genevieve McCarthy when both of them were in ill health. Within a year of them celebrating their Golden Jubilee together they were both dead. Mother Xavier Arthur died on the 27th July 1867 in her 88th year after a long illness.

Mother Mary Xavier and
Eliza Arthur

<u>MOTHER MARY JANE ARTHUR:</u> *(Sister Mary Theresa).*

Mother Mary Theresa Arthur O.S.B. was a granddaughter of Francis Arthur and a great granddaughter of Patrick the father of Francis. Her father was Francis Arthur's son Patrick Edmund. She was born in Limerick in 1813 and she was the niece of Mother Xavier Arthur her father's sister. Her father died while she was very young and her sister had not yet been born. Patrick Edmund left large fortunes to both of his daughters. Some years later her mother married again and she and her husband a Mr. Galway went travelling to France and Italy and the two children went with them. After arriving in Rome the two girls were sent to the school at Latrinita Dei Monti where the nuns of the Sacred Heart had opened a school. They were sent there to finish their education and the time they spent in the convent left an indelible impression on the two Arthur girls.

After Mr. And Mrs. Galway returned to Dublin with the two Arthur girls they found that both had a strong desire to enter the religious life however they wished the two sisters to see something of the world before taking the decision to become nuns. Mary Jane could not be persuaded and she ran away to her aunt (Mother M Xavier Arthur) at Princethorpe where her family were persuaded to allow her to stay. At her profession on October 9th 1837 she gave a gift of costly vestments of gold and silver to the church. She lived to celebrate her Golden Jubilee on October17th. 1887 and several of her relations present at the celebration. However two and a half years later she died on March 4th 1890 when she was 77 after an attack of influenza.

<u>ELLEN ARTHUR:</u> *(In religion Sr. M. Aloysia of the Loreto Order).*

Ellen Arthur was the sister of Mother Mary Jane Arthur and they were both the daughters of Patrick Edmund the son of Francis Arthur. Ellen was the niece of Sr. Mary Ignatia. She had travelled extensively with her family and spoke both French and Italian fluently. She entered Loreto Abbey in Rathfarnham on 24th June 1836 aged 25, receiving the habit on 26th July 1836 and she was professed on 18th October 1837.She died at Loreto Abbey, Rathfarnham on 13th 1895 after being a nun for 60 years. It is interesting to note that nearly one hundred years after Sr. M. Aloysia entered the order there was another descendent of Patrick Arthur who joined the community at Rathfarnham and this person was Lucy Flatly.

<u>ELLEN FRANCES ARTHUR:</u> *(In religion Sr. Mary Ignatia of the Loreto Order).*

Ellen Frances Arthur was the youngest daughter of Francis Arthur. She was born in 1792. As with her sister her father tried to prevent her from entering the church but she entered the Bar Convent in York on September 2nd 1819 aged 27 and on October 15th 1821 she was professed in Dublin. Ellen died at Rathfarnham, Dublin on January 5th 1842.

In August 1820 Mary Ignatia accompanied Rev. Mother Teresa Ball and Sr. M. Baptist Therry to found a convent of the institute of the B.V.M. in Ireland. So along with Mother Teresa Ball she was co-founder of the Loreto order in Ireland. Unlike her relations who became nuns she did not have a long life in the order and died quite young.

<u>THE VERY REV JAMES ARTHUR O.P.:</u> *Prior of the Dominicans, Limerick.*

Fr. James Arthur studied in Portugal and after his ordination remained in London for a long period as the chaplain to the Portuguese Embassy, under the protection of which he ministered to the Catholics of London. This was only possible because he was protected by being a member of staff of the Portuguese Embassy in London. A church was attached to the embassy and it was considered part of the embassy grounds and so it had diplomatic protection. In this way some Catholic churches survived in London throughout the reformation. James returned to Limerick where he died in 1689.

REV. LUCIUS ARTHUR: *Of Glenomera*

The Rev. Lucius Arthur 1810 – 1887 was 76 years of age when he died having packed a lot of living into his 76 years having had a large family. His wife Harriet Smith died before him, as sadly did many of his sons who served in the army.

He served in many parishes from Leeds to Suffolk, Cornwall, and Derbyshire as well as in the north of Ireland. Newspapers of the time mention that he was well known for upsetting other clergy. It would seem that he had a forthright manner and said what he thought without giving what he was saying enough thought.

When he died his daughters were all around him.

SISTER CECILY ARTHUR *Sister of Charles William Augustus and Desmond Arthur.*

Sister Cecily seems to have been the sister of Charles William Augustus Arthur and Desmond Arthur of Glenomera. She told my great uncle Brother Charles (Firmin Arthur) this in a conversation she had with him when he visited her in in her convent in the 1930's. She said that they were her brothers although as of yet we have not found a birth record for her. Br. Firmin believed her story and he may have had access to records we do not have now. Here we should note that the descendants of the Glenomera family have no doubt that she was a sister to both Charles and Desmond. Indeed it is quite possible that Br. Firmin was told about Sr. Cecily when he met with

Charles William Augustus in Dublin. She told Br. Firmin that when she was very young she was sent as a boarder to an Anglican girl's school run by an Anglican order of nuns called The Community of St Mary the Virgin and as a result of going to boarding school so young she had very little contact with her family. When she finished school there she joined the order. However her memories of her brothers and her family were very sparse as she had been sent away at such a young age. This may have been to protect her from her father who was known to have mental problems or perhaps she was Charles older twin sister and in order to protect the male succession she was sent away to school as being the oldest child she may have had a claim on the estate of her father. The fact is we do not know why she was sent away and neither did she so we can only speculate. The order she joined was based at St. Mary's house, Pembroke Park, Ballsbridge, Dublin 4. The community of St. John the Evangelist is now based there having taken over from the previous order when they were down to two nun's sister Cecily being one of the two still alive at that time. Cecily stayed on with the new order giving them any help she could. As she knew all the Church of Ireland people in that area of Dublin she was of great help in raising finance for the new convent. Sister Cecily died on the 22nd June 1962 when she was 81 years of age and she was buried in Mount Jerome Cemetery, Harrold's Cross in Dublin which then was the main cemetery in Dublin for members of the Church of Ireland.

<u>THE ARTHUR CHALICE OF COROFIN:</u> *Co Clare.*

In Corofin there is a Chalice with the following description in Latin, which reads as:
"Calix benedictionis cui benedicimus, none communicatio
Sanguino Christi est. (1 Corinthians x)
D. Robertus Arthur at Margerita, soror eius
Deo optimo maximo Dicant"

This translates as:

The chalice of the benediction, which we bless, is the communication of the blood of Christ.
Robert Arthur and his sister Margaret Blake to the Most High dedicate it.

The date on the chalice is 1670.

# Chapter 5

*A little about the Arthur's who were banished to Co. Clare by Cromwell.*

By 1653 the Cromwellian military conquest of Ireland was complete so now they turned their hand to the civilian conquest of Ireland. To this end an act was passed in the British Parliament which set out in detail a scheme by which a survey was to be made and lots were to be drawn by the soldiers for the best estates and lands. This scheme was also applied to the Renegade Irish (Catholics who had supported Parliament with money etc. in the war against the Irish. Believe it or not there were some Catholics who had supported Cromwell).

Much of Co. Clare like Connaught is comparatively poor land and so was of little interest to Cromwell's settlers as they were only interested in good land. So a decision was taken that this poorer land should be handed over to those Catholics who had not taken up arms against the English and Cromwell or who indeed had actively supported Cromwell. The Arthur's of limerick and many of the Arthur families who farmed along the Limerick/Tipperary border were among those Catholic families who were known to the government as "Innocent Papists" (they supported neither side in the war). Many of these were dispossessed of their homes and estates and transplanted into Clare and Connaught (at this time Clare was considered by many to be more part of Connaught than Munster) to make room for planters approved by the government. Most of the dispossessed Arthur families in Clare came from the Arthur families who had farmed along the Limerick/Tipperary border and were not of the

Limerick family. However a number of the Limerick family were transplanted to Clare but it would seem that they were not long in Clare when they began finding their way back to Limerick. However one section of the Limerick family does seem to have settled in Ennis rather than return to Limerick.

According to the census of Co. Clare taken by Sir William Petty in 1659 there were seven Arthur families in the Barony of Tulla. Even in 1642 there were Arthur's in Clare. Raids on houses were quite common in Clare at this time and amongst the names of the rebels we find the name of John Arthur of Inniscarthy. Ann Webster of Ennis complained that Dominic Arthur had rifled her house and she also made a complaint against him in 1642. This Dominic was a merchant from Ennis and in this case it would seem that Dominic was trying to recover his property as Ann Webster does not seem to have paid her rent on time.

In 1703 Francis Arthur, a gentleman, living at Ballyquin was accused of treason and his estates sold because he supported James II in the Williamaite war. In 1684 Sir Donough O'Brien lent this Francis £60 for which he got the lands of Shanbor. Sir Donough received his interest regularly until 1691 when the rebellion broke out. From then until 1695 the land was laid waste by Francis Arthur and since Francis was accused of High Treason this land was given over to O'Brien. He in turn let them back to another member of the Arthur family along with other lands. This of course was Thomas Arthur from Limerick and this estate was in time to become known as Ballyquin or the Glenomera estate.

The lands of Creevagh and Caherkelly, a total of 440 aces were set out to Nicolas Arthur in 1665 and Nicolas then mortgaged them to a Patrick Arthur after this the lands were then mortgaged to a Dr. Mar for £500 however as Nicolas Arthur was then outlawed for high treason Sir Donough O Brien got all the of the lands that had belonged to Nicolas Arthur for £10.

Now the following names are recorded in the Public Records Office in Dublin as having conformed to the Protestant religion between the years of 1702 and 1789. In other words they converted to Protestantism each for reasons of their own.

Thomas Percy Arthur, gentleman – 1740.
Elizabeth Arthur - 1741.
Thomas Arthur, Clooneycorney – 1750.
John Arthur, gentleman – 1753.
Catherine Arthur, Ennis – 1754.
Ann Arthur, Ennis – 1780.

It would seem likely that most of the names above allowed their names to go forward as converting to Protestant in order to keep possession of their property and keep the vote. Of course to pretend to convert was illegal but as long as they made a show of honouring their conversion they were left alone.

In 1773 Thomas Arthur of Ballyquin has the Freedom of Ennis conferred upon him of course his family had converted to Protestantism by then as no Catholic could have had such an honour conferred on them at that time.

The following members of the Arthur family served as Justices of the Peace in Clare.

Nicolas Arthur – 1687.
Thomas Arthur – 1766.
Walter Arthur – 1796.
William Arthur – 1801.
Augustus Arthur – 1846.

It seems likely that all the above were Protestant as all served after the time of Cromwell and it was difficult for a catholic to hold any public office. Nicolas Arthur was an exception as he served during the reign of James II who was the last Catholic King of England and Nicolas was a Catholic.

The following members of the Arthur family served on the Clare Grand Jury.

Thomas Arthur - 1799
John Arthur – 1874

Thomas Arthur who was from the Arthur family who owned the Glenomera estate would have been a Protestant. John however not so certain, he seems to have come from the Arthur family of Ennis most of whom were Catholic (although some had converted) so he may have been a Catholic. When James II was king a man called Thomas Arthur held the post of "Clerk of the Hanoper" in trust for Robert Arthur's wife, Tyrconnell's niece.

In 1747 in the Regiment de Roth that was part of the Irish Brigade in the service of France there was a Lieutenant

Colonel Arthur who to the best of our knowledge seems to have been a descendant of one of the wild geese who left Limerick after the Williamaite war.

# Chapter 6

*Old Limerick Arthur family records*

Over the next number of pages there is information extracted from various Arthur family wills which were still in existence in the 1600's when Dr. Thomas Arthur (His story is being told in the next chapter) did his research and recorded his findings. It is because of his research and recording his findings that we now have the records recorded over the next few pages. If he had not recorded what he did, we would have none of these records as virtually all Irish wills from before the 1800's were destroyed during the Irish Civil war or to prevent them falling into the hands of the English establishment during the penal laws. These pages give a genealogical picture of the Arthur family at that time but they do not give a complete picture but still more than most families have from those centuries. All of this information comes courtesy of the work done by Noel Murphy and his study of what we call The Arthur Manuscript and The Arthur Fee Book which are now in the British Library. I have only included the entries that relate directly to the Arthur Family.

There is some information from civil survey 1640 which gives the values of the land and properties held by members of the Arthur family in Limerick.

# The Arthur Family Tree,

## Taken from the wills in the Arthur Mss.

By Noel Murphy

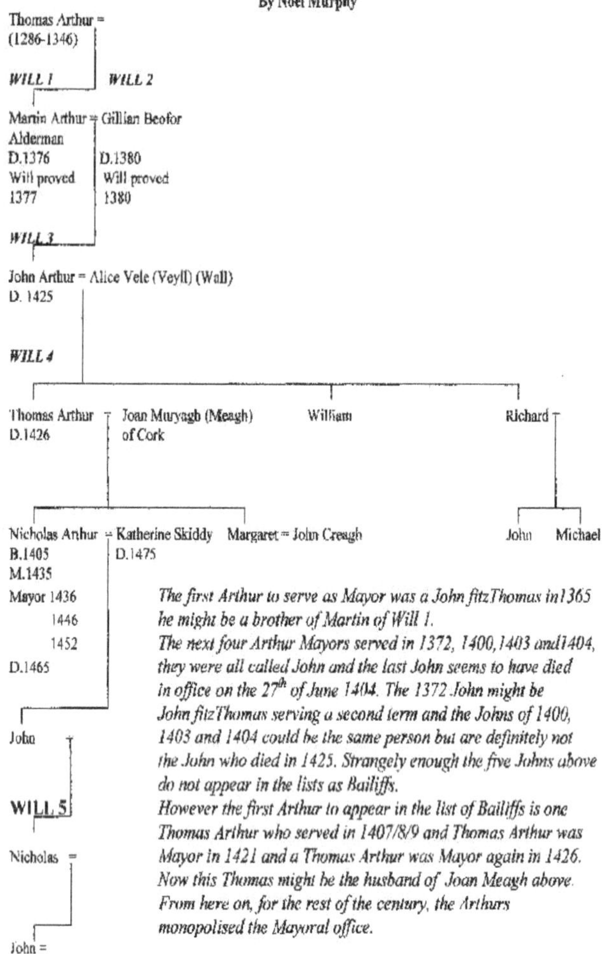


*The first Arthur to serve as Mayor was a John fitzThomas in1365 he might be a brother of Martin of Will 1.*
*The next four Arthur Mayors served in 1372, 1400,1403 and1404, they were all called John and the last John seems to have died in office on the 27th of June 1404. The 1372 John might be John fitzThomas serving a second term and the Johns of 1400, 1403 and 1404 could be the same person but are definitely not the John who died in 1425. Strangely enough the five Johns above do not appear in the lists as Bailiffs.*
*However the first Arthur to appear in the list of Bailiffs is one Thomas Arthur who served in 1407/8/9 and Thomas Arthur was Mayor in 1421 and a Thomas Arthur was Mayor again in 1426. Now this Thomas might be the husband of Joan Meagh above. From here on, for the rest of the century, the Arthurs monopolised the Mayoral office.*

# Patrick Arthur.

## Of Cloonanna, Pubblebrien. His Will dated 1675

By Noel Murphy

**The will identifies the following people:-**

| | |
|---|---|
| Son and Heir | **Patrick Arthur** |
| Daughter | **Margaret,** unm. |
| Daughter | **Catherine,** unm. |
| Son-in-law | **Daniel O'Brien.** |
| Son-in-law | **William Lysaght.** (Married to Barbara Arthur) |
| Sister | **Elinor,** married to a Mr. Lysaght. |
| Cousin | **Dr. Thomas FitzPatrick Arthur.** (See T-Certs for Dr. Tom Jnr.) |
| Brother-in-law | **John Sexton.** |
| Brother-in-law | **David Cantillon** |
| Nephew | **Philip Cantillon** |
| Brother | **Daniel Arthur** of London. (Is this the Daniel Jnr. in Arthur Mss. Fee Book) |
| Cousin | **Patrick Arthur** of Limerick. |

---

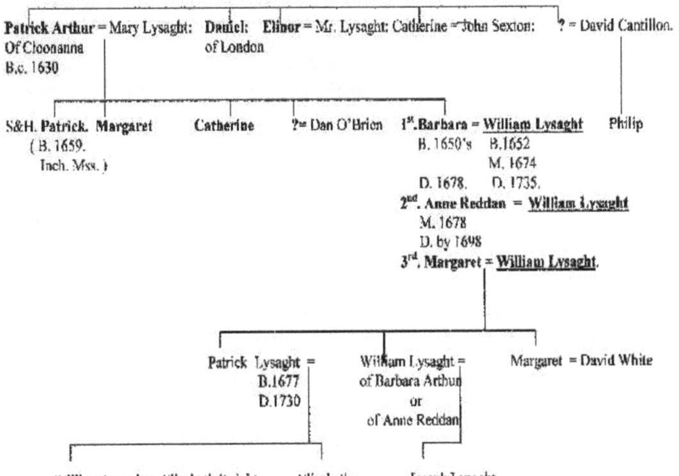

# Dr. Thomas Arthur Jnr.

By Noel Murphy.

**Source:- T-Certs.**

| Dr. Thomas Arthur = | Ellinor | Pierce | Margaret |
|---|---|---|---|
| Of Ballynacarrigy | B. 1629 | B. 1632 | B. 1635 |
| B. 1623. | | | |
| *L. 1675. Age 52.* | | | |

Pierce and Margaret were Thomas's siblings.

---

There can be no doubt that the two Dr. Toms were closely related. Tom Snr. In 1675 names Tom Jnr. as his third choice for heir general after - 1st. William Arthur FitzJohn of Dublin who was not a close relative.- 2nd. his reluctant choice, at his wife's request, his grandson Thomas, son of his disinherited daughter Dymphna. From this it is evident that Tom Jnr was alive in 1675.

---

**Source:- Short Study of a Transplanted Family, by E. Lysaght. Dublin 1935.**

There is another Will which mentions a Dr. Thomas Arthur and that is the Will of Patrick Arthur of Cloonanna in Pubblebrien also written in 1675. Patrick mentions his cousin Dr. Thomas FitzPatrick Arthur and another cousin, Patrick Arthur of Limerick.

---

When Dr Tom Jnr. was transplanted, he was accompanied by his new wife and his own siblings. There is no mention of him having any children in December 1653, even though he was now 30 years old and his wife was 24 years old.

**The Civil Survey** gives Dr. Tom Snr. Holding land in Clanwilliam. The Jnr. Dr. Tom's address of Ballynacarrigy in Clanwilliam, was actually owned by Capt. George Ingoldsby and that would have been in right of his wife Mary Gould, the daughter and heir of James Gould and his wife Annabella Browne of Hospital. James was killed in action fighting on the protestant side in 1641. James was the son of Thomas Gould and became the ward of Edmond Sexton and Dominick Roche in 1624. Judging by the list of the lands that Ingoldsby came into possession of, through his wife, Thomas Gould, Mary's grandfather, must have been the son and heir of James Gould, the Justice and would be Undertaker of the Denzil lands in Tarbert.The last named James died in 1600. (Thomas Gould D. 23rd Jan. 1623. Sexton Diary.)

Tom Snr. and his brothers seem to have left no heirs male behind them so that would rule out the likelihood of Tom Jnr. being Snr's nephew. The next possibility is that Jnr was the son of a cousin of Snr. So now we must search for a cousin of Dr. Thomas Snr. called Patrick. One possibility is the Patrick who was Mayor in 1608/9 and who died in office. He has to be ruled out because Jnr. was born in 1623. ( His sister Margaret was born in 1635 ). Dr. Tom Snr. and the mysterious Patrick must be contemporaries as they were both became fathers at the same time. It is possible that Tom Snr. was uncle to Tom Jnr. through Tom Snr's sister Kathleen who was married to a Patrick Arthur. Tom Snr. also had another Nephew called Christopher Arthur fitzPatrick, a Doctor of Divinity.

Two Patrick Arthurs signed a petition in Limerick City in 1642. For which they must have been mature and important citizens of the City.

# Dr. Thomas Arthur.

**Details from his will.**

**Dated:- 31 Dec 1674.**

**By Noel Murphy**

Details from other sources in italics.
**Source N.M.A.J. Vol 1. P. 163 on.** Old Limerick Wills

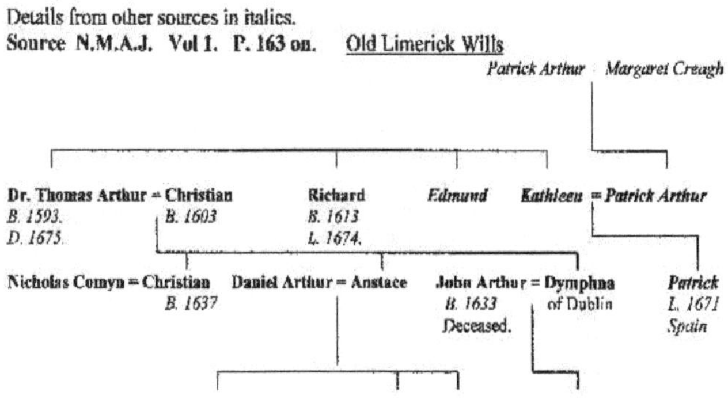


Dr. Tom appointed **William Arthur FitzJohn** of Dublin to be his heir. If William died before Dr. Tom,
Then **Thomas FitzJohn,** son of his disinherited daughter Dymphna, was to succeed and if he died before Dr. Tom,
Then **Dr. Thomas Arthur fitzPatrick of Limerick, B. 1623** was to be the heir.

---

Dr. Thomas Arthur and his two brothers Edmund and Richard seem to have left no male heirs to succeed to their estates. Dr. Tom makes no reference to his eldest daughter Mary and her husband Bartholomew Stackpoole and their son James. Mary was dead already by 1653, young James died before his father and Bartholomew might have died before Dr. Tom.

## Limerick Names from Dr. Arthur's Fee Book.

By Noel Murphy

A 1619 Andrew **Arthur** FitzWilliam.
1619 Richard Arthur FitzGeorge's wife.
1619 Stephan Arthur's wife, Maria.
1623 Stephan Arthur.
1620 Edward Arthur FitzGeorge's wife Catherine.
1620 Edward Arthur fitzGeorge.
1620 Daniel Arthur, Jnr.
1623 Daniel Arthur. Jnr.
1620 Johanna Arthur FitzThomas.
1619 Gerald Arthur.
1620 The widow Arthur, widow of Patrick **England**.
1620 Walter Arthur.
1621 Hector Arthur's wife.
1621 Patrick Arthur FitzRichard.
1623 Patrick Arthur FitzRichard.
1621 Peter Arthur FitzChristopher.
1621 Thomas Arthur FitzDominick's wife Margaret.
1621 Oliver Arthur FitzRobert.
1622 John Arthur FitzRichard.
1623 Margaret Arthur FitzDaniel.
1623 Richard Arthur fitzGeorge's wife.
1623 Joan Arthur, widow of George Sexton.

1623 George **Andrews** wife.

---

B 1620 Richard **Bourke** of Killonane.
1619 Charles Bourk.
1620 Charles Bourk's wife.
1619 Ellis Bourk, widow.

1620 John **Brown.** Merchant.
1619 Oliver Brown.

1619 George **Bently.**

1619 Mrs. **Bonefield,** widow, for son.
1620 Gregory Bonefield.

1620 Edmond **Baggott.**

1621 Henry **Barckley's** daughter. ( of Ballycahane. Pubblebrien Barony. )

1

# Dr. Thomas Arthurs cash transactions.

By Noel Murphy

A

1631 Patrick **Arthur** (brother-in-law)
1636 Patrick Arthur
1631 Hector Arthur
1632 Hector Arthur
1633 Hector Arthur
1634 Hector Arthur
1635 Hector Arthur
1636 Hector Arthur
1632 John Arthur
1633 John Arthur fitzChristopher.
1636 John Arthur
1633 Christopher Arthur fitzDominick. (A nephew)
1634 Mrs. Ellin Arthur, (aunt)
1635 Ellyn Arthur, (sister)
1631 Anstace Arthur (daughter)
1636 Mary Arthur (daughter)
1644 Dymphna Arthur (daughter) to marry John Arthur fitzRobert of Dublin.
1620 William Arthur (Tom's Father)
1643 Mary Arthur wife of Bartholomew Stackpoll.
1631 Catherine Arthur (sister-in-law) not yet married.
1629 Edmund Arthur ( brother) dead by 1644.
1630 Richard Arthur (brother)
1636 Richard Arthur (brother, 20 years younger)
1620 Sir Nicholas Arthur (distant cousin)
1652 Thomas Arthur
1652 Thomas Arthur fitzGerolt
1653 Thomas Arthur

---

B

1631 James **Bourke**
1631 Henry Bourke of Kissiquirk
1632 William Bourke of Caherconreefy
1632 Richard Bourke fitzWilliam of Williamstown.
1634 John Bourke fitzThomas
1635 Walter Bourke fitzJohn of Williamstown
1636 Walter Bourke fitzJohn

1632 Mr. **Bryen**
1635 Daniel Bryen (singing lessons for daughter Mary)

---

C

1631 Leonard **Creagh** fitzPatrick
1630 Andrew Creagh fitzAndrew Alderman.
1631 Andrew Creagh
1633 Andrew Creagh
1634 Andrew Creagh

# Arthur

By Noel Murphy

## Source:- 1574 Visitation, Pos 8286. G.O. Ms, 47. Page 19.

Master Thomas Arthur – Christian Creagh.
Mayor of Limerick
1573-4

3 sons | 4 daughters

Nicholas = Martin, James, Katherine, Elenor, Jenet, Joan.

(Thomas was Recorder for the Corporation for many years. A Legal Position.)
A Thomas FitzMartin was Mayor in the year 1635. ( Correct generation gap. )

---

Nicholas =
Alderman.
Mayor 1592 &1607.
Held Reboge and Rathmisteall in 1615. ( Inquisition to identify the Corporations 40 Townlands in the Liberties and who held them and what rents were being paid and to whom. ) Begley Vol. 1.

Thomas Arthur –
Alderman.
D. 1640/1
Held Rheboge, 89 acres and Rathmisteall, 36 acres , when the Civil Survey was being taken. Alderman Thomas is recorded as being deceased at this time.

**The 40 Townlands of the Liberties held by the Arthurs.**

| Name | 1615 | 1640 – 1654. |
|---|---|---|
| Ballyclogh | Christopher Arthur | John Arthur |
| Ballygadynan | John Arthur | |
| Ballygrenane | | William Arthur, deceased. |
| Ballyinaghten Mor | William Stritch, Alderman | John Wolfe |
| Ballyinaghten Beg | John Arthur | James Bourke |
| | | James White |
| | | William Arthur |
| | | Thomas Fanning |
| | | John Comyn FitzDavid |
| Moylish | James White, Merchant. | James White FitzJames. |

From Transplanter Cert. 1653.

Dr. Thomas Arthur = Elinor, Pierce, Margaret
Of Ballynacarrigy
B. 1623 B. 1629 B. 1632 B. 1635.

# Arthur

**By Noel Murphy**

From Betham's abstracts.

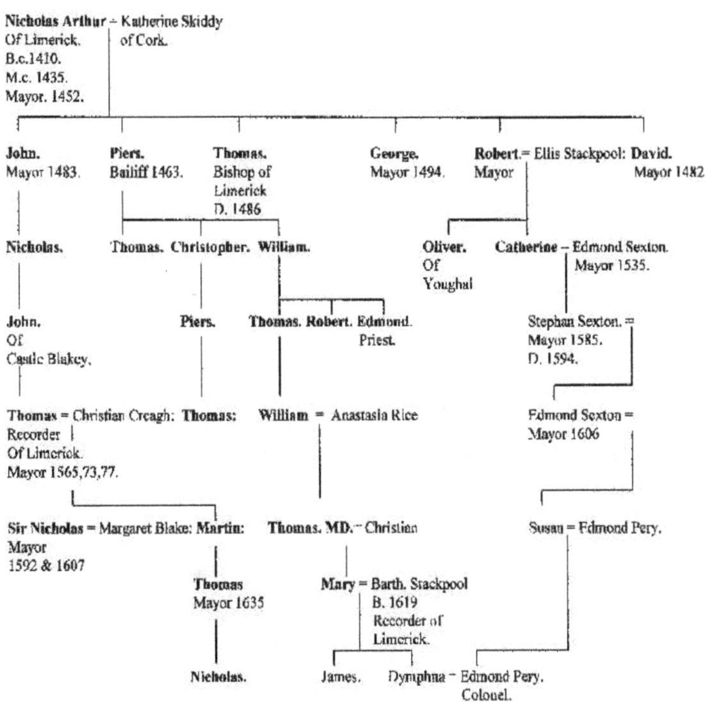


A Nobility claim in Spain in 1671. From Irish Roots Magazine No. 54. The Familytree submitted by Patrick Arthur.

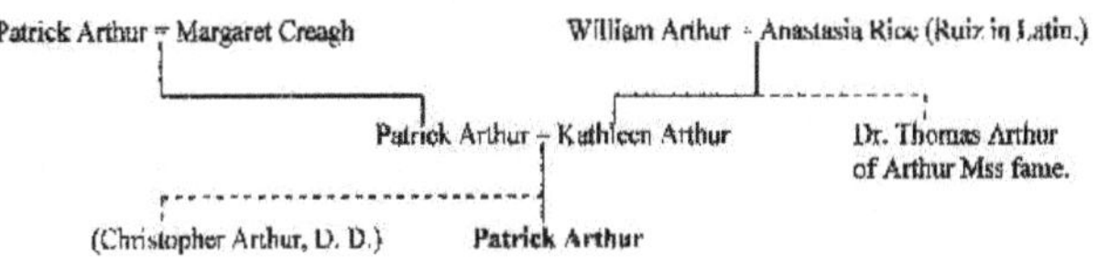


Kathleen was the sister of Dr. Tom. So Dr. Tom had a brother-in-law called Patrick Arthur and a nephew called Patrick Arthur.

The Pedigree chart above, submitted by Patrick in 1671 to support his claim for Hildago status omits his brother the Protestant Devine as this would ruin his case. Claimants had to be of Pure Catholic stock without any trace of Jewish, Muslim or Lutheran blood in their family tree.

# ARTHUR

By Noel Murphy

## Source:- Fiants Elizabeth.

| Year | Fiant. | |
|---|---|---|
| 1564 | 666 | Thomas Arthur, Recorder of Limerick. |
| 1571 | 1846 | " " |
| 1576 | 2758 | " " |
| 1576 | 2771 | " " |
| 1576 | 2862 | " " |
| 1577 | 3156 | " " |
| 1583 | 4186 | " " |
| 1584 | 4499 | " " |
| 1570 | 1470 | Edward, of Kilmallock. |
| | | Patrick, of Kilmallock. |
| 1578 | 3287 | Christopher. |
| 1583 | 4186 | Richard, Precentor of St Marys. Limerick. |
| 1597 | 6170 | Christopher FitzEdward of Co. Limerick |
| 1601 | 6569 | Anthony, of Tralee, Merchant. |

## Source:- Begley, Vol. 1, P. 317.

Nicholas fitzThomas Arthur = Katherine Skiddy.
B. circa 1405. of Cork.
1428, Captured by Pirates
1430, Ransom paid.
M. circa 1435
Issue 6 sons; 4 were Mayors, 1 was Bailiff and Thomas was a Bishop.
Buried in St. Marys.

Note: - Nicholas offered one of his daughters as a bride for the Archbishop's brother to marry if the Archbishop would arrange for Thomas to be appointed to a position in the Cathedral which would guarantee Thomas the Bishop's position when the old Bishop died. The offer must have been taken up as Thomas was ordained the next Bishop. Not much thought was given to the unfortunate young girl who was handed over to the Archbishop's brother who cannot have been anything but an old man of similar age to his unscrupulous sibling.

In an Inquisition taken in 1576, these Arthurs are mentioned,

Thomas, Recorder of Limerick
Myles. Merchant.
Richard FitzMiles, Merchant.

# ARTHUR FAMILY

By Noel Murphy

**In Dr Arthurs Fee Book.**

**Source:- Kilkenny Arch. Journal. 1867.**

| | |
|---|---|
| 1619 & 1622. | Richard FitzGeorge Arthur |
| 1619 & 1620 | Edward FitzGeorge |
| 1620 | Edward FitzGeorge Arthur's wife Catherine. |
| 1619 | Stephan Arthur's wife |
| 1619 | Andrew FitzWilliam Arthur |
| 1620 & 1623 | Daniel Og Arthur. |
| 1620 | Joanna FitzThomas |
| 1620 | Walter |
| 1621 | Hector |
| 1621 & 1623 | Patrick FitzRichard |
| 1622 | John FitzRichard |
| 1621 | Peter FitzChristopher |
| 1621 | Thomas FitzDominick |
| 1621 | Thomas FitzDominick's wife, Margaret. |
| 1621 | Oliver FitzRobert ****** |
| 1622 | Margaret FitzDaniel |
| 1623 | Joanna, widow of George Sexton. |

# Arthur

By Noel Murphy

**From various sources.**

Fiant 1470. Edward Arthur Merchant of Kilmallock, 26th Jan. 1570.N.S.
Patrick Arthur, same.

---

William Arthur = Beatrice Creagh

James Arthur.
B. 1587. Entered Salamanca to study for priesthood.

---

Nt. Mun. Antiq. Journal. T – Certs. Lenihan.

William Arthur = Anastacia Rice | David | John. | Walter Arthur
B. 1562 | B. 1570
M. 1587, 25 YRS. | M. 1587, 17 YRS.
D. 1622, 60 YRS. | D. 1640, 70 YRS.

*From Arthur Mss.*

******* Dr. Thomas Arthur = Christian. | Richard = Miss Arthur
B. 1593 | B. 1603
M.c. 1620
D. 1675 age 82.
Buried, Dublin.

Mary = Barth. Stackpool. | Anstace = Daniel Arthur. | Christian. | Dymphna
Eldest dau. B. 1619 | B. 1633 of Mungret | B. 1637
M. 1641. | M.c. 1645
D. by 1653.

---

Frost. A Thomas Arthur was deeded Doonbeg in Co. Clare, by the Earl of Thomond in 1622. Thomas died 25th. Mar. 1635.

---

C.S.P.I. 1608 - 10 Patrick Arthur, Mayor of Limerick died in office between 23rd. July and 4th Aug. 1609. (A Patrick Arthur's pension ceased at the same time. This pension was granted to Patrick for services rendered to the Lord President of Munster, Sir George Carew. This Patrick was arrested in Spain, accused of being a spy for Carew.)

---

Admiralty High Court. Patrick and Richard Arthur, Merchants of Limerick, were taken by English Pirates in 1598. they were on board the "Nicholas Bonaventure" sailing from Limerick to Lisbon.

---

Pac. Hib. Anthony Arthur, Merchant of Limerick, used Glyn Castle as a base to deal with the rebels in 1599.

Fiant. 6569. Anthony Arthur, Merchant of Tralee was pardoned in 1601.

# Arthur

By Noel Murphy

Source:- The Irish Ancestor, Vol viii, No. 1. 1976. P48.
Family Search, (in Brackets)

**The Will of Patrick FitzOliver Arthur. Dated 19 Feb 1652.**

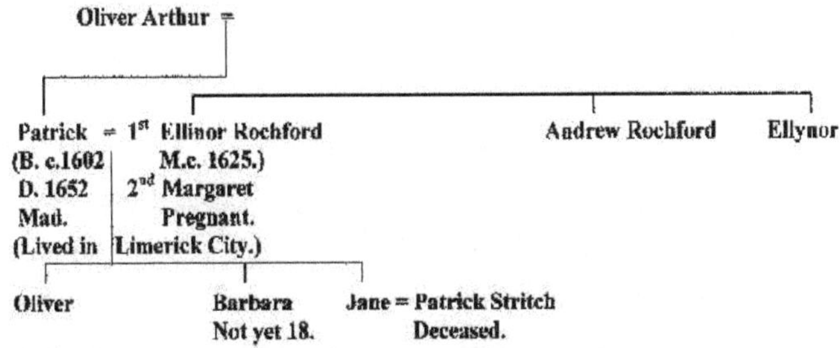


Also Mentions cousins Steven White and Francis Casey.

# Arthur

By Noel Murphy

## In Civil Survey.

| | |
|---|---|
| Dr. Thomas Arthur lived in a house beside Tom Cor's Castle in Irish Town. | |
| Its yearly value in 1640 was | £ 15-0-0 |
| He had a waste plot in Kilmallock worth | £ 0-5-0 |
| He also held Rochestown's 140 acres worth | £ 40-0-0 |
| The biggest land and property holder in the Arthur Family was Alderman Thomas Arthur who was recently deceased. His holdings in the city and in the Liberties were worth | £324-5-0. |
| The next biggest player was Nicholas FitzThomas holding property worth | £162-0-0 |
| Nicholas was son and Heir to Thomas above | |
| Piers Arthur had houses and gardens valued at | £ 37-0-0 |
| Walter Arthur, recently deceased, held a Mill and a stone house nearby worth | £ 40-0-0 |
| The Mill and house were on the North side of the Abbey river. | |
| George Arthur had a stone house valued at | £ 10-0-0 |
| William Arthur of Ballygrenane, recently deceased, held it and a share of Ballynantybeg. | £ 24-0-0 |
| In the North Liberties | |
| John Arthur held Ballyneclohy in the South Liberties worth | £ 40-0-0 |

## Transplanter Certificates. 1653.

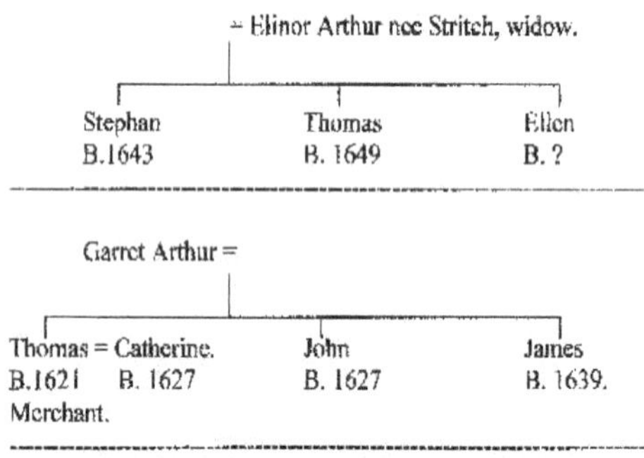

2

Pierce Arthur =

John Arthur = wife dead
B. 1617.

Patrick
B. 1648.

---

= Margaret, widow.

Pierce Arthur = Mary ( 2nd wife )
B.1613 B.1625.
Merchant.

Walter B. 1635 | Thomas B. 1636 | Jenny B. 1637 | Ellen ( by 2nd wife ) B. 1648.

---

Thomas Arthur = Catherine Woulfe, widow of Mr. Woulfe
B.1613 B. 1613

Thomas Woulfe.

---

*************

Dr. Thomas Arthur = Christian
B. 1593. B. 1603

Anstace B. 1633 | Christian, B. 1637 | Also Richard Arthur. ( Dr. Tom's brother ) B. 1613.

---

R.C.Simington's, *The Transplantation to Connacht* gives the names of four daughters of Alderman Thomas Arthur. Tom died shortly before 1653, the sisters were
*Katherine, Margaret, Mary and Jennet.*

Nicholas FitzThomas, who got land in Connought but for whom there is no Transplanter Cert., is most certainly the heir of Alderman Thomas, deceased and brother to the four girls above. Thomas was Recorder of Limerick from at least 1564 to 1584 and possibly longer. (Fiants)

The descent should be thus:-

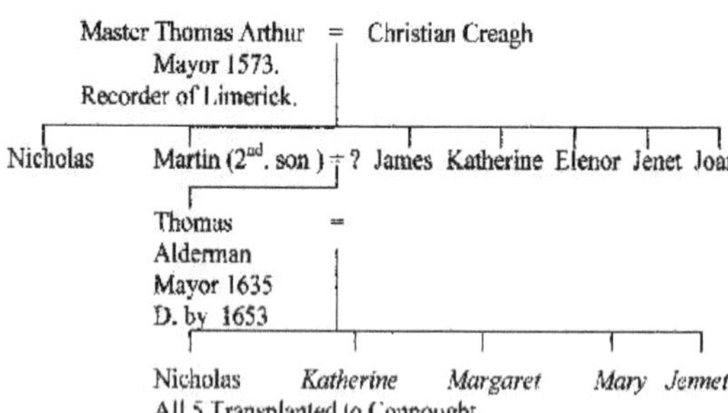


Ormond's list should be checked for claims by the Arthurs for restoration.

A Richard Arthur of Limerick left a will dated 1684.
A John fitz Pierse of Limerick left a will dated 1698

# Arthur Family

By Noel Murphy

| YEAR | MAYOR | BAILLIFF | NOTES |
|---|---|---|---|
| 1407 | | Thomas | |
| 1408 | | Thomas | |
| 1409 | | Thomas | |
| 1421 | Thomas | | |
| 1423 | | Richard | |
| 1426 | Thomas | | |
| 1431 | William | | |
| 1436 | Nicholas | | |
| 1440 | William | | |
| 1441 | William | | |
| 1442 | Nicholas | | |
| 1444 | Nicholas | | |
| 1445 | Richard | | |
| 1446 | Nicholas | | |
| 1449 | William | | |
| 1450 | Thomas | David | |
| 1451 | Richard | | |
| 1452 | Nicholas | | |
| 1454 | Nicholas | | |
| 1457 | Nicholas | | |
| 1458 | Nicholas | John | |
| 1460 | Richard | John | |
| 1462 | Nicholas FitzThomas | | |
| 1463 | Nicholas | Peter | |
| 1464 | Nicholas | John FitzWilliam | |
| 1466 | Thomas | | |
| 1467 | Thomas | Patrick | |
| 1469 | Thomas | Daniel | |
| 1471 | John | | |
| 1472 | Patrick | | |
| 1474 | John | | |
| 1475 | | Edmond | |
| 1476 | Patrick | Edward | |
| 1477 | | Edward | |
| 1478 | Thomas | | |
| 1479 | Thomas | | |
| 1480 | John | David | |
| 1481 | | Walter | |
| 1482 | David | | |
| 1483 | John FitzNicholas | | |
| 1486 | John | Myles | |
| 1487 | John | Myles | |
| 1489 | Thomas | Christopher | |

| | **MAYOR** | **BAILIFFS** |
|---|---|---|
| 1431 | William | |
| 1436 | Nicholas | |
| 1440 | William | |
| 1441 | William | |
| 1442 | Nicholas | |
| 1444 | Nicholas | |
| 1445 | Richard | |
| 1446 | Nicholas | |
| 1449 | William | |
| 1450 | Thomas | David |
| 1451 | Richard | |
| 1452 | Nicholas | |
| 1454 | Nicholas | |
| 1457 | Nicholas | |
| 1458 | Nicholas | John |
| 1460 | Richard | John |
| 1462 | Nicholas fitzThomas | |
| 1463 | Nicholas | Peter |
| 1464 | Nicholas | John fitzWilliam |
| 1466 | Thomas | |
| 1467 | Thomas | Patrick |
| 1469 | Thomas | Daniel |
| 1471 | John | |
| 1472 | Patrick | |
| 1474 | John | |
| 1475 | | Edmond |
| 1476 | Patrick | Edward |
| 1477 | | Edward |
| 1478 | Thomas | |
| 1479 | Thomas | |
| 1480 | John | David |
| 1481 | | George and Walter |
| 1482 | David | |
| 1483 | John fitzNicholas | |
| 1486 | John | Myles |
| 1487 | John | Myles |
| 1489 | Thomas | Christopher |
| 1490 | Patrick | |
| 1491 | | Christopher |
| 1494 | George fitzNicholas | |
| 1501 | Christopher | |

# ARTHUR FAMILY

By Noel Murphy

**In Dr Arthurs Fee Book.**

**Source:- Kilkenny Arch. Journal. 1867.**

| | |
|---|---|
| 1619 & 1622. | Richard FitzGeorge Arthur |
| 1619 & 1620 | Edward FitzGeorge |
| 1620 | Edward FitzGeorge Arthur's wife Catherine. |
| 1619 | Stephan Arthur's wife |
| 1619 | Andrew FitzWilliam Arthur |
| 1620 & 1623 | Daniel Og Arthur. |
| 1620 | Joanna FitzThomas |
| 1620 | Walter |
| 1621 | Hector |
| 1621 & 1623 | Patrick FitzRichard |
| 1622 | John FitzRichard |
| 1621 | Peter FitzChristopher |
| 1621 | Thomas FitzDominick |
| 1621 | Thomas FitzDominick's wife, Margaret. |
| 1621 | Oliver FitzRobert ****** |
| 1622 | Margaret FitzDaniel |
| 1623 | Joanna, widow of George Sexton. |

# Chapter 7

*Thomas Arthur (1593-1674)*

Thomas Arthur was one of the most eminent doctors of his time not just in Ireland but in Europe and below is told the story of the life of this amazing member of the Arthur family.

Thomas Arthur was a member of the eminent Arthur family of Limerick. He was the son of William Arthur a wealthy merchant and Anastasia Rice. William Arthur died in 1620 and as far as we know it was his wife Anastasia Rice who donated a chalice to the Franciscan Church in Limerick. This was done in her maiden name after the death of her husband. Maurice Lenihan makes the point that the practice of medicine was not prohibited to Catholics by the penal laws although the training in medicine in Ireland was banned was banned for Catholics. Now since most other professions were prohibited to them Catholics were often in the first rank of physicians and surgeons in Ireland at that time. However since Catholics were not allowed at this time to study physic (medicine) here in Ireland Thomas Arthur studied arts in Bordeaux and then medicine in Paris. He took his doctorate in Rheims after which he returned to Limerick where he commenced practice in 1619.

He was a meticulous note-keeper, recording all kinds of autobiographical details e.g. family genealogy, and various interesting facts relating to life in the city of Limerick. He kept strict accounts, keeping notes of all financial details of his practice and his dealings in money and property. This manuscript is known as the Arthur Manuscript and it is written partly in English and partly in what Lenihan termed "contracted Latin". It is quoted on many occasions and at length in Lenihan's History of Limerick. Lenihan originally owned Thomas Arthur's manuscript, but when he fell on hard times when he sold the manuscript to the British Museum who later gave it to the British Library which is where it now is.

The first case recorded concerns a gentleman with venereal disease. This does not cause any great difficulty in translation. "Charolus Bourk, a gonorrhoea simplici liberatus, dedit mihi pro-honorario, 20th May 1619, £2". It is interesting that Widdess quotes a French visitor, Le Gouze, who noted, "there are a large number of profligate women in the city, which I would not have expected on account of the climate"! Now why would the climate have had an effect on the number of profligate women in the city of Limerick I do not know? Did he think that this only occurred in places with warmer climates or possibly just in France.

Shortly afterwards Thomas relieved a lady of breathlessness and he cured the son of a Peter Stacpoole of an obstructive liver problem. He relieved a certain Nicholas Cromwell from pleurisy and after this he had a major diagnostic triumph, which was to boost his practice considerably. A lady named Anna Gould, who was aged over 50 at the time, and living with her second husband, consulted him. She had always been barren and she consulted Dr. Arthur for abdominal swelling and discomfort. Dr. Arthur says that as she had the usual signs of pregnancy he predicted that she was expecting a child. However, "some senior doctors in whom she had more faith" disagreed with him and prescribed an offensive mercuric compound, which eventually killed her in the eighth month of her pregnancy. Arthur relates that he dissected the dead lady's uterus and extracted a female child which proved his assertion. He records that this case brought him "no minima laudem".

Naturally his name spread, and by the end of the year he had treated several of Limerick's most distinguished citizens including Donough O'Brien, the 4th Earl of Thomond, and George Sexton, who owned extensive estates in the neighborhood. He actually accompanied Donough O'Brien on a trip to Dublin and collected a large fee for doing this.

Early in 1620 there is the following entry: "The amount of my fees for this year past is £74. 2s 8d, for which, and other gifts conferred upon me am unworthy, I return boundless thanks to the Almighty God who had deigned to bless the beginnings of my medical practice".

Encouraged by his success, he embarked on the building of a large stone house in Mungret Street, which took a considerable time to complete. By now he had begun to achieve national as well as local acceptance, and from then on he traveled widely and his practice included a large number of titled persons.

On 3 May 1620 he was called to Dublin to treat a gentleman for gonorrhea, who being "thoroughly cured, gave him a horse valued at £8 as well as £5 in gold" (a lot of money in those days). Lady Chichester, Sir Randall McSaurley, and the Protestant Bishop of Killaloe were also listed as needing his services. Incidentally, he always referred to a Protestant bishop as a "Pseudo Episcobus".

In November 1620 he records in the manuscript that he attended a "Thadeaus Derleo qui asumpta infusione emetica vitri antimony tineam trigeinta pedas longa per alva deiecit quibus dudu cruciabutur", to whom he gave a strong emetic dose of antimony. Thomas Derleo passed a worm 30ft long which had crucified him for some time and for this he received a fee of £1.

The turning point of his career occurred in March 1625, when he was asked to go to Drogheda to see Archbishop James Usher who was the Archbishop of Armagh and Primate of All Ireland (Pseudo Primatus). The era was not known for ecumenism, and Usher, in public at any rate, was an extreme opponent of Catholicism. However, as J. B. Lyons has said, "The most rigid sectarian barrier can be breached by an effective therapist" (*Brief Lives of Irish Doctors*, p. 32). Still it is a remarkable tribute to Thomas' reputation that Usher asked for a Catholic doctor to come to him and trusted him to look after his health when you take into account his well-known anti Catholic stance.

The ensuing drama was a complete triumph for the Limerick doctor, and it is a superb tale. Usher had developed a serious illness in England and had been treated by many doctors including the Royal physicians at very great expense. Now we will let Thomas himself carry on the story: "Having heard his statement and weighed the options of the eminent physicians, I seriously studied the symptoms, which arose throughout the whole history of the disease. From these I thought I had explained the cause of this doubtful disease which every day grew worse, and which had hitherto escaped the observation of several eminent men. When I was sensible I had perfectly ascertained, after making an experiment to try my conjecture, I was confident that I could cure him; nor did my hopes deceive me. The cure of this disease, which baffled the physicians of England, Royal and most eminent, made me famous and acceptable among the English to whom I had been hateful". He had of course been hateful to them because of his religion.

After this it was becoming clear to the people of his time that Thomas was indeed one of the foremost physicians of his time not just in Ireland but anywhere in Western Europe.

As a result of this spectacular success he was entertained by the Viceroy, Lord Falkland, who in the words of Thomas "inquired about the history of the whole disease and in what points the Royal doctors had been mistaken. He then appointed me physician both to himself and to his nearest and dearest". As a result of this meeting Thomas Arthur was appointed doctor to the vice regal household.

Around 1630 Thomas felt it would be more profitable for him to move to Dublin, where he stayed for the next ten or eleven years. His practice flourished in the capital and his fee book contained notes on members of the Usher family, Sir James Weir, Thomas Luttrel of Luttrelstown, the Countess of Fingal and other notables.

In 1633 he was called to see Sir Basil Brooke it was a grim attendance the story of which is worth telling. Sir

Basil Brooke of Ulster was afflicted with a severe blockage of the neck of his bladder by a thick fluid, some unwise doctor had prescribed cantharides (sometimes known as Spanish fly). This putrid prescription had caused a most painful and malignant inflammation of the neck of his bladder and destroyed the whole penile duct. He had a fever and intolerable pain. Thomas saw him on 24 July and gave a prognosis of impending death. He urged him to put his finances in order and attend to his spiritual affairs and then he left him.

By 1640 the political climate had changed. Falkland, who had appointed Arthur as doctor to his own household, followed a policy of "connived indulgence" with regard to the penal laws (he did not enforce them with any great diligence). Wentworth, whom Thomas described as "a grim visaged Satan", then replaced him. Even though it would mean a reduction of income he felt he would be safer in Limerick, and he returned there to continue his practice.

In 1651 the parliamentary forces under Ireton besieged Limerick and after the city fell Thomas was probably imprisoned briefly as well as losing all his properties. He bitterly recalls that he had to pay a fine of £172 as well as losing all he had. Much of his lands and properties that were seized at this time were returned after the restoration. He partly offset this reduction of his assets by treating some British officers who had been bombarding him a short time previously, and his journal records attendances to Colonel Ingoldsby, Major Maye and other military worthies.

Among those successfully treated by Thomas after the capitulation of Limerick was Dr. Credanus, who was severely injured by a shell during the siege, and Dominick Fitz David Rice, one of the outstanding defenders of the city had to have a leg amputated. These were two special cases which illustrate Thomas' surgical skills.

After the Cromwellian victory, about two dozen people were executed, including six army personnel, four priests and the Bishops of Limerick and Emly. One doctor, a Dr. Higgins, was on this list and Thomas may have been fortunate to escape with his life. Subsequently, he continued to practice as a doctor until 1666 and he died in 1675.

Thomas Arthur was a difficult man to understand for people of our time as he seems to have been simultaneously an Englishman and an Irish man in his own mind. He seems to have been particularly well disposed towards the Duke of Ormond who was the leader of the Royalists in Ireland. The Duke of Ormond was a man whom most Irish at the time did not trust as he seemed disinclined to fight the parliamentarians despite repeated guarantees that he would do so (It should be noted here that Ormond was in command of a large army at that time and this force did very little fighting against the Cromwellian forces when they arrived here). Because Thomas was a Catholic who seemed to favor the English side he was placed under a ban of excommunication. However after King Charles II was restored to his throne Thomas sent a petition along with other Catholic renegades (those who had not opposed English rule who were nevertheless dispossessed and sent to Clare and

Galway) to King Charles II and he had some of his lands and properties restored to him. He was at times referred to as a castle Catholic. But he was a supreme diplomat as well so when Father Scarampi the Papal Legate was refused permission to enter the city by the then Mayor who feared the Legates presence might cause a popular uprising. As a result of this refusal to allow the legate permission to enter Bishop Arthur placed the Mayor and his followers under interdict for the affront they had offered to the representative of the Holy See. It was Thomas Arthur who was employed by the Mayor and the corporation to draw up a humble letter of apology. This illustrates how torn between both sides the people of Limerick were. It is clear that many of the leading citizens did not want to oppose Cromwell and Thomas seemed to be one of those who did not want to oppose Cromwell.

It should be noted that I have reproduced the language in which the will was written and I know it can be a little difficult to follow and understand at times but this was the legal language of the day which does not seem to have changed very much in the meantime.

**Here is a copy of the will of Thomas Arthur.**

*PREROGATIVE WILL: THOMAS ARTHUR M.D. 1674.*

Thomas Arthur Doctor of Physic. I appoint my wife Christian Arthur sole executrix. I bequeath unto said wife all my lands of Tullaghedy containing two ploughs in Ormond (a plough was the amount of land a man with a horse and plough could plough in one day) in the county of Tipperary and the lands of Mayne Co. Galway and all other lands in said county of Galway now in lease to Henry Davis and enjoyed by him and his assigns by virtue thereof for several years past. To hold the same to said Christian for and during her life and after her decease to her admons or executors for the space of two years immediately following her death the lands in Tipperary and Galway I have already by deed executed conveyed to the use of said Christian for he jointure during her life. I also bequeath and devise to my wife Christian Arthur all the benefit and advantage, which I have or may expect in any lots tenements and heredits by virtue of any clause or provision to Act of Settlement or Explanation in my behalf as nominee, or otherwise the same to be held by said Christian during her life.

To my brother Richard Arthur £6 annually. I remit and release to my son in law Nicholas Comyn whatever debts are due to me by him by bond or otherwise. I further bequeath to my daughter Christian wife of said Nicholas the moiety of Newtown in Co. Carlow and debt and mortgage thereof due from the Duke of Ormond. Whereas I owed unto my son in law Daniel Arthur (the banker) the sum of £100, which remained of my daughter Anastace Arthur his wife's portion to which sum I paid by order for said Daniel unto John Arthur of Dublin deceased my son in law and took his bond for the same I do hereby appoint my executors to deliver said bond to said Daniel Arthur. To grandchildren the younger Elinor Arthur and Anastace Arthur children of said Daniel Arthur my son and of my daughter Anastace deed the other moiety of said debt and mortgage of Newtown due from the Duke of Ormond to my wife all other goods and chattels.

Signed: Thomas Arthur 31[st] December 1674.

*Hen. Lynch J Fitzgerald, Matthew Nangle, William James Der Donnelly, Francis Lange.*

*A Codicil to his will.*

My further will is that William Arthur Fitz John of Dublin in case he be living be my heir and that after the death of my wife and executrix and after the time before my last will limited to hold and enjoy all of my state of inheritance within this kingdom of Ireland to him the said William Arthur and the heirs male of his body and for want of such heirs said estate of inheritance shall descend to my grandson Thomas Arthur Fitz John and his heirs male and for want of such heirs to my grandson Daniel Arthur Fitz Daniel son to my daughter Anastace Arthur deed and his heirs male and for want of such heirs.

To Thomas Arthur (his nephew) of Limerick doctor of Physic and his heirs male and for want of such heirs my said estate of Inheritance shall descend and come to the right heirs of me the said Thomas Arthur Fitz William and their heirs forever and do declare for the several injuries done unto me by my son John Arthur and Demphna his wife and her disrespect unto me that I was intended not to transfer any of my estate upon their issue but by the earnest entreaty of my now wife Christian I have been induced to make their provision for them I will that my will be recommended as my last will and request to favor and kindness of the Rt. Honorable the Countess of Mount Alexander doubting not but she will answer her in all her just demands and reasonable desires.

Dated 2nd January 1674.
Proved 27th January 1674 by Christian Arthur widow and sole executrix.

As you can see from reading this will Thomas held lands in many different areas of the country and so must have been well off.

# Chapter 8

*Daniel and Robert Arthur*

It seems to me that during their own times members of the Arthur family were driven to excel in whatever field they chose in whatever place they made their home and this was certainly true in the case of the members of the Arthur family discussed in this chapter.

## Daniel Arthur 1620- 1705

Sir Daniel Arthur was born in Limerick circa 1620 and he died in Paris in 1705. He was a talented and well-connected banker on the continent and even in England. His role in Ireland was very pronounced as the forces of King William of Orange dealt with King James II who was the Catholic claimant to the British throne. During the siege of Limerick with many Irish Catholic landlords trying to preserve as much of their wealth as they could, Daniel Arthur was *"found to have 2 million livres of their wealth in his possession"*, according to a French commander at the siege, the Marquis d'Albyville.

The Treaty of Limerick spurred the emigration of Catholic landowners and soldiers who came to form a majority (some 60% of the total, according to Nathalie Genet-Rouffiac) of the Jacobite population that settled around the court of James II in the old castle of Saint Germain-en-Laye outside Paris. Daniel Arthur who was knighted by James in 1690 was already well established in Paris by this time, having been exiled there in 1679. He had been implicated in the obscure 'Popish plot', also called 'Oates plot' (the plot was fictitious) against King Charles II. He settled first in Rue Mauconseil (1st arrondissement) and from then until his death he was close by in the rue du Petit Lion (now called the rue Tiquetonne in the 2nd arrondissement). As further proof of Sir Daniel's close connections with the court in Saint Germain-en-Laye, two of his daughters married Jacobite officers. One of these officers Patrice Fitzgerald was the son of Richard Fitzgerald of Waterford and he was staying at the Hôtel de la Rivière in the Rue Aux Ours (3rd arrondissement) at the time of his marriage to Sir Daniel's daughter Elizabeth, in January 1704.

The English and Irish Jacobite's were only too happy to leave their financial affairs to Daniel Arthur and a small number of Irish bankers like him, including one Richard Cantillon who was an uncle of the Richard Cantillon discussed elsewhere in this book in another chapter. But Daniel Arthur was possibly the most successful and influential of all these bankers at that time with a client list that extended to the extensive and wealthy Irish merchant community established on France's western seaboard.

In spite of his deep Jacobite connections, he was able to maintain a banking house in London that was run by one of his sons. This cross-Channel network enabled the Arthur's *Père ET Fils,* to run a money transfer operation between Great Britain and the continent for wealthy British travelers. Another relative of Daniel Arthur, Francis Arthur, ran the Arthur & Crean bank in Madrid, ensuring that the British government turned to the Arthur family when they needed to funnel money to British prisoners of war in Spain who were captured during the War of The Spanish Succession. According to the

*Dictionary of Irish Biography*, "*All his employees in Paris were from the same part of Ireland as himself, particularly Limerick and Kerry*". One of these employees, Edmond Loftus, subsequently turns up as a banker in his own right at rue Quincampoix ($3^{rd}$/$4^{th}$ arrondissements). The Cantillon to whom Daniel Arthur was related also belonged to this Kerry/Limerick mafia.

Not surprisingly, both Richard Cantillon's were given a helping hand in their banking career by Daniel Arthur's circle. The older *chevalier* Richard Cantillon ending up as banker to the British ambassador in Paris and the younger Richard becoming a conduit for the money sent to Spain for British prisoners held there during the War of the Spanish Succession.

Sir Daniel Arthur's son by his second marriage, Daniel 'Mannock' Arthur continued as a banker in Paris after his father's death in 1705 at first out of rue Saint Denis (1st/2nd arrondissements), and then out of his father's premises old in the Rue Du Petit Lion. After a dispute over his father's inheritance was decided against Daniel 'Mannock' Arthur and in favor of another son, Daniel 'Smith' Arthur, the latter settled in Paris and took over the family business in 1713.

Daniel 'Smith' Arthur established a premises first at Rue de la Chanvrerie (absorbed by a section of the modern-day rue Rambuteau in the first arrondissement) and then (in 1715) in Rue des Vieilles Etuves (now Rue Sauval, $1^{st}$ arrondissement). But the Arthur banking empire went into decline after Sir Daniel's death, with most of Daniel Arthur's clients turning to the talented Richard Cantillon the younger.

Daniel 'Mannock' Arthur was a keen art collector, building up a substantial collection before his death in Spain. Mannock's collection which included paintings by Van Dyke, Michelangelo, Tinteretto, Veronese and Titian was left to his wife, who then married a Mr. Bagnall. The collection was subsequently sold to King George II and now forms part of the Royal Collection in Windsor.

Daniel Arthur was responsible for getting the wealth of those who fought for King James out of Ireland after the fall of Limerick. These people who went mostly to France to be with King James were very wealthy and while there are various estimates of how much of the wealth of Ireland went with them it is likely that as much as half left the country at this time sending the country into an economic decline which took over a century to begin to recover from. Indeed there is a case to be made that it was only in the 1960's that Ireland finally begun to recover from this mass exodus of its wealth and real economic growth begun again.

## Robert Arthur 1761 – 1794

Now I will move on to tell the story of another remarkable member of the Arthur who rose to prominence in another country i.e. France and this member of our family was to be one of the leading lights in the French Revolution yet outside of France most people have never heard of him. The man of whom I speak is of course Robert Arthur.

Robert Arthur's father was a watchmaker from Limerick who moved to Paris to make a living and Robert was born in Paris in 1761.

Robert amassed a considerable fortune in the paper making business and in Paris he was better known as Jean Jacques Arthur because he was known to idolize Jean Jacques Rousseau. (A namesake of his Captain Robert Arthur was promoted to the rank of Colonel on the battlefield of Laffelt where the Irish Brigade had distinguished itself).

Robert Arthur going to the guillotine.

Robert became deeply immersed in the boiling politics leading up to the French Revolution and in the reign of terror afterwards. He became a very close friend of Robespierre, so much so that he became known as the "Little Robespierre". He was a true idealist because he was a wealthy man who had nothing to gain from the revolution yet he was one of the most ardent supporters of the revolution. In fact it could be said that he had everything that a man could wish for, a beautiful estate outside Paris, a prosperous business employing more than 200 people and above all youth and good health.

The Club of the Jacobean's was the home of all the revolutionary enthusiasts, especially those who were attached to Robespierre. It was here that the burning questions of the day were argued and Robert Arthur took part in the debates there. His activities however were not just confined to the more academic discussions as he was one of the moving spirits of the Revolutionary Committee de Place Vendome, the district in Paris where he lived. Robert was a leading member of the mob that helped in the sack of the Tuileries.

There is a story that was part of Limerick lore which says that Robert rescued a young student called Patrick Hogan from a murderous mob at the Irish College in Paris during the reign of terror. This Hogan was afterwards parish priest of St. Michael’s in Limerick and he died in 1839. By a curious coincidence, the only two memorials in St. Michael's were to Patrick Hogan and Patrick Arthur.

The Insurrectionist Commune became the real ruler of the France which was established on the ruins of Royalty. This Commune undertook to guard the King and his family while they were prisoners. Robert Arthur was a member of this new body and as such was one of the 12 commissioners selected from its number to carry out this task. Shortly after assuming the duties of his office he accused one of his colleagues of having secret interviews with the queen.

His uncompromising attachment to the principles of the Revolution earned him the title of” Little Robespierre” from his enemies. He denounced vigorously the speculators who were smelting money for its copper and he attacked Pitt's English agents who were hatching schemes to slaughter cows and sheep in order to starve France.

At this time too when Royalist intriguers and anti-revolutionaries were lurking in large numbers in Paris a decree was pronounced by him that compelled all citizen householders to affix on the door of their residence the names, ages and occupations of everybody who was living there.

Spring 1793 saw the death struggle between the two political factions the Gironde and the Mountain growing more intense. The crisis was reached with the insurrection of June 2nd 1793 when the former went under and twenty two of its deputies who included the most illustrious of the National Convention were proscribed by that body under the influence of the Commune. Included in the 22 was the minister of finance Clavierre whom Robert Arthur had long been attacking. The patriots of the Place Vendome Revolutionary Committee placed him under arrest, but it was not until six months later that his trial before the Revolutionary Tribunal began.

On the eve of that event he was handed a list of witnesses who were to give evidence against him, and on finding Robert's name among them, he quietly retired to his cell and committed suicide. Clavierre's fellow prisoner Reouffe tells the story in his memoirs and describes Robert Arthur as a "foreigner who became a member of the Commune, and was more factious and blood-thirsty than Herbert and Chanmette

Robert was one of the witnesses listed to swear against Danton at his trial, but in the course of the proceedings he was informed that the jury had quite enough evidence.

Robert Arthur, who was very successful in business, owned a beautiful chateau and park outside Paris. Robespierre was often a guest there and to him Robert was most affectionately attached.

After the arrest of his idol Robespierre, Robert Arthur signed his own death warrant when he put his name to the proclamation calling on the people to rise in defense of their leader. There was no response to this call and he was arrested for his action. On 30th July 1794 Robert Arthur was executed on the guillotine two days after Robespierre,

## Members of the Arthur family who fought for King James II.

This is an account of Mayor Thomas Arthur and the Irish officers named Arthur who served in the army of King James who fought at the siege of Derry and at the battle of Aughrim.

> In King James' charter to Limerick in 1689 Nicholas Arthur was named one of the Aldermen while James Arthur and Thomas Arthur were Burgesses and this Thomas would appear to have been Mayor Thomas Arthur. At the parliament in Dublin in 1689 he sat as one of its representatives for the Borough of Newcastle, Co. Dublin. An early

> notice of this Thomas appears in the "Correspondence of the Earl of Clarendon" 6th May 1686. When writing to the Earl of Sunderland he recommends, "Captain Thomas Arthur a Roman Catholic who lately brought the employment (in those days if you were wealthy you could but yourself promotion in the British army, promotion was rarely on merit but rather on who your family were and could they afford to buy you a promotion). So Captain Thomas Arthur became a Lieutenant Colonel of the guards by purchasing the promotion".

Early in September of that year he was sent to Connaught to raise recruits, but not having the Earl of Clarendon's written order he was recalled.

Apart from Thomas Arthur there were other members of the Arthur family in this regiment, Captain John Arthur, Ensign Edward Arthur and Ensign John Arthur. There was also a Captain Patrick Arthur in Major General Boislean's infantry. One of these Captain Arthur's was wounded at the siege of Derry while Major Thomas Arthur fell at the Battle of the Boyne. Dean Story in his "Imperial History Vol 2 page 138 records the death of a Colonel Arthur at the Battle of Aughrim. This Colonel Arthur was married to a niece of Richard, Earl of Tyrconnell" Another Irish officer who was recorded as a prisoner and who died of his wounds at Aughrim was a Major Arthur. The Arthur's mentioned above belonged to the Kings Regiment of Infantry. The above is taken from "King James' Army List 1689" by John D'Alton.

Lieutenant Robert Arthur of Hackett's Town Co. Dublin is also recorded as being an officer in the Army of King James.

There was a Patrick Arthur who was one of the Aid de Camp's to Patrick Sarsfield and it is likely that this Patrick Arthur is the Captain Patrick Arthur in Major General Boislean's infantry. While difficult to prove this Patrick Arthur was most likely the Grandfather of the Patrick Arthur who along with his son was to build Arthur's Quay. This Patrick Arthur is recorded in in a genealogy that is in the possession of the Ryan family of Limerick.

# Chapter 9

*The Arthur family of Limerick in the Eighteenth Century*

From the first member of the Arthur family to be mayor of Limerick until Patrick Arthur finished his term in 1648 as the last member of the Arthur family to hold the mayoral chair in Limerick a period of 478 years passed. The Arthur family together with a small number of other Limerick merchant families were the rulers and prince merchants of Limerick. After this the penal laws begun to come into force and the Arthur family paid a terrible price for the majority of them remaining Catholic as they began to have their lands and properties confiscated.

You may remember that Abbess Margaret Arthur and her family left Limerick for France in 1690 and that she died there in 1743. However the last member of the Arthur family to be buried in St. Mary's Cathedral was Thomas Arthur who was interred there in the year 1729. The Arthur family had a right to be buried in St. Mary's and most of them were but after it became a Protestant cathedral this ceased. A monument was erected above the family grave in the Arthur chapel in the Cathedral.

In a will dated 1765 made by a Thomas Arthur his brother is mentioned as living in Mungret Street and the garden of his house was said to run to the city walls. Thomas was a brewer by profession and his uncle was a Patrick Arthur.

There is a record of a marriage agreement between William Arthur of Limerick (ancestor of Ennistymon Arthur's) and Margaret Considine of Ennis, in this agreement there is a mention of a Joseph Arthur, this Joseph seems to have been either an Uncle or a great uncle of William Arthur who was a merchant in Limerick.

In a will dated 1765 a Joseph Arthur is mentioned, this Joseph had three sons named John, Martin and Thomas. Joseph's sisters were Anstorce and Mary. Mary Arthur married David Callinane and both he and Joseph Arthur were executors to the will of Thomas Arthur. Thomas, Andrew and John were the sons of David Callinane and Mary Arthur.

A daughter of Patrick Arthur was married to the brother of Very Rev. Thady Lynch who was most probably P.P. of St. Michael's. Ellen the daughter of Patrick Arthur was buried in the graveyard of St. Michael's in a tomb near one of the walls. The inscription on the tomb reads, "Here lies the body of Ellen Arthur and her niece Elizabeth Lynch, July 9th 1805".

Now perhaps it is time to talk about one of the most famous Arthur's I speak of course of Patrick Arthur 1717 – 1799 (Also known as **Patt Arthur** of Limerick).

## Patrick Arthur 1717 – 1799

It seems possible that the Patrick Arthur whose will is set out below was the great grandfather of the man I refer to as Patrick Arthur of Limerick. His son also called Patrick is known to have lived in Limerick city at that time. It would seem that he was the Patrick Arthur who was an Aide De Camp to Patrick Sarsfield one of a number who served Patrick Sarsfield in this position (this information came from a genealogy in possession of the Quain/Ryan family). It is known that Patrick lived on lands at Cluananna that were later known to be in the possession of Francis Arthur, Patt Arthur's son.

There is no documentary evidence to prove this beyond a reasonable doubt however there is a lot of circumstantial evidence. It is definite that other members of the family also had land in that area where they built their summer houses and one of these is still lived in today (not by a member of the Arthur family I hasten to add, I was asked not to publish a photo of the house to preserve the anonymity of the family living there now) although it has had its second story removed and is now a single story house looking out on to the Shannon river, this house was in the possession of Thomas Arthur who bought the lands at Glenomera. There are a number of other houses in the area now sadly in ruins that were the summer residences of the merchant families of Limerick. The merchants of Limerick built houses on the banks of the Shannon outside the city in the late 1600's and early 1700's. These were the places they would escape to during the summer to escape the heat and smells of the city which the summer heat accentuated.

Below I have transcribed the will of Patrick Arthur of Cluananna (the spelling of this place name seems to have been a little flexible) and once again the language may seem a little old fashioned but that is the language of the will.

**Prerogative Will of Patrick Arthur of Cluananna:**
Will made 25$^{th}$ June, 1675; Codicil 29$^{th}$ June, 1675. Proved 27$^{th}$ Nov 1675.

Patrick Arthur of Cluananna, Co. Limerick, gent, to be buried in St. Francis Abbey in Adare, son Patrick Arthur; unmarried daughters, Margaret and Catherine; son-in-law Daniel O'Brien; son-in-law, William Lysaght; mortgage of Cluananna to son-in-law, Wm. Lysaght, as trustee for testator; sister Elinor Lysaght, alias Arthur; cousin, Dr. Thomas Fitzpatrick Arthur (nephew of the Dr. Arthur spoken about earlier); brother-in-law, John Sexton; brother-in-law, David Cantillon; nephew, Philip Cantillon; brother, Daniel Arthur of London (this Daniel Arthur was the banker mentioned in the previous chapter)

| | |
|---|---|
| Executors | Daniel Arthur of London brother<br>Patrick Arthur of Limerick cousin<br>Philip Cantillon nephew |
| Overseers | David Cantillon brother-in-law<br>Dr. Thomas Fitzpatrick Arthur cousin |
| Witnesses | William Lysaght, Jn. Sexton, Thomas Arthur, Laur Creagh |

(The names above are all from the great families of the city at that time)

Codicil, 29th June, 1675: Kilderry, Kilkerily and Boherown in Small County and Pobblebrien baronies in Limerick County to nephew, Philip Cantillon.

Witnesses: John Lysaght, Christopher Lysaght, Dan Brien. Probate to Patrick Arthur and Philip Cantillon's, saving right of 3rd Executor.

The above is extracted from the Prerogative Will cited, and indicates the sort of information in regard to the relationship existing between the people in whom we are interested which can be elicited from such a source.

Richard Cantillon to the left with Mary Anne O'Mahony his wife to right.

The Cantillon's mentioned in the will were the nephews of Richard Cantillon the banker and merchant in Paris and London. Richard's nephew also called Richard Cantillon was the first man to write a proper thesis on national economics as we now understand the subject so you could say that he was the father of modern economics. He was in effect the first monetarist. His treatise was written in French and was only published many years after his death. There have been many questions asked about what happened his treatise between his death and the time it was published many years later, It seems that it was available to a number of people who based their writings and ideas on Richard's ground-breaking work. His work was paid attention to because he predicted the collapse of the Mississippi company (In 1716, the French government granted John Law permission to found the *Banque Générale* and virtual monopoly over the right to develop French territories in North America, named the Mississippi Company. In return, Law promised the French government to finance its debt at low rates of interest. Law began a financial speculative bubble by selling shares of the Mississippi Company, using the *Banque Générale*'s virtual monopoly on the issue of bank notes to finance his investors. In this John Law was working in co-operation with Richard Cantillon) even though he was one of the original promoters of the project he could see that it would collapse and sold his shares when they were at their height and made a fortune although this did annoy many of the investors as they had borrowed from him to buy their shares and when it collapsed they owed Richard a fortune with many of them thinking that he in some way cheated them Their own greed had cheated them.) One of the Cantillon's mentioned in the will was Philip who was a nephew of Patrick Arthur his son also called Philip lived in London and he published a work based on Richards work before the original was published but it lacked Richard's insight into how economics worked especially under the monetarist system. While we cannot be certain it does seem probable that Philip of London was in possession of Richard Cantillon's original manuscript when he was writing his as the similarities between the two works are too close to be coincidental. What does come across however is that Philip did not fully understand the thinking of his uncle from the way he interpreted Richard's writings and so his publication was totally lacking in any real insight. Philip's work was published well before Richard's which again raises the question of where he got his information and was he trying to hide Richards work and gain recognition for himself for his uncle's work, or was he in effect trying to pass off Richards work as his own.There were a couple of other publications around that time on economics that were published before Richards was and they seem to have drawn inspiration from Richards work so it seems likely that somebody must have had access to Richards original manuscript.

In 1653 after Cromwell's victory in Ireland the Arthur's of Limerick had all their estates and worldly wealth confiscated and they were banished to Co. Clare. They were dispossessed because they refused to convert to the protestant faith and they were banished to Co. Clare where they were given new lands etc. in lieu of those confiscated. The new properties were given to them because most of them had not as Cromwell saw it backed the rebels. Those who had backed the rebels lost everything and were not compensated. It seems likely that in spite of Cromwell's efforts to banish the Arthur family from Limerick some of them must have remained in the city or returned to the city soon after they were banished.

Thus it was that in the year 1717 to the best of our knowledge Patrick Arthur was born in the city. I have been able to find no information about his early years but it seems probable that his family were well to do as it would have been very difficult for him to have gone on to do all the things he did if he had to build up his fortune from scratch. It is certain that he was a very wealthy man indeed when he died in 1799.

After the Williamaite siege of 1691 when conditions returned to normal, it was agreed that the City Wall of Irishtown, which ran along the east side of Michael Street behind the present town hall and down to the river, should be pulled down. This opened up the slob land that was there on which there were very few buildings however this land was subject to flooding when the Shannon overflowed and so that would have to be dealt with before the lands could be developed. The walls were finally demolished in the 1760's.It would seem that the first family to move out to develop this new land was the Roche family but they were closely followed by the Arthur family i.e. Patrick Arthur who was soon to be joined in the enterprise by his son Francis. It is likely that Patrick bought the land he was to develop from the Roche family.

Patrick Street Limerick

St. Mary's Church Limerick.

Patrick and his son Francis were very quick to take advantage of this development opportunity and they acquired much of the slob land. They built a quay for the dual purpose of carrying out this development scheme and the berthing of their ships. Among the numerous different businesses they were involved in they were timber merchants based in Denmark Street and this business required ships and a quay to berth them at.

When the old mediaeval city walls were pulled down in the 1760s, work began on expanding and building Georgian Limerick, and the Arthur family played an important role in the early development of the new town.

Patrick Arthur built Arthur's Quay in 1773 to provide

harbour facilities for his timber ships. His son and business partner, Francis Arthur, became involved in property development and financed the building of triangular block of Georgian terraced houses on the site now occupied by the Arthurs Quay Shopping Centre.

A house built by Patrick Arthur around 1780
The shop front was added in the 1890's.

Whether intentional or not, this triangular block was in the shape of the letter A for Arthur, so that the Arthur family could be said to have left a permanent mark on the shape of Limerick's streetscape. There is no documentary evidence that I have seen to say that the streets were deliberately laid out in the shape of the letter A but to me it seems unlikely that it was an accident.

The housing development was completed by 1791, and the houses were rented out or let, with the terraces becoming the homes of many comfortable merchant, professional and middle class families.

One of the main reasons why they were happy to develop this slob land was because it was outside the old city walls and because of this they were not subject to the same taxes they would have been subject to if they had built within the old city walls. So it was much less expensive for them to develop this land than to develop an area that had been inside the old city walls.

They laid out streets and lanes' starting in the 1770's which they named them after themselves e.g. Patrick Street, Francis Street and Ellen Street. Francis his son was his partner in all his enterprises and Ellen was Ellen Sexton the first wife of Francis. The fine row of residential houses Patrick Arthur had erected along the quay facing the river were very prominent. These houses quickly became the popular residences of the elite and wealthy of both the English and Irish towns of Limerick.

The position was superb, looking out on the river Shannon, which when the tide was in looked like a beautiful lake or when the tide was out there was the musical roar of the Curraghgower Falls. The quay itself was enlivened with sailing ships coming and going. Across the river (remember there were no rows of houses on the Clare side at that time) the view stretched away over woods and hills to the beautiful old mansion of the Arthur's at Glenomera which was backed by the Broadford hills and the great horseshoe forest reaching nearly to the mountain top.

Patrick and Francis built the houses to get the full benefit of the afternoon sun and when they were viewed from the Clare side on a summer afternoon the houses presented a fiery red no artist could do full justice to.

The houses that Patrick and Francis built were tall, narrow with stately hall doors and of Spartan simplicity. It is thought that the Arthur family was the only one to build this style of house and so their houses were somewhat different to the other Georgian houses being built in Ireland at that time. It has been noted that the three streets built by the Arthur family seem to be laid out to form the letter A but nobody knows for sure if this was deliberate of an accident. Note the photo on the front cover of this book with the streets apparently laid out in a letter A.

Until he built the new houses Patrick had lived in a house in Nicolas Street which was very similar to the new houses that he built so this may have been the inspiration for the new houses that he was building. Patrick moved to a house he built on the quay at the corner of Francis Street where he remained for the rest of his life.

Arthur's Quay in 1870's.

However, with the development of Georgian Limerick by the Perry family in the late 18th and the early 19th century, Arthurs Quay quickly became an unfashionable address.

Further damage was done to the area one evening 180 years ago on the 3rd January 1837, when a store of gunpowder exploded at Richardson's gun shop at No 1 George's Street, killing 15 people, injuring many others and damaging the houses in the area. The site of the gun-shop is now a corner on O'Connell Street, opposite the main entrance to the present Shopping Centre.

By the middle of the 19th century it was unfashionable to live in the houses on Arthurs Quay. According to Limerick historian Maurice Lenihan, by 1866 the houses on the quay were occupied by petty dealers and turf vendors.

By the end of Queen Victoria's reign, the terrace houses had fallen so badly into disrepair that they had become tenement slums.

A Michael Comerford (1870-1907) who was a Limerick carpenter, his wife Mary Ann (O'Dea), and their children lived at various addresses in Limerick that included 18 Arthur's Quay (1903-1904). Michael Comerford died in 1907 at the age of 36, and his widow Mary was living at 11 Arthur's Quay on the census night in 1911. They seem to have had 13 children, although the 1911 census said they were the parents of 12 children, six of whom were still alive.

The high level of infant mortality in a family like this shows the abject poverty and frightening living conditions in a place like Arthur's Quay little more than a century ago.

In *Angela's Ashes*, the Limerick writer Frank McCourt recalls the night he spent in a tenement in Arthur's Quay in the 1930s. Before entering the squalid tenements, he was warned by a friend to mind yourself because some of the steps are missing and there is shit on the ones that are still there. He says that's because there's only one privy and it's in the backyard and children can't go down the stairs in time to put their little arses on the bowl.

In the 1950s, many of the houses were crumbling away and eventually had to be demolished.

By the early 1970s the harbor area in front of Arthur's Quay was filled in by Limerick Corporation to form a car park. This area is now more occupied by a public park, and a cafe and arts center, as well as serving as a stop for buses.

The triangular site once occupied by the terraced houses built by Francis Arthur was developed as the Arthur's Quay Shopping Center that stands today. The concept is mainly credited to Limerick's civil engineer, Michael Tiernan, and the center was built by John Sisk & Son, who began work in May 1988 this ensured that virtually all of the original Arthur's quay no longer exists.

Here is a description of what life was like on Arthur's quay while it was still the address to be seen to be living at in Limerick, it said, "Gaiety was the life of the residents. A military band played every afternoon on the quay and the handsomest of women in all Ireland strolled about on the quay with the English officers. A favorite occupation was to drive to the Spa generally in a coach then to Castleconnell, where they met other members of the Castleconnell club".

An old record says "The Castleconnell Club was composed of the first persons of rank, fashion and landed property in the country. They were of the prime class of bon-vivants and played high and drank deep. They wore a uniform of scarlet with gilt buttons, green silk waistcoat and breeches, a green ribbon on the breast with three C's in gold which stood for Castleconnell Club. They never quarreled among themselves, which in those days of claret and swords would have proved fatal if they had been inclined to quarrel".

There were some sad sights on the quay as well, cruel exhibitions of dancing bears, performing dogs, monkeys and jugglers. Perhaps the worst sight of all on the quay was during the cholera outbreak of 1832 and 1833 when the dead cart made its daily rounds accompanied by the terrible cry “any dead here, any dead here”.

The Arthur family had the right to be buried in St. Mary’s Cathedral, as mentioned previously; this had become the Protestant cathedral so no member of the family had been buried there since 1729. Patrick who donated the land on which St. Michael's is built was buried in St. Michael’s when he died on the 16th of December 1799 at the grand old age of 82. Patrick’s probable second wife died on 20-08-1804 at the age of 84 years in Patrick Street. It was said that he died of a broken heart because of what happened to his son Francis of which more anon.

The marble memorial over his grave reads thus: “To the memory of Patrick Arthur Esq. Who died on the 16th of Dec. 1799 in the 82nd year of his age. In him the poor have lost a liberal benefactor and society an example of every Christian value, and his affectionate family a kind and tender parent. R.I.P.”

Ellen Flynn (nee Arthur) Patrick’s daughter was buried there in 1805.

## The Children of Patrick Arthur of Limerick.

*Patrick Arthur*

1743 – 1841 While not definitively proven it seems likely that this Patrick Arthur (I call him Patrick of Ennistymon as that is where he lived and died in his old age) was the son of Patrick Arthur of Limerick from a first marriage. If he was the son of Patrick of Limerick it is likely that his mother died giving birth to one of Patrick's daughters who seem to have been his sisters who are also not recorded in the official history. It was quite common for women to die in child birth at that time. After this it seems that Patrick of Limerick married for a second time which was also the norm especially in well to do families as a marriage was usually made for monetary or property purposes rather than for love. Now when a man got married for a second time it was usual for the second wife to want to protect the interests of her children and to this end she would try make sure that the children of any first marriage were disinherited. The father if he were wealthy would usually see that the children of his first marriage were set up in life before cutting them off. The boys were usually set up in business, in one of the professions, in the army or in the Church. The girls were usually expected to go into the church as finding a husband for them without a big dowry was very difficult although some did find husbands because of the family name. This usually happened when a family who were trying to climb the ladder of success wanted to have an association with a family further up the social ladder than they were and so they would marry a daughter who was not being given a dowry as she was from a first marriage. Some of these daughters were given a small pension to live on condition that they did not marry but they had few other choices. As we will see the Howley family of Limerick made one of these marriages to a daughter with little of or no dowry because of the name she carried.

Patrick of Ennistymon seems to have married a Mary Roche on the 11th December 1766 in Limerick City. I have not yet found out for certain if there were any children of this marriage but Br. Charles Firmin Arthur believed that there were although no record of any has yet been found. It is known that Patrick of Ennistymon married twice and his second wife was Mary Mulqueeny from Ennistymon and this is where his connection to Ennistymon comes from. Mary was much younger than Patrick (again not unusual at that time) and she died on the 10th July 1846 at the age of 62. Patrick had died at his house in Ennistymon in 1841 at the age of 98. The children of Patrick of Ennistymon that we know of are the children of his second marriage. In the registry of Deeds there is a document where one of the people referred to is Patrick Fitz Patrick Arthur which of course means Patrick the son of Patrick Arthur and the date on this document is 1781 so this document does seem to refer to Patrick Arthur of Ennistymon as being the son of Patrick of Limerick. In another document Francis Arthur is referred to as Francis Fitz Patrick Arthur mirroring how Patrick is referred to in the first document and as both documents are about deeds to properties that belonged to Patrick of Limerick it seems likely that that the Francis Fitz Patrick and Patrick Fitz Patrick were half-brothers. Another unusual thing that may tie the two Patrick's together is that they were both referred to as Patt not by the more usual Pat. Patrick had two houses that I know of in Ennistymon and at least one in Ennis and more in Limerick. I know that he was in the wines and spirits business although it is likely he had other business as well. The house in which Patrick lived and died in Ennistymon was built in the same style as the Limerick merchants summer houses that were built along the Shannon and as far as I know this style was very unusual in that part of Clare at that time.

## *Patrick Arthur*

I have a death cert for a child called Patrick Arthur who died on the 11th February 1851 in St. Johns Limerick. He may have been a son of Patrick of Limerick's second marriage but I am far from certain that he was a son of our Patrick. However if he were it might explain why Francis was not called Patrick as it was the tradition in the family to call the first son Patrick (it did sometimes happen that the first children of first and second marriages would have had the same name e.g. Patrick by first wife and another Patrick by the second wife especially when the name was as important as it was in the Arthur family.

## *Margaret Arthur*

Margaret was born in 1744 and died in 1781. She married John Howley (one of the rising merchant families of Limerick at that time) of Ballintogher, Killenaule County Tipperary and Limerick City. They had three daughters the first was Catherine Howley who married Daniel O'Connell (Kilgorey County Clare who was a cousin of the Liberator), the second Helen Howley married Thaddeus Ryan of Ballyvestia and Scarteen Knocklong County Limerick and the third Margaret Howley who married Henry O Shea of Limerick. The Ryan family archive contains a hand written note in Helen's handwriting listing the birth date and date of death of her nineteen month old son Thea as well as the date of death of her Grandfather Patrick Arthur in 1799 and the date of death of her mother in law Elizabeth Ryan So as the death of her grandfather Patrick Arthur is the same as the date of the death of Patrick of Limerick it is safe to say that Helen's mother Margaret Arthur is a previously unknown daughter of Patrick of Limerick from well before the known children of Patrick of Limerick and she was likely the younger sister of Patrick of Ennistymon.

*Ursula Mary Arthur*

The Ryan archive also contains a letter from a Sister Ursula who was an aunt of Helen Arthur exoring Helen to teach her grandnieces and grandnephew their catechism and to lead by example in the ways of Life. This letter was sent from the Palatinate in Germany where she seems to have been a nun in a convent. This note proves as near as possible that Sister Ursula was another daughter of Patrick of Limerick. Ursula seems to have been born around 1745.

*Nancy Arthur*

I have a death cert for a Nancy Arthur the daughter of Patrick of Limerick for the 7th October 1749 in St. John's Limerick. It seems possible that Patrick's first wife may have died trying to give birth to Nancy.

*Anne Arthur*

Anne was born in 1752 and she married Jordan Meade of Cork in 1772. Their daughter married Andrew Morragh

Glissan of Limerick on Monday 27th June 1794. They had a daughter but I do not know the name of Anne's daughter.

*Mary Arthur*

I have a death cert for a child called Mary Arthur the daughter of Patrick Arthur of Limerick who died on the 10th April 1753 in St. John's Limerick again I have no birth certificate for Mary.

*Unknown Arthur*

I have a death certificate for an Arthur child with no name who died on the 2nd Of June 1762 and once again the child's father was Patrick Arthur of Limerick. Again this record comes from St. Johns Limerick and it would seem likely that this child either died at birth or was still born.

*Catherine Anne Arthur*

She was the daughter pf Patrick Arthur of Limerick merchant and she married Michael McCormick of Dublin on the 5th Of April 1783.

*Ellen Arthur*

Ellen married a man called Edmund Flynn on the 8th July 1783 and she died in the 5th July 1805

## *Francis Arthur.*

Francis was born in 1758 (it is thought) and died in 1824 in Dunkirk. His father would have been 42 at the time of his birth which was I believe unusually old for having a first family. Francis married twice the first time to Ellen Sexton with whom he had all his children, Ellen died around 1815 and then Francis Married Ellen Barrett on the 11th February 1819. This Ellen was the daughter of the late Michael Barrett of Edendale County Clare and there some question as to whether it was Francis idea to marry Ellen Barrett or was he encouraged into it by his legal representative a Mr. Leahy of Cork whose son was married to one of Francis daughters). Ellen Barrett died in Dublin on the 15th January 1831. In 1792 Francis was the chairman of the Limerick Catholic Meeting one of his many activities on behalf of the Catholic community that he was involved in that got him into trouble with the authorities. Eventually they had him falsely tried for treason (of which more in the next chapter). Francis died in Dunkirk in France in 1824 far from his beloved Limerick.

# Chapter 10

*Francis Arthur 1758 – 1824*

Photo of Arthur's Quay in the 1800's

Francis Arthur the son of Patrick played as big a part in the development of Limerick in his time as did his father; in fact he worked with his father to develop the city and to further the Arthur family fortune.

## The Children of Francis Arthur.

*Catherine Helen Arthur*

Catherine was born on the 20th March 1780 and died on the 27th July 1867. She became Mother M Xavier a Benedictine nun at Princethorpe Abbey in England. She joined the convent against her father's wishes although he did eventually agree reluctantly to her becoming a nun.

*Unknown*

A child of Francis Arthur was baptized on the 27th March 1781. No name was recorded neither was it recorded if the baby was a boy or a girl.

*Patrick Edmund Arthur*

Patrick Edmund was baptized on the 26th February 1783 at St. Michael's in Limerick. According to that useful source book "Admissions to Kings Inns" it has an entry, Arthur, Patrick Edmond, son of Francis Arthur Middle Gardiner St. Dublin( this was Francis Arthurs house in Dublin), merchant, admitted Hilary term 1811, qualified Easter term 1814. Patrick Edmund was in Stonyhurst College (this was one of the first secondary schools for Catholics for boys to open in England after the reformation) in England at the same time his father was put on trial for treason in Limerick. Patrick Edmund married Susannah Grainger the daughter of John Grainger of Causetown County Meath on the 22nd June 1812 in the Pro Cathedral in Dublin. They had a daughter on the 29th September 1813 and she was called Mary Jane Arthur. Mary Jane Arthur (Mother Mary Teresa Arthur) became a nun at Princethorpe Abbey where her aunt Mother M Xavier was a nun. On the 2nd November 1814 Ellen was born and Ellen went on to become a Loreto nun in Rathfarnham. It should be noted that she was born after Patrick Edmund had died on Wednesday the 26th of October 1814. Another thins that should be noted is that four days before Patrick Edmund died his mother died on Monday 22nd October of a fever at her husband's house in Middle Gardiner Street in in Dublin.

*Ellen Arthur*

Ellen was born on the 24th October 1784 and she died on the 14th August 1785. Francis was to have another daughter whom he called Ellen in 1793

*Eliza (Alicia) Arthur*

Eliza was born on the 24th November 1786. She married Jeremiah Scully of Mt. William, County Tipperary at Middle Gardner Street (Francis house in Dublin), on the 7th January 1809. As you will see later Francis was not allowed to come to Ireland without a special license and this wedding seems to have been one of the few occasions he was allowed to return after he had been expelled. Jeremiah died in 1840 and sometime after this Alicia became a Carmelite nun having first spent some time with her sister at Princethorp. She died at Darlington in 1859 and had no children

*Miss Margaret Jane Arthur*

Margaret was born on the 31st of August 1789 and she married Patrick Green of Green Abbey at her father's house in Middle Gardener Street in Dublin on the 26th September 1806. (Another occasion Francis was allowed to return but note the girls had to get married in Dublin as he was still not allowed to return to Limerick even with a special license however he does seem to have received a special license on one occasion to return to Limerick in order to marry Ellen Barrett his second wife). Patrick Green died at his house in Green Abbey, Tipperary in 1813. Margaret was married again on the 20th November 1818 to David Leahy of Shanakiel (he was the son of Francis legal representative) in the county of Cork by the Arch Bishop of Dublin the Most Reverend Dr. Troy in the house of John Scully Middle Gardner Street. Not sure if Francis was present for this wedding but I think he was not. The Leahy and Scully families had many ties especially in the Clerical and legal professions just as the Arthur family had. The warren Darley family are descendants of the marriage of Margaret Jane and Patrick Green. Lilly warren Darley whose photo is on the right and her sister Francis Warren Darley whose photo is on the left both became nuns.

Francis Warren Darley

Lily Warren Darley

*The Warren Darley's descendants of the Arthur family.*

Mr. Arthur Warren Darley was the son of Henry Warren Darley (Henry had been a protestant but he had converted to Catholicism) who was a land-owner with property in Donegal, Limerick, and other parts of the country. His mother was a member of the Green family of Castleconnell. He came from a musical family, his father being an accomplished player of both the violin and the Uilleann pipes. He was a close relation of Dion Boucicault, the actor and writer of Irish plays. George Darley, the poet, was another relative. His grandfather was a close friend of Thomas Moore, and frequently sang the famous Irish melodies to Moore's own accompaniment.

The late Mr. Arthur Warren Darley started to study the violin at the age of eight, and pursued his studies In Dublin and London. He took a keen interest in Irish folk music, especially music for the violin. An accomplished violinist himself, he specialized in the playing of unaccompanied violin music and in the early days of the Abbey Theater the musical interludes were provided by Mr. Arthur Warren Darley.

A successful performer on the concert platform both in Ireland and in England, his ability as a solo violinist at a recital at the Steinway Hall won the highest praise from the London critics. He was a keen student of chamber music, and took part in chamber music recitals at the Royal Dublin Society from 1893 for a number of years.

While he was Leader of the Dublin Musical Society from 1897 until 1902 he lectured before the Royal Dublin Society. In 1900, he was appointed professor of violin at the Royal Irish Academy of Music, and held the appointment for some years. Later, he became keenly interested in the Municipal School of Music of which he became Director.

He was a great collector of unpublished Irish airs, and published a collection himself. He was also responsible for the collection of hitherto unpublished Irish airs, which from time to time were submitted for competition in the unpublished Irish air section of the Dublin Feis

AN ENGINEER'S HOLIDAY

THE Easter holidays have [illegible] number of our friends [illegible] Dublin for a few days. I [illegible] Thomas Darley, the young engine[illegible] other day. He always avails of a [illegible] of coming home to Dublin.

Mr. Darley, who is the second [illegible] the late Arthur Darley, is engag[illegible] important constructional works [illegible] harbour of Goole, in Yorkshire.

The big dam which is being [illegible] there has, he tells me, given him [illegible] experience during the past two [illegible] He says he was most fortunate in [illegible] ing under the distinguished en[illegible] Mr. J. Pettigrew, who is a W[illegible] man.

Mr. Darley returns to Yorksh[illegible] Tuesday after a visit to his moth[illegible]

Two of the Warren Darley boys.

Arthur displayed great activity in the promotion of feiseanna and musical competitions, and for many years adjudicated at the Feis Ceoil in the Irish fiddle and pipes competitions, as well as in the unpublished airs section. Along with this, he adjudicated at the Oireachtas competitions and other feiseanna around the country. He was a co-founder with the Reverent Father Aloysius of the Father Mathew Feis.

He was President of the Irish Musical Fund - a fund which was established around the end of the eighteenth century for the support of necessitous musicians

Arthur Warren Darley died in 1929.

### *Ellen Frances Arthur*

Ellen was born on 1st July 1793 and she was the youngest daughter of Francis Arthur. At the age of 27 on the 2nd September 1819 against her father's wishes she entered a convent. She took the habit in York in May 1820 and she was professed in Dublin on the 15th October 1821. Ellen died at Rathfarnham Dublin on the 5th January 1842. Ellen was one of the nuns who helped establish the Loreto order in Ireland.

As was previously mentioned Francis has for long been thought of as Patrick's only son but as the man I call Patrick Arthur of Ennistymon who was born in 1743 before any records exist is I believe the first son of Patrick of Limerick by a first marriage. There is a document referring to a Patrick Fitz Patrick as mentioned previously and this would make him a half-brother to Francis as Francis would have been from a second marriage. Patrick of Ennistymon was born when Patrick of Limerick was 26 years old a normal age for a first family and Francis was born when Patrick of Limerick was 41 to 42 years old very late for having a first son and the tradition in the family was that the first son was always called Patrick so the question must be asked if Francis was a first son why was he not called Patrick as was the tradition in the family.

Francis was born about the year 1758 and as he grew up he showed himself to be a clever and sensible businessman. He married Ellen Sexton from a well-known Limerick merchant family and soon became a partner in his father's business. He soon came to possess large estates of his own made up of both land and houses. He was a man with a social conscience and he always took a deep interest in the welfare and upkeep of his city of Limerick. He was one of the leading Catholic citizens in the city of Limerick and in the year 1796 he raised a corps of Yeomanry Artillery at his own expense to help the Government of the day, defend Limerick against the French forces that were at that time on the Shannon threatening Limerick. As a reward for raising this corps at his own expense he was given the rank of Captain, a feat in those days when many of the penal laws were still in force. Here it should be noted that Francis was a Catholic and no catholic was ever promoted beyond sergeant in the British army at that time. Francis being elevated to the rank of captain seems to have caused a lot of disquiet among a number of the Protestant ascendancy in Limerick and Clare (only a small number it must be said were upset but the ones who were upset at his promotion were among the most powerful people in that area at that time) that a mere Catholic should be given a commission in the army regardless of the fact that Francis was paying for the corps from his own resources. On the 15th On May 1798 the corps was disbanded as a result of the machinations of these people behind the scenes spreading rumors that Francis was in some way involved with the United Irishmen.

It was at this time that the Catholics as a result of the restrictions on them because of their faith decided to summon a great meeting in order to appeal to the King of England for redress. The delegates were to meet in Dublin in early 1798 but some members of the Protestant ascendancy feeling threatened by this did all they could to stop the meeting and intimidate the delegates. However in spite of their best efforts, the delegates did meet and they sent their petition to the King.

As a result of this petition many of the restrictions on Catholics were lifted. The Earl of Clare (John Fitzgibbon the first of his family to hold the title was to prove a great enemy of Francis Arthur. Fitzgibbon's father had been a Catholic who converted in order to become a barrister) was a leading member of the group that opposed any lifting of the restrictions on Catholics. He was one of those responsible for calling a meeting of magistrates and freeholders in Limerick. Francis Arthur engaged a counselor, a Mr. Powell to attend this meeting and to plead the cause of the Catholics. Although counselor Powell was there at great personal risk, he did all he could to plead the case of the Catholics, but his efforts were in vain. An anti-Catholic resolution was passed and it was published in the public press of the day in large type. The Catholics met again with Francis Arthur as chairman of the meeting. They drew up another statement in opposition to the Protestant resolution and Francis as their chairman signed it after which it was sent to the press and it was published. It is said that the Earl of Clare, who was also the Lord High Chancellor was wild with rage and anger that Francis Arthur a mere Papist should dare to act so. One Stephen Roche (he was an agent of the Earl of Clare) and Sir Christopher Knight came to Francis to point out the enormity of his "crime" and to tell him how he had angered the Earl of Clare. They also warned him to be careful in the future as the Earl of Clare had learned many things about him that could be seen as disloyal to the crown. Francis simply declared his innocence.

Matters became much worse for Francis when shortly afterwards he proposed a Mr. Maunsell for election as M.P. in the coming general election. This action only served to make his enemies even more determined to deal with this upstart and some who previously no strong opinion on the matter had begun to turn against him.

Below is a report on the trial for treason of Francis Arthur and what happened after the trial this report is taken from a manuscript held in Stonyhurst School in England where Patrick Edmund Arthur the son of Francis was a student at the same time his father was on trial. There is another manuscript of the trial held in The Limerick City Museum and it is on this account I believe that a printed version of the trial that appeared in the 1870's was based. There seems to be little difference between the two handwritten versions. It seems reasonable to assume that the manuscript in Stonyhurst was left there by Francis son Patrick although they have no record of who left it there.

On Thursday May 12th 1798 Francis was speaking to a friend in the presence of a British officer when the latter remarked "On Tuesday next everyone will be surprised at some of the arrests that will be made". On Tuesday May 29th while Francis was at breakfast with his family, a number of British officers entered the dining room and told him that they wanted to speak privately with him. He was immediately informed that he was under arrest and he was ordered to give up his keys. The officers next approached his wife, took her keys and ordered the family to quit the house immediately. Mrs. Arthur protested to the British officers but to no avail and she and the children had to leave and seek shelter at her father's home. Francis was then handed over to Sheriff Lloyd just as Major General Morrison arrived at the scene. Francis told Morrison that he would hold him personally responsible for a thousand guineas in gold and a quantity of valuables and papers that were in the house. The military placed seals on the doors and presses of the house and Francis was removed to the prison in Mary Street. He was placed in a foul and stuffy cell. He petitioned for air and his father Patrick, then 81 years of age came to see him. He too asked that air might be allowed to his son with the result that the jailer broke two panes of glass in the window. Francis then demanded to be told of the charges that were being brought against him but the only answer he got was that he was being arrested by order of the Government. His wife applied to have a doctor sent to her husband but her application was refused. She then sent some food and refreshments to Francis but the jailer and sergeant assaulted the messenger and he returned covered in blood.

I was told that this was Francis Arthur's house in Dublin.

On June 22nd 1798 while Francis lay ill he was told that he would be tried the next day. He asked about having a legal counsel but he was refused permission to have any legal representation.

On the following day the court martial sat and the Judge Advocate read out the charges against Frances. (here we should note that as he was no longer a captain in the army and his corps had been disbanded he should not have been brought before a court of military discipline but rather before a civil court, the state of martial law overriding civil powers had not yet been declared either so his being brought before a military court was even by English law illegal). What The Judge Advocate read out was "Francis Arthur you stand charged with having aided and assisted in the present rebellion" He was also charged with: - [1] having offered money to Lord Edward Fitzgerald for rebellious purposes [2] for having employed one Figgin's for raising men in the west and [3] with having firearms and pikes hidden in hogs head's in the city.

The only witness the prosecution had was a Mr. William Maum a man who had long been a notorious vagabond. He had been convicted of treasonable practices and was at that time under sentence of transportation for life. He had been on his way to Waterford to be shipped off with other convicts to Botany Bay, when he was stopped by order of the Government at Clonmel. How he was tampered with there, it is impossible to be certain other than that the names of Hargrove and Arthur were there suggested to him. It is certain that he had not the least knowledge of either of them and neither had he ever even met either of them. Francis was now on trial for his life (if found guilty of treason the only penalty would be death). It appears also that some assurance was given to Maum by the High Sheriff of the County of Tipperary (Thomas Fitzgerald) or so he told Hare, which made him (Maum) see he had an interest in convicting some people he did not know by describing them as his accomplices. Maum was a doubtful character who should have been legally incapable of giving testimony in a court of Justice (this is because he was a convicted and unpardoned felon). This then was the man they called up to accuse of high treason, a respectable gentleman, whose loyalty to the crown he had proved many times, and had always enjoyed an unimpeachable reputation.

The accusation being made against Francis was obviously upon the face of it a wild and absurd fabrication. Maum said that on the day he met Lord Edward Fitzgerald and

Counselor Sampson in Dame-street, and walked with them to the Printing Office of a Newspaper called The Press, a Peter Finnerty was set in the pillory in Dublin. There Lord Edward gave him two letters directed to Francis Arthur at Limerick, one was a circular letter which was open, merely notifying, that there would be an insurrection in March to supersede the present Government and elect another Government more on the principles of liberty. The other was sealed and in manuscript form which spoke of money or contracts for money, for the use of the Rebels or United Irishmen. Maum left Dublin shortly afterwards on the two day couch to Limerick, where he put up at a house belonging to Mr. Anderson. After arriving there from Dublin he went to Ward's a Silversmith on Balls-bridge, to purchase some articles. In the course of a conversation, Maum inquired of him, where Mr. Arthur lived, and Anderson showed him the house. Maum then left Anderson to fetch a bundle he had left at the mail coach office, and on his return knocked at Mr. Arthur's door, which was opened by a manservant who told him his master was at home. A person came to the door, received the letters, read them and when Maum said he knew the contents, he promised to comply with them asking Maum to call again in the morning. The next morning Maum went to the same house, and asking for Mr. Arthur, was told, that Mr. Arthur was at the review with his artillery corps. Maum, together with Ward, went to the review and after his return from there to Limerick, he immediately set out for county Cork, without calling on Mr. Arthur. Sometime after however he received a letter by the post at Charleville which was signed Francis Arthur and in this letter he was offered any sum of money he might want on for Lord Edward Fitzgerald.

It was at this stage the prosecution realized that the dates Maum had given for being in Dublin did not include the day on which Peter Finnerty was in the pillory in Dublin and the days and dates he said he was in Limerick and Cork did not match the evidence he had given. If Maum's evidence of where he was and when he was there were investigated it would be simple to prove that he had been lying as while he had been in those places he had not been there when he said he was. When Maum was asked whether Mr. Arthur's were a corner or a middle house or one that he could find again he answered that he could not tell, nor could he find the house again, for it was dark when he called there, and he had never been in Limerick before or since till he was brought there to testify for the prosecution. When he was asked if he called at Mr. Arthur's house more than once, he distinctly said that he had not.

The Court asked Maum, is the prisoner the person, to whom you delivered the letter? He answered without hesitation "yes that is he" but when asked again, "Are you sure?" he reduced his positive answer to the more cautious reply of, "why it was dark, I cannot be sure." Maum having sworn, that Mr. Arthur had promised to comply with the request contained in Lord Edward Fitzgerald's letter, if Maum would call upon him "the next morning. It was natural to suppose, that some important reason could be given by Maum for omitting, when he came back from the review, to call upon Mr. Arthur, and proceeding without the money to County Cork, the Court therefore asked Maum to explain this conduct. His answer was, I was in a hurry to get to County Cork, where I expected to get larger sums than I would get from Mr. Arthur. He was then asked what it was he expected from Mr. Arthur and he replied twenty guineas. Twenty guineas, ejaculated the President in a tone of surprise and dissatisfaction.

There were also two others who came forward and all they had to add was that they said that they had heard the story from others. William Ward was a silversmith where Maum was supposed to have bought some items but he had no record of him having been there. Joseph Anderson was the man with whom Maum was supposed to have stayed with while in Limerick and to have shown him Francis Arthur's house. Anderson said that he had not shown Maum Mr. Arthur's house, however Colonel Cockell and Captain Brand said that Anderson had told them that he had pointed out Mr. Arthur's house to Maum.

Here the first charge closed. In support of the two remaining charges, viz. raising men and concealing arms, the only witness produced was Edward Sheehy, a man who had been master of a country school and was then a prisoner in custody to be tried by the Court martial for treasonable practices. Sheehy said, "That he had heard from a man called Hogan, that someone called Higgins had been employed by a Mr. Arthur to raise men in the West. Farther, that one Carsidy of the Longford militia also told him, that one McMahon of the Artillery had informed Carsidy that a Mr. Arthur had guns and pikes concealed in hogsheads. When asked about Mr. Arthur, Sheehy replied I can't tell, I don't know him and with this the interrogation of Sheehy ceased.

Two other witnesses were produced on the part of the prosecution, not to give witness to one or other of the charges specifically but to give such corroborating testimony in general as they could furnish. One was called Saunders, the other was called Shee and both were from Charleville. When they were sworn in they each gave the same answer, "that they did not know the prisoner or anything about him." This drew an expression of surprise from the court, and the President said significantly, "they were both friends of Maum". It was now beginning to become clear that according to the proverb, what was every body's business has been a little neglected and that the organization of the evidence had not been as well arranged as they had thought. The president now declared the prosecution closed. Mr. Arthur was ordered to be ready with his defense for Monday the 25th June. Then it seems that although Francis was ordered to prepare his defense they did all they could to prevent him preparing it. This they did by denying him the means to prepare it and even though he was locked up before, from now on he had two additional guards placed at his door, and access was denied to every person including his guard and turnkey. On the next day, Sunday, Colonel Cockell called upon Mr. Arthur with the printed proclamation of martial law from the Lord Lieutenant, and pointed out the part, which directed trials to be conducted in a most summary way adding, that the General was very angry the court had not closed the business on Saturday.

You could ask why Sheehy's evidence was brought up in court, as what Sheehy could say must have been known before the trial and indeed there are grounds for believing that the Sheehy evidence had been previously investigated by Colonel Cockell. McMahon and Carsidy were described as" being in the King's service", consequently could have been brought forward, and it would seem that Hogan and, Higgins could also have been produced. What they could have told must have been known, and its quality may be judged by their evidence not being introduced into Court.

Now in order to prepare his defense Francis gave Colonel Cockell a list of the witnesses he wanted to be summoned, in order to prove his absence from Limerick at the period Maum said he was there. "They will be of no use to you replied Colonel Cockell, "since we know from the Mail Coach-book, that you were absent from the 5th to the 23rd of February so you will find the time very different to-morrow. Francis then asked what time would now be fixed for his supposed interview with Maum, that he might prepare his defense accordingly. Yet even this was refused him even though this information would have been of little use to him as he was prevented from communicating with anyone except the Colonel himself. Francis persevered, in saying that the attendance of those witnesses was necessary for him, particularly Cassidy, McMahon, Hogan and Higgins. The answer he received from the Colonel was, "We have no power to compel the attendance of any witness". Surely replied Mr. Arthur, Carsidy and McMahon at least may be obliged to attend. On that point the Colonel said we have inquired, and we find that there is not, nor has there been a man of the name of McMahon in the detachment quartered here. The city and district being under martial law, it is very clear, that the professed inability to compel the attendance of witnesses was a cruel excuse.

Eventually Colonel Cockell consented to transmit the list of witnesses to Mrs. Arthur. On Saturday evening, after the Court had adjourned, Mrs. Arthur, by accident, heard that Maum had been an usher under the Rev. William Dunn, master of the public school in Charleville. When she got this information she sent Mr. Peter Arthur (he seems to have been a cousin of Francis) to Charleville and he returned on Sunday with a written document, stating, that Maum was in Charleville at the time, when he said he came from Dublin to Limerick. He also got information about a number of other things relative to Maum, which would satisfactorily refute many parts of Maum's evidence. He brought a promise that many respectable persons would attend on Tuesday, if the trial could be put off till that day. The reason being that they had to go to the Spancillhill fair on Monday (it was a fair where the principal people of both County Limerick and County Clare negotiated their business affairs, For their business they could not afford to not be there without suffering great financial loss as they would have missed out on deals with the people who were there and who would have done their deals with other people who were there) this prevented their voluntary attendance on Monday. Since Colonel Cockell refused to summon them, Mr. Arthur did not have the power to compel them to attend. Mrs. Arthur (Francis wife) spoke to the President of the Court, and petitioned for one day's delay, his answer was that it depended not on him, but that General Morrison was the person, to whom the application should be made. Having failed in this application, Mrs. Arthur went to the Bishop of Limerick who was a Doctor Bernard He agreed to deliver her petition to the General and to testify as to the truth of the representation respecting the occupation of the witnesses at the fair. Still the General remained inflexible. Early on Monday morning Mrs. Arthur again went to see him and he sent his Aid-de-camp a Captain Brand, to tell her, that he could not see her as it would not be consistent with his duty. She replied that the favor she asked was in writing and she would rely on his humanity to comply with the contents. The Aid-de-camp replied that alas duty must take place of humanity and the General could not grant her request as Mr. Arthur had been charged as a rebel and this obliterated all other considerations.

Before the defense opened, John Creagh Esq. a gentleman and a lawyer by profession as well as being an alderman of Limerick and the oldest magistrate of the County expressed a wish to assist Mr. Arthur in his defense. Mr. Sheriff Lloyd told him that if he were a friend of Mr. Arthur he had no business there. The Sheriff then planted himself opposite the prisoner to see that nobody should communicate with him. Soon after this he made a formal complaint to the Court that Mr. Arthur's father had delivered to the prisoner the names of Peppard, Hare and Shee along with those of other witnesses. It was under these circumstances that the Court opened. The President began by declaring that Maum, having had time to recollect himself was cooler and could now better ascertain the time of delivering the letters. It should be remembered here that according to Colonel Cockell's acknowledgment, the Court had been told how Maum's needed to correct his dates. We should not be astonished that the President of the court wanted to bring this change of evidence before the Court because if Maum’s original evidence stood it would be clear that Maum had sworn falsely. It was clear; that in the correction he was about to make he would perjure himself again in changing the times he had first given. The president of the court continually intervened in Maum's second deposition to help him to remember the evidence he was supposed to give although this was not his job as he should have been impartial.

Soon after the Court met to hear Mr. Arthur's defense, Joseph Andersen who had been one of the witnesses for the Crown appeared standing on the Pillory close to the Exchange and opposite to the Council Chamber, where the Court Martial sat. He appeared to be placed there as a scarecrow to intimidate any witnesses, who might appear against the prosecution.

It was now observed by the Court, that frequent notes were from time to time delivered to the prisoner to enable him to cross examine Maum.

A note was passed to the President of the court, which said that a revolutionary committee was sitting in the adjoining tavern. This revolutionary committee consisted of Mr. Arthur's witnesses, who were about ten in number, all respectable inhabitants of Limerick. They were not allowed to be in Court during the examination of other witnesses, and could not remain in the street, which was kept clear by the military that were there on the pretense of attending the punishment of Anderson. The military surrounded the Court in great numbers on every side so the witnesses had to wait at a hotel near the court, until they should be respectively called to give their testimony.

Because of the note the trial was stopped and the Judge Advocate was sent to secure those persons who were to be witnesses for Francis. To which purpose he placed guards at the front and rear of the hotel, with orders to let none of them out. The Judge Advocate also seized all the documents and papers, which Mr. Arthur's friends had been able to collect in the short interval since Saturday, when the nature of the charge first became known to them. Among others he seized the authenticated papers brought from Charleville by Mr. Peter Arthur who was himself one of those witnesses so detained. These documents were intended to be used in the prisoner's defense, but the Judge Advocate would not now suffer them to be used, retaining them in his possession, on his return to the Court. This contempt of justice which they barely tried to hide shows in part the state of Ireland at that time. Francis now found himself without the information and evidence his friends had worked so hard to gather in such a short time, but his problems did not end there here. Mr. Sheriff Lloyd, who had planted himself opposite to the prisoner during the trial, actually complained to the Court that the aged father of Mr. Arthur had communicated to his son, the names of Hare, Peppard and Shee along with some others. These people were capable of bearing important testimony, and who fortunately had not been with those, who were just taken into custody. The Court again strictly forbade any communication with the prisoner, and ordered that no document or paper should be handed to him, without having been first submitted to the perusal of the Court.

From the steps that had been taken it seemed little was left in Francis power to produce in his defense yet less than little appeared sufficient. For nothing seemed necessary to destroy the credit of such a confused and contradictory narrative, as Maum had offered, especially when the recorded infamy of that witness was entirely known to the Court. Still the wisdom and solicitude of Mr. Arthur's friends made them deem it advisable, not to leave the prosecution a semblance of probability to shelter itself under and from this wish, rather than from any apprehensions of his own, he called the witnesses who had been indicated to him.

Mathew Hare a permanent Sergeant of the Clanwilliam Cavalry swore that he received Maum into his custody at Clonmel from the High Sheriff of the County of Tipperary, Thomas Judkin Fitzgerald. His orders were to treat Maum well with indulgence as he was a person, who would give material information to the Government. At General Morison’s lodgings in Limerick Maum wrote a letter to a Mr. Richard Peppard, which letter he gave to the witness (Matthew Hare) who read part of it and he then forwarded it. It was at this time that the letter was produced to the Court. Maum being questioned if it was his hand writing, acknowledged that it was and said in great confusion to the President, "You know, Sir that it was but lately, that I gave information against Mr. Arthur, and that I did not wish to do it." It was of great importance that the meaning of the word lately should be defined and that Maum should explain how he was compelled or induced against his wish to give his testimony on this occasion.

If you think about it, it does not seem likely, that Maum could have had scruples about working out his own pardon by incriminating another person. So that his reluctance to accuse Mr. Arthur seem to have rested solely on his realization, that his lack of knowledge of anything, relating to Francis would leave his tale so liable to detection, that it could not be borne through with any chance of success. Cross-examination might have found this out.

Maum wrote a letter from his detention in Limerick to a Mr. Richard Peppard,

The letter was as follows.

Dear Sir,
I had not an opportunity this morning of informing you of the circumstances, which brought me from Waterford to this town they are as follows. I was remanded to Limerick by an order from the Government, my name being found on Lord Edward Fitzgerald's roll and intimating that I was to hold a very excellent command in the Counties of Cork and Limerick. I cannot conjecture what is now to be done with me. 1 was asked if I knew Mr. Hargrove, I declared I never spoke to him in my life, much less to Mr. Arthur, who it seems was likewise nominated in his Lordship's muster. 1 hope 1 may be sent to Cork, that I may have a second interview with the lads of Charleville.

W. Maum.

Maum was asked, when, and why he wrote that letter, his answer was I wrote it at the General's lodgings. This letter probably saved Francis from a sentence of death, as it made clear that Maum did not know Mr. Arthur.

Sylvester Shee a prisoner then in custody and to be tried by the Court Martial, was now called for by Mr. Arthur at which the Court seemed very much surprised. Major Carlisle, addressing himself to the prisoner, asked him to what point he meant to call Shee. Francis replied to prove the infamous character of the witness Maum but the Major answered that the Court was already fully informed in this matter and you need not take any trouble to confirm it. Mr. Arthur however, persisted and Sylvester Shee was produced and sworn. He said that he had lodged information against Maum, which was then in General Morison's hand. This was strong proof, that Maum could not be an unbiased witness. It is scarcely credible, that such information which must have gone to protect Maum's life he being already under sentence of transportation could be made use of to intimidate him to come forward as prosecutor of Mr. Arthur. Yet it would be difficult to account otherwise for his expressions to the President "You know, Sir, it is but lately I gave information against Mr. Arthur and I did not wish to do". Mr. Arthur was proceeding with his cross examination, when Major Carlisle again solemnly assured Mr. Arthur it was totally unnecessary for him to proceed as the Court were fully apprised of the infamous character of Maum. Francis naturally believing, that the Court were satisfied on this material point relinquished the farther examination of the witness Shee.

Then two servants of Mr. Arthur said that Mr. Arthur slept after dinner when he had no company, never allowing himself to be disturbed at that time and that he was not called out to any person whatever during any evening of the last winter or spring. This was-confirmed by Mrs.

Arthur who added that Mr. Arthur had always talked of Lord Edward Fitzgerald as a madman, who wanted to excite a rebellion in the kingdom. The rest of Mr. Arthur's witnesses being in custody and he not having had the means of learning what facts they meant to substantiate no other defense could be offered.

While Francis was cross-examining Maum the president of the court addressed Francis saying you yourself admitted on Saturday that Maum did call at your house an accusation that was not true. Since Francis had not been allowed to keep notes of the proceedings he could not immediately recall if he had ever said such a thing. This was intended to make Mr. Arthur look guilty and Mr. Arthur's attempts to answer the question were continually interrupted by the judge advocate who put a different interpretation put upon his replies which he had to give in writing. It was now clear to Francis that no matter what the truth of the matter was the court martial was determined to find him guilty.

He was removed from the court and sent back to prison where all his belongings were taken from him including the contents of his pockets. At 9 o'clock in the night the Assistant Adjutant General Cockell brought to him the sentence of the court martial. The sentence was as follows. "You are to be transported to Botany Bay for life; to be sent off to-morrow morning; and you are to pay a fine of £5,000 plus 1000 guineas that was held in Francis house to the King forthwith, or your entire property will be confiscated. Immediately after the trial closed those witnesses for Mr. Arthur, who had been kept under a strong guard during the trial were ordered into court, the

President, telling them, he regarded them as a revolutionary committee assembled to overawe the court. He menaced them for having dared to harbor so traitorous a purpose and then after much insulting language and boasting of his own leniency in not subjecting them to punishment he finally dismissed them.

Mrs. Arthur was permitted to see her husband in goal, provided it should be in the presence of the General's Aid de Camp, Captain Brand. This permission was given on the express condition that she should not attempt to give her husband any information about any steps that were been taken, in attempting to get his sentence reversed or to give him any hope of being pardoned or released. In order to be allowed to see her husband she had to agree to these restrictions. Captain Brand sat between her and her husband all the time of her visit in the prison, and Francis was kept in the cruelest suspense till the moment of his final liberation.

It seems that the prosecutors were aware of the possibility that Lord Cornwallis might interrupt their proceedings. They had reason to suspect that representations would be instantly made to his Excellency about the course they were pursuing. Mr. Gorman the prisoner's nephew(I think he was his wife's nephew) was present at the trial on Saturday and fearing from the violence of the proceedings, how it might finish set off for Dublin and arrived there early on Sunday morning. He presented a petition to the Lord Lieutenant stating that Mr. Arthur was an eminent merchant of Limerick, father of a large family and a man of independent property who had made great exertions for Government. When the enemy appeared on the coast he formed a corps of artillery, and whose loyalty was never impeached except by one Maum a convict for his treasonable practices who was under sentence of transportation. That the prosecution had been closed on Saturday, and the defense ordered to be ready for Monday, Therefore praying, that, even if the prisoner was sentenced the execution of it might be delayed until his Excellency should see the minutes of the Court Martial. In answer his Excellency was pleased to inform Mr. Gorman, though the medium of Mr. Cooke (the under Secretary of State) "that the prayer of his petition was granted, and that a King's messenger had been dispatched that moment for the purpose to Major General Morrison. The messenger arrived in Limerick at 5 o'clock in the morning of Tuesday the 26th of June, and immediately delivered the orders for suspending the execution of any sentence on Mr. Arthur, and to transmit the minutes of the Court Martial to the Lord Lieutenant. This order came in time to prevent Mr. Arthur's being sent off that morning for transportation.

But notwithstanding the express direction of the Lord Lieutenant that the execution of the sentence should be delayed until he saw the minutes of the Court Martial, General Morrison levied the fine of five thousand pounds as previously imposed by the Court. Mr. Gorman returned on Tuesday, and on hearing of the General's determination to levy the fine he went to him to remonstrate against this demand, so contrary to his Excellency's orders. To which the General replied, "I have received Lord Castlereagh's letter respecting Mr. Arthur, and shall use my discretion for the contents. I order the money to be paid. Colonel Cockell attended by the Collector of his Majesty's Revenue, George Maunsell, Esq. who left his station in the

Custom-house for this purpose came to Mr. Arthur's house, took out of his desk a bag containing 1,000 guineas (£35,000approx ) and then sent for Mr. Arthur's father who was obliged to give another £5,000 (£170,000 approx. It would appear that since General Morrison was going to be prevented from exiling Francis to Botany Bay (Mr. Maum's inconsistent evidence prevented his execution) he would at least extract the fine from him

The General transmitted the minutes of the Court Marshal by the King's messenger to Lord Castlereagh. The Chief Secretary of Ireland in his answer to the General's letter conveying the minutes, wrote: "I am directed by his Excellency, to acquaint you that his Excellency desires, that the sentence of the Court Martial held upon Mr. Arthur of Limerick be remitted and desires, that you will take security for his quitting Ireland, and not returning until the present troubles have subsided and he receives license for that purpose".

Soon after this letter Lord Castlereagh wrote another, from which the following is an extract: "Upon further inquiry from Major General Morrison, his Excellency desires "the fine paid be returned, and that Mr. Arthur may "be allowed to go to Great Britain, or any other part at "peace with his Majesty." The above note is underwritten, by order of Major General Morrison.
Henry Brand, Aid de Camp.

This change or commutation of sentence of transportation to Botany Bay to that of general and indefinite banishment especially in the case of an eminent merchant with a large family, from the place of his birth, his residence, his friends and extensive commercial concerns appears to import that the full minutes of the Court Martial had not been fairly transmitted-to Government, otherwise such sentences could not have been inflicted on any innocent and oppressed man.

Sir,
Dublin Castle, 30th June 1798.

Mr. Arthur received through Mr. Gorman the above extracts from General Morrison as the final order of Government for his quitting Ireland. On Tuesday the 3rd July. Mrs. Arthur sent a petition to his Excellency praying either a reversal of the sentence or such farther inquiry as might enable her husband to prove his innocence, upon a full dispassionate and cool investigation of his case. In support of this petition, she enclosed a short abstract of the trial, and some few general and obvious remarks together with the affidavits copies of which are subjoined, confirming the several facts stated in her petition.

Though Mrs. Arthur had been led to expect from the strength of these affidavits either a reversal of her husband's sentence or a re-investigation of his case, no answer was given by his Excellency. But on Friday, the 6th of July, five days after, General Morrison received his Excellency's order for liberating Mr. Arthur. Colonel Cockell gave Mr. Arthur the first indication of any disposition in Government to relieve him from suspense by informing him, that Government directed, that he was to be liberated and his fine to be returned on his giving security for quitting Ireland, and not returning until the present troubles had subsided, or that he received license for so doing.

Therefore was Mr. Arthur was not only closely confined, and all intercourse with him strictly forbidden for five days contrary to the order of Government, but his mind was kept on the rack during this period by the uncertainty of his fate. Colonel Cockell then added you must not stir out of your house and in twenty-four hours you must quit Limerick. Francis left Limerick accordingly and on his arrival in Dublin where he waited on Mr. Cooke, the under Secretary of state who asked him to remain in Dublin, as he intended making farther inquiries and that he would send down for Maum.

On the 16th of September, Mr. Arthur wrote to Mr. Cooke, praying that as Maum was now brought up the investigation might take place, and offering at the same time to prosecute him for a conspiracy against his life. To this letter Mr. Cooke did not honor Mr. Arthur with an answer and Francis therefore took the liberty of representing his situation by letter to the Lord Lieutenant; humbly praying something might be done, as his wish was to go to England on the reversal of the sentence against him.

Hubert Taylor, Esq. private Secretary to the Lord Lieutenant, informed Mr. Arthur the next day that his Excellency would speak to Lord Castlereagh and Mr. Cook about Mr. Arthur, and Mr. Taylor was pleased to add that he considered his case a very difficult one. Francis feeling himself disappointed at last, on the 28th of September presented a petition to the Lord Lieutenant, acknowledging the remission of his sentence on the condition of his quitting Ireland with liberty to reside in any other place at peace with his Majesty.

But as Maum was now brought up from Cork by Mr. Cook's order and Mr. Arthur by the same order was restrained from going to England pursuant to his sentence. He therefore prayed a complete reversal of the sentence, or an investigation of the particulars of the trial with liberty to prosecute Maum for perjury. To this petition Mr. Arthur annexed copies of Mrs. Arthur's petition and the affidavits laid before his Excellency, on the 4th July, together with copies of his letter to Mr. Secretary Cooke, requesting investigation.

On the 3rd October, Mr. Arthur received the following letter from Mr. Secretary Taylor.

Sir, Dublin Castle, 3rd October 1798,

"Having laid before the Lord Lieutenant your memorial and the enclosures. I am directed to acquaint you that his Excellency's opinion, with respect to the nature of Maum's evidence against you, has already sufficiently appeared from his decision in your cause. Nor does he consider, that any further advantage can result from the prosecution of a man actually sentenced to be transported to Botany Bay, independent of which, as such prosecution must necessarily be carried on before a civil Court of Judicature, the delay of attending it would bring I will agree with your wish to proceed as soon as possible to England.

I have the honor to be,<br>
H. Taylor.

Francis decided to address the Lord Lieutenant by letter, stating that from the tenor of Mr. Secretary Taylor's letter, he was induced to think his Excellency must have alluded to a total reversal of the sentence against him, though such had not been communicated to him. He therefore, requested his Excellency to direct that an authentic copy of his Excellency's decision would be given to him. Mr. Taylor informed Francis the next day, that his Excellency could do no more, than he had already done in his case, and referred him to Mr. Secretary Cooke. Francis applied to Mr. Secretary Cooke for a copy of the Lord Lieutenant's decision, who told him his Excellency's decision was verbally given, and not in writing. Thus Mr. Arthur could obtain no satisfaction on this very important point. At length, after many applications, Mr. Arthur was honored with the following letter.

Sir, Dublin Castle, 10th October 1798,

I have examined William Maum, whose evidence, I am clear is false. He will be sent off and transported, and there cannot be any objections to your going whither you think most eligible. As far as 1 can give testimony to your character, I shall ever do it by saying, that I think it by no means implicated from any lying asserted by Maum, and I certainly never heard any aspersion upon you from anyone else.
To Francis Arthur,
I have the honor to be, Esq. E. Cooke.

For, though according to Mr. Secretary Cook's letter Maum was to be sent off and transported soon after Mr.

Arthur's sailing for England, Maum was set at liberty, and publicly walking the streets of Cork, where he continued till the middle of January 1799. At that time he was again arrested not apparently because of his former sentence of transportation, but for having advertised his intention of publishing an account of Mr. Arthur's trial. Yet even under this arrest he was only sent to the guard house and kept in the Officers sitting room, with orders to be treated civilly, and there he was frequently visited by the late High Sheriff of the County of Tipperary, Colonel Thomas Judkin Fitzgerald. Maum was at last sent on board the transport ship Minerva whose Captain was Joseph Salkeld, and sailed with other convicts for Botany Bay on the 24th August, 1799.

Francis was very distressed because the government would not allow a new investigation of his case, and prosecute Maum for perjury, or allow him to obtain a public reversal of his own sentence. He decided to make a final effort toward a public exculpation and he again took the liberty of addressing both Mr. Taylor and Mr. Cooke by letter, asking that he be allowed to insert in the Dublin Newspapers copies of Mr. Secretary Taylor's and Cooke's letters to him. Mr. Taylor did not honor him with an answer, but he received the following letter from Mr. Cooke.

Sir, Dublin Castle, 18th October 1798.

To Francis Arthur, Esq.

I have received the honor of your letter. I should rather wish under the present circumstances that no publication should appear. 1 think a time more eligible than the present may arrive for any publication and I shall be willing on a future day to assist your wishes. As you have been so good as to defer to my opinion I have taken the liberty to give it you without specifying all my reasons. I have the honor to be E. Cooke.

Francis realizing that Government was determined to shut up every avenue for his justification for the moment and to leave him under the impression that he was liable to be arrested, if he remained in Ireland. He obtained the necessary passport and embarked for England with his family on the 25th October 1798.

In 1799 a letter was received in Limerick by Thomas Francis Wilkinson Esq. by the regular post from Cobh near Cork. This in effect said that Mr. Maum wished to make a full confession of his part in the persecution of Mr. Francis Arthur. As a result of this letter Mr. Wilkinson, Mr. Martin Arthur, and Mr. Peter Arthur, left Limerick post haste, for the Cobh of Cork, on the way they were joined by Kilner Brasier, Esq. late High Sheriff of the County of Cork and Thomas Holmes Esq. of said County. These gentlemen received from Wm. Maum the promised confession hereunto annexed directed to Mr. Wilkinson near the Exchange, Limerick.

Here is the text of the letter received by Thomas Francis Wilkinson from Maum.

Sir, Minerva, Cove, 5th August, 1799,

I suppose you will be surprised at receiving a letter from me. I desire you, if you value the interest of your friend, Mr. Arthur to come instantly to Captain Salkeld here, who will give some information which will not only surprise you but the entire kingdom. I have fully delineated every matter which contributed to his arrest, his trial, and the conduct of every officer who has been concerned. The villainous manner I have been compelled to be concerned on that trial, carried on by every species of dishonor. When you have every part of the proceeding your mind will be immersed in astonishment and you will likewise assert that Maum was not a villain, no, Mr. Arthur owes life to him notwithstanding the different opinions to the contrary. When you see my account of the business you will look on some of the gentlemen in Charleville, with these associates in Limerick, with merited detestation as Mr. Arthur owes all his unmerited confinement and temporary embarrassment to their little suspected villainy.

You may imagine I was concerned in Mr. Arthur's arrest. I assert the contrary; he was arrested by reason of his acquaintance with Mr. Hargrove and on no other charge. I stood firm against all their intrigues, until the 17$^{th}$ of June, and you will be surprised at the manner they then compelled me to accede to Anderson's oath, which I made him retract afterwards by a conversation I had with him in the council chamber which saved Mr. Arthur's life. Come to me therefore, or write to Captain Salkeld, or to me and you shall receive the entire proceedings, they are of the greatest importance to Mr. Arthur. I request you, or some friend of his to come off without delay and you will find, that Maum instead of being an object of detestation by reason of that villainy, should be rather an object of surprise. You will, when you see the proceedings readily acknowledge that you will in my account find an accurate account of the conduct of every officer, and private gentlemen in Limerick, who (to my knowledge) were concerned in this trial, expecting your speedy arrival.

I am, Sir,
Your obedient humble servant,
Wm. Maum.

P. S. I wish my account of the business may be published before I leave this kingdom as I defy any of the officers, or Gentlemen mentioned, to contradict any assertions from me I should have no objection to your publishing this letter.
Admitted to be his letter, in presence of us, on board the Minerva, in the Cobh of Cork, the 12th day of August 1799,

Joseph Salkeld,
Kilner Brasier,
Thomas Holmes.

Francis sent the following letter to Marquis Cornwallis along with a copy of Maum's declaration of Mr. Arthur's innocence.

To the most Noble Charles, Marquis Cornwallis, Lord lieutenant General and General Governor of Ireland, &c.
May it please your Excellency, having had the honor of so lately laying before your Excellency my petition, stating, in a plain impartial manner, the particulars of my late unjust prosecution and praying to be either again examined touching all the parts of the charges exhibited against me or permitted to return to my native country, with honor, and reputation. I should have waited with

becoming resignation the result of your Excellency's determination, did not a fresh corroboration of my innocence providentially start up totally unexpected or solicited by me or my friends, in the voluntary confession of Wm. Maum, my late principal prosecutor. I suppose he was stung by the reproaches of his own conscience, has now done all in his power, to make amends to me, by his voluntary confession not only of his own guilt, but of the means by which he was seduced to attempt my life and character his confession. I therefore take the liberty of laying this before you in order that your Excellency might receive this additional proof of the several affidavits, a correct copy of which I have also the honor to enclose, stating the several facts relative to my trial. How unjustly and with premeditation I have been singled out as a victim of private and public malice, trusting to the nobleness of your Excellency's nature, who I am confident must feel for the oppression's and disgraces heaped upon the head of an unoffending man. I commit the record to your perusal, waiting with all becoming loyalty and expectation for that period when you're Excellency, in your wisdom and humanity shall think proper finally to reinstate me in my former situation of life.

I have the honor to be,

With the most profound respect, Your Excellency's most obliged, And most grateful humble servant, London, 15th May, 1800. Francis Arthur.

The letter above, was laid before His Excellency together with the following declaration from Mr. Maum.

Voluntary declaration of William Maum, an accurate account of the trial of Francis Arthur, Esq. and the cause of his confinement prior to his being arraigned. Many opinions being in circulation relative to the guilt or innocence of Mr. Arthur, I think it incumbent upon me to give the following account of the iniquitous proceedings practiced against him, in which I have been in the most unprecedented manner compelled to be concerned. I was escorted from Donerail, (on I believe the 25th of May) to Clonmel by a detachment of yeomanry commanded by Captain Evans, whom I told that on that day there was an insurrection in some part of the kingdom. On my arrival in Clonmel my prediction was verified, upon which every person entertained great ideas of the importance of the contents of my mind, by reason of the priority of my knowledge to that of the public relative to the intended insurrection. I had a conversation with Colonel Fitzgerald, then High Sheriff of the County Tipperary at the house of Mr. Ryall, and another at the inn, he told me, that if I informed him or General St. John of the plans I had formed, that he and the General would exert themselves in favor of me and my friends, whom he found by my examination were peculiarly dear to me.

I desired some time to consider, and the next day informed him of my accession to his offer. The principal matter required of me was, to give an accurate account of my last conversation with Lord Edward Fitzgerald, which I did, in no part of which was Mr. Arthur's name mentioned, as may appear by the same in the possession of General Morrison. Colonel Fitzgerald then sent me to Limerick, that I might inform the General there how he should order relative to the King's stores in Charleville, and likewise as some parts of my conversation with Lord Edward relative to some parts of his district. I had the honor of dining with Colonel Foster in Tipperary, he gave me an unsealed letter to General Morrison, which I gave him the next morning in Limerick.

In my conversation with Lord Edward the name of Mr. Hargrove happened to be mentioned, indeed, with diffidence. Mr. Hargrove was arrested and Mr. Arthur, by reason of his acquaintance with him. When Mr. Arthur was arrested, there was no charge whatsoever against him, save his acquaintance with Mr. Hargrove. After his arrest General Morrison, Assistant Adjutant General Colonel Cockell, and Colonel Darby came to me at the General's lodgings and asked me if I could possibly bring any charge against Mr. Arthur. I firmly asserted it was not in my power in the smallest instance to traduce the character of that gentleman. I met that morning Richard Peppard in the coffee-room, who I imagined might form a bad opinion of me by reason of the arrest of Mr. Arthur.

I then wrote a letter, mentioning the questions put by the General, and my answers. I was then given in charge to Colonel Darby, who conducted me to his barracks where I received an officer's apartment. I from thence reported in a letter, which I addressed to General Morrison the entire of my conversation with Lord Edward, in no part of which was Mr. Arthur's name mentioned. Colonel Garden came to me frequently and said that the General was very angry because he should liberate Mr. Arthur and asked me if I could not bring a charge against him, I affirmed positively in the negative. He then asked me if nothing more could be brought against Hargrove; I asserted not, as his name was always mentioned with diffidence. After this I received some rest, but on the 4th of June, Lieutenant Louis of the 54th Regiment, brought me a letter from Colonel Darby.

This was but a silly pretext to arrest Mr. Arthur. He had no intercourse, connection or conversation whatever with Mr. Hargrove, for more than twelve months previous to his arrest. At the same time it will but be justice here to observe, that respectable man was put on his trial in June, 1798, before the same Court-martial, and honorably acquitted. Is it not to be supposed that General Morrison, knowing, that Government had interfered in Mr. Arthur's case and that he had not just grounds for detaining Mr. Hargrove in prison, was induced thereby to bring him forward and by a verdict of acquittal restore him to society?

Knowledge of my being possessed of information, the importance of which they were assured of which if I gave, I should receive a still greater share of their patronage. This letter I answered, in which Mr. Arthur's name was not mentioned. On Sunday, the 17th June, Colonel Darby brought me a letter from General Morrison requiring information from me against I. Barry, Joseph Littes, Dennis Linehan, and two gentlemen of my acquaintance in Charleville. I answered his letter directly saying, that I thought it a dishonorable infringement on my condition to injure my friends, who owed their liberties to my exertions and that he could not by any means influence me to my friend's injury.

The same day Colonel Darby came to me with another letter, viz. "to whom were the papers sent and what they contained, which were brought privately by you into this town about six months ago. A direct answer is required." Colonel Darby desired me to consider my situation I informed him I was fully acquainted with it. I answered the General's letter, peremptorily denying any papers being brought by me to any person in that town, but that I was in possession of papers, which Mr. Robert's negligence when I was arrested, gave me an opportunity of destroying. The General wrote me then letters on account of the following information Saunders in Charleville, swore in the presence of a gentleman of the same name in Charleville and other prejudiced gentlemen there that I in his presence, wrote letters to Mr. Arthur which John Barry was to deliver. Anderson an Inn-keeper in Limerick, swore, that I came to his house in a Nenagh chaise and that he conducted me to Mr. Arthur's house and saw me deliver a letter. After dinner on the above mentioned day, Lieutenant Louis came to me and told me, it was the General's "wish I should remove from my present apartment, they then placed me in a tent under a sentinel, he informed me of the arrest of my friends, and read me a letter from the General desiring him to send me to goal and confine me to a cell, that I might be whipped the next day. That I should likewise witness the execution of my friend Barry who I since learned was never arrested. Captain Brand, Aid-de-camp to General Morrison, came to me, and took me back to my former apartment, and desired me to leave the decision of the fate of my friends to the General's humanity and acknowledge to the letters sworn to by Anderson.

My wits were then put to the rack. I after many endeavors to send Richard Peppard a letter paid the waiter three guineas for carrying a letter from me to Richard Peppard, with instructions for Mr. Arthur's conduct on his defense, particularly about Saunders testimony and that of Anderson which I found afterwards was never delivered and was I suppose intercepted. On the 23rd of June, Captain Brand came to me and told me that Mr. Arthur was put on his trial and that I should be subject to the severest punishment if I did not stand firm. He had me brought to Assistant Adjutant General Colonel Cockell to the Council Chamber when the General made me repeat what I had to say, to refresh my memory. I there saw Saunders and Anderson whom I told I would injure for immersing me in such an abyss of trouble.

I said I would entirely disavow everything they had to say. I was called to the Court and asked relative for the above-mentioned letter and no question relative to Saunders and Anderson, as the President and the other officers fully knew what I would say. When I came out I told Saunders and Anderson that I fully did away their evidence, upon which, when they were examined they totally disavowed their former oaths, for which they suffered accordingly. I assert, that had it not been for my conduct in that respect, Mr. Arthur would have been hung at his own door, according to premeditation.

The principal cause of the dislike the officers in Limerick conceived against Mr. Arthur originated from some reports which General Sir James Duft" heard in 1796, purporting to report on Mr. Arthur's political principles, and his determination of injuring the General. This information was frequently conveyed to the General in anonymous letters and 1 believe those reports contributed to his being superseded in his commission. This information I derived from the President, Colonel Darby inquired of Maum in the course of the trial, whether he had sent a letter by the servant to Richard Peppard Maum replied he had done so and paid him three guineas to deliver it.

This seems to account for the pillorying of Anderson on the flimsy pretext of prevarication in his known evidence. It appears (if we may credit Maum) to have been merely to cover the real cause and it also seems to account for the President's evident surprise when on Saunders being sworn he declared he did not know the prisoner or anything about him.

Likewise there was absolutely a faction raised against him in Limerick, by some of the gentlemen in that town, particularly such as had acquaintances in Charleville. As may be well inferred from Saunders's testimony before some of the Magistrates in that town which I assert to be false in every instance. I rest assured, that the same gentleman excited that unfortunate man to swear against Mr. Arthur, and when Colonel Garden showed me his testimony written by Mr. Saunders, a Magistrate there. I informed him of the falsity of it, and the circumstance, which excited Saunders to swear in that manner. In my memorial to Mr. Cooke, I mentioned particularly every part of the officer's conduct in Limerick towards Mr. Arthur, which I gave General Meyers and in another memorial to his Excellency which 1 showed to Captain Judge of the Westmeath Regiment.

To conclude I assert, that Mr. Arthur's destruction, by every circumstance which can appear to me, was premeditated and that the methods adopted were villainous in every particular. I likewise assert that had it not been for my conduct on his trial, respecting the evidence of Saunders and Anderson he would have inevitably been hanged. Sir Christopher Knight contributed to Mr. Arthur's embarrassment, he made use of his Charleville acquaintance in procuring Saunders's testimony. I also assert, that, when my eyes were looking about for Mr. Arthur, Colonel Darby very positively pointed him out to me.

On the 17th of June, the day above alluded to Colonels Darby, Cockell and Garden dined with the General, who I am confident with the gentlemen in Limerick, who had Charleville acquaintances on that day settled Mr. Arthur's trial and also his death. On my going to the trial, Lieutenant Louis informed me after asking me some questions about his person and age, "that he was a very well looking man, and of a florid complexion." On the evening of the 17th of June, when Captain Brand came to me and took me back to my former apartment, he found, that I could not on that evening bring any charge against Mr. Arthur. He told me he would ask me no more questions until morning and said it was nearly contrary to the General's orders but to confine me together with Barry. Colonel Garden, after coming from the General's, came to my room, and asked me, if I could not give a positive charge against Mr. Arthur.

After many hesitations he said that I was perfectly able, by reason of the abilities I possessed, to bring a decisive charge against him and that my friends should be saved. And what is a stranger to you when compared to your own friends? The next morning he brought me the bundle of English Newspapers, which the mess had and a part opened. Wherein Perigord's address to the French Directory relative to England was published, which I suppose he was reading that morning and laid it before me, from which I derived the charge of the circular letter to Mr. Arthur. In consequence of such materials and the regard I had for the lives of my friends, I drew out the letter from those papers brought and left open by Colonel Garden, As Captain Roberts, when he came to me in company with Colonel Garden, likewise told me, that my friends were all in arrest and particularly mentioned Shee and Barry.

On the Sunday preceding his defense, Colonel Darby and Garden came to me and told me that Arthur was preparing his defense, and intended to prove an alibi, which we prevented by writing to the General about the review. Colonel Garden desired me to mention the orderly book of Jocelyn's dragoons to be produced on the trial which would totally counteract the alibi. My memory being strong, and having read about it, I fully recollected the time of Finnerty's pillory from Lord Edward's activity on that business which should be a favor-able time for his circulating seditious papers.

That circumstance occasioned me to mention that time in particular. The morning of his trial Captain Brand, after the threats, which he brought me from the General desired me take down notes of the leading points in the information. I did not, by reason of my good memory, I was not shown the information the day of the trial but I believe I would, had I not repeated to Colonel Cockell the lie.

It will be recollected that Maum in his direct evidence said he inquired for Mr. Arthur at his house and was there informed, he was gone to the review with his corps, where he certainly was on the 9th January. He had borrowed Cornet Lidwell of Jocelyn's horse-furniture his own not being made, but this date was widely different from the middle of February.

I assert that nothing whatever could induce me to injure Mr. Arthur, but the great intimidation's made use of and the earnest desire I had of saving my friends who I was led to imagine, were to be executed. I am now with a clear conscience ready to leave this kingdom after disclosing the iniquitous proceedings practiced against this innocent, devoted and truly injured gentleman, and I with readiness, and happy for having the favorable opportunity most willingly subscribe my name to it.

On board the Minerva, Cove of Cork, 12th August 1799.

This delivered as the voluntary declaration of William Maum not biased I am confident, by any motive, save his wish to repair the injury done Mr. Arthur.
Blaster of the Ship Minerva, Joseph Salkeld,
Kilner Brasier.

Kilner Brasier, Esq. High Sheriff of the County of Cork in the year of 1795, makes an oath upon the Holy Evangelists of Almighty God and says that the foregoing contains a

true and faithful extract of an original declaration, voluntarily made and delivered by William Maum, on board the Transport Ship Minerva in the Cobh of Cork, bearing date the 12th day of August, 1799. This is an accurate account of the trial of Francis Arthur, Esq. and the cause of his confinement, prior to his being arraigned with which said original declaration, now unto him this deponent produced he hath carefully examined and compared the said foregoing extract and found the same to agree. This deponent further deposes and says that he, this deponent and Joseph Salkeld, Master Henry Harrison first mate of said transport Minerva, Thomas Holmes of the County of Cork, aforesaid, Esq. Thomas' Francis Wilkinson, Martin Arthur and Peter Arthur of the City of Limerick, Merchants, were present, and did see the said William Maum sign and deliver the said original declaration. The names Joseph Salkeld, Kilner Brasier, Thomas Holmes, Henry Harrison, Thomas Francis Wilkinson, Martin Arthur, Peter Arthur, thereunto likewise set and subscribed, are the respective signatures and of the proper handwriting of the said William Maum, Joseph Salkeld, Thomas Holmes, Henry Harrison, Thomas Francis Wilkinson, Martin Arthur, Peter Arthur, and him this deponent. Sworn the 8th day of May, before me, in London.
Kilner Brasier. H. C. Coombe, Mayor.

I John Mitchell of London notary public, by royal, authority duly admitted and sworn do hereby certify and attest unto whomsoever it may concern that the signature, H. C. Coombe Mayor set and subscribed to the Jurat's at foot of the above affidavit is the true signature and of the proper handwriting of the Right Honorable Harvey

Christian Coombe, Lord Mayor and one of His Majesty's justices of the peace for this City of London. Who on the day of the date thereof administered oath according to due form of law (in presence of me notary) unto Kilner Brasier the deponent in the said affidavit named and thereupon signed the same in conformity, in manner as thereon appears, whereof an act being required of me I have granted these presents under my notaries firm and seal of office to serve where needful, thus done and passed in London, the 8th day of May, 1800.
Intestimonium veritatis,
John Mitchell, Notary Public.
Notaries Seal.

We the under named do hereby certify, that Mr. John Mitchell, whose firm is foregoing, is a sworn notary public, practicing in this City lawful and of trust, and to all acts and writings by him signed, faith is given in court and there out Witness our hands, London the 8th of May, 1800.
David Gillonneaa, Notary Public.
Robert Gibson, Notary Public.

Now why have I devoted so much time to the trial of Francis Arthur? The reason quite simply is that I believe that this trial and the reasons why it happened at all are at the root the beginning of the decline in the fortunes of the Arthur family. At a meeting of the Aristocratic Club in Limerick of which he was a member, it was resolved that Francis be expelled from the club for taking part in the rebellion and resolved that his name be erased from the list of subscribers to the house by order of Maurice Crosby Chairman.

Francis went to London when he finally gave up on being totally vindicated by the Lord Lieutenant although he was told that he could return to Limerick when the troubles of 1798 were finished. In London he purchased a large property where much of Piccadilly now stands.

Later he went to France where he died at Dunkirk in June 1824. Much of the Arthur estates that had not already been given to the various girls who entered convents ad dowries were left to the Leahy family of Cork. Daniel Leahy who was Francis' son in law acted, as executor under Francis will.

After going to England Francis rarely got a license to return to Ireland but he did return for the wedding of his daughter to Mr. Green in his house in Dublin. As Francis was no longer personally present to look after his business due to his banishment, his business that had been thriving went downhill as those who were looking after it for him were not as wise in the ways of business as he was and did not keep as close an eye on it as he would have.

An account book in the Special Collections section of the Glucksman Library at the University of Limerick gives details of rents received from Francis Arthur's ownership of property in Limerick city, mainly dating to the 1820s. His properties included 149 acres at Coonagh (this may have been his great grandfathers), land in the North Liberties of the city, property at Arthur's Quay and many other city locations. Copies of 18$^{th}$ century deeds show his title to these properties. Details of Francis Arthur in account there accounts show that Francis did business with such persons as Thomas William Roche, Lord

Glenworth, Patrick Greene of Abbey, the executors of P.E. Arthur, Luke Callaghan of Paris and many others. Arrears rentals for Arthur's Quay and other Limerick premises, 1821, statements of yearly outgoings, copies of deeds in connection with a conveyance Francis Arthur, Ellen Arthur and Daniel Leahy are also included in these records.

Here is an advertisement that was in the Limerick Chronicle on March 9th 1805.
Mr. Arthur's Houses. To be let the house in Georges Street, No 4 next to Mr. Lyons's house, for lives renewable forever. It is now in great condition and is ready for a tenant on the first of May next. Details to Francis Arthur or Mr. Thos. O'Brien, Broad Street.

Here is another article that was in the Limerick Chronicle on the 31st March 1804

Sheriffs Sale. Francis Arthur Plaintiff and Laurence Durack Defendant.

To be sold by public Cant on Thursday the 12th day of April next at the Tholsel of Limerick, by virtue of his Majesty's writ of Fieti Facia, to us in this cause directed, marked to the sum of 219 pounds 18 shillings and 10 pence all the defendants interest in two houses in Patrick Street, in the liberties of Limerick, now tenanted by Messer's Creagh and Hartnett, being for a long term for years; the cant to begin at two o'clock on said day. Dated this 31st. day of March 1804.

H.P.Carroll, A.C.Stretch, Sheriffs.

I have told how Francis was very involved in the work to get Catholics equal rights with their Protestant neighbors as well as working for the commercial betterment of the city. It must have been some source of pleasure to him to see that members of the Arthur family continued his work after he was banished from these shores. Below are to instances that were found in the Limerick Chronicle of members of the Arthur family still being involved in the commercial life of the city as well as in the quest for Catholic rights..

The following appeared in the Chronicle on March 26th 1806.
Yesterday at a meeting of the proprietors of the commercial buildings in this city the following were elected a committee of directors for the ensuing year: John McNamara, John Howley, John Kennedy, Walter Martin White, George Maunsell, Martin Arthur, William Roche, William O'Shea, John Kelly, Dan Gabbett, R Westropp Jnr, Jasper Whit, Dennis Lyons and William Norris. Messrs. Maunsell and Kennedy - Treasurers, Daniel Gabbett - Law Agent and D.G.F. Mahony – Treasurer.
Note here that John Howley, Martin Arthur and William O'Shea. Indeed William O'Shea was an ancestor of the Captain O'Shea whose wife Kitty O'Shea (nee Woods) was instrumental in bringing down Parnell.

This notice appeared in the Limerick Chronicle on the 31st July 1813.
Catholic Meeting.

We the undersigned request a meeting of the Roman Catholics of the County and City of Limerick at one O'clock on Thursday the 13th August next at St. Michael's Chapel to prepare their petitions to Parliament and an address to the Throne for the ensuing session as well as to take into consideration such other matters as may be connected with the Catholic cause.
Thomas Roche, Thaddeus R Ryan, William Roche, William Howley, John Kennedy, Gerald Griffin, Roger Scully, Martin Creagh, John Evans, Francis Mahony, Bryan Sheehy, Michael Arthur, John Howley Junior, Michael Ryan, James D Lyons, James Griffin Junior, Henry Lyons, James B Curtained.
The Limerick Catholic Board will meet at their board room William Street on Monday the 2nd August at one o'clock to organize proceedings for the above meeting which every member is requested to attend.
Note the number of surnames on this committee were the same as on the previous one.

David Leahy of Shanakiel, near Cork city married Catherine O'Sullivan and they had two sons Daniel and John. Daniel married twice and his second wife was Margaret daughter of Francis Arthur of Limerick. Their son David inherited the Arthur estate in Limerick from Francis Arthur and he took the additional name of Arthur, becoming known as David Leahy Arthur. The Leahy estate passed to the second son Francis Robert in 1855 and later to his brother Daniel Francis. John and Daniel Leahy held land in the parishes of Clonfert and Knocktemple as well as in the barony of Duhallow at the time of Griffith's Valuation. In the 1870s Daniel Francis Leahy of Shanakiel was the owner of over 2300 acres in county Cork and Mrs. Leahy of Shanakiel owned 675 acres

So between Francis leaving Limerick and relying on others to administer his estates and his enemies making it as difficult as they could to do business a lot of damage was done to the family fortune. His daughter Margaret inherited much of his fortune and as she was married to Daniel Leahy of Shanakiel House Co. Cork so the fortune passed out of the hands of the Arthur family. (Francis only son Patrick had died before his father)

Here is a list of some of the properties held by David Leahy Arthur who took the name Arthur because his mother was Francis Arthur's daughter and he inherited much of Francis' wealth. This list is dated 1850 and comes from Griffith's valuation.

Here are some of the properties in Limerick that were owned by David Leahy Arthur because he has inherited them from his grandfather in law Francis Arthur. In 1849 he has numbers 13 and 14 Francis Street, he had number 1 and 2 Arthur's Quay as well as the above he also had numbers 27 and 28 Lower Denmark Street. In Cork he had the following properties; in Georges Quay he had number 9, number 29. Now the above Limerick properties are just a few of the properties owned by Francis Arthur in Limerick. I put in the Cork ones to show that the Leahy Arthur's had their own property portfolio in Cork. These are just the ones for which I have found definite records there were many more.

Below are accounts for some of the properties some of the properties that David Leahy inherited from his grandfather Francis Arthur. The dates involved are from September 1869 to September 1864. These properties were in Denmark Street, Patrick Street and Arthurs Quay in the city of Limerick and the name of the tenant is given for each property

| Name | One Year Rent | Five year rent | Rent paid | Poor rate allowance | Income tax allowance |
|---|---|---|---|---|---|
| Mrs. C Sexton | £20 | £100 | £100 | | |
| D. L Arthur | £4 | £20 | £20 | £2-11-04 | £0-6-9 |
| Mick Egan | £65 | £325 | 325 | £25-2-06 | |
| Mrs. C Blake | £5 | £25 | £25 | | |
| M Hanley+ Holihan | £3 | £14 | £14T | | |
| Thomas Mahir | £25 | £125 | £125 | | |
| Mrs. O'Brien | £22 | £110 | £110 | £6-10-0 | |
| Mrs. Dixon and I Keane | £24 | £120 | £120 | | |
| A Cooney and J Hayes | £27-10-0 | £137-10-0 | £137-10-0 | | |
| J Casey and E O'Toole | £11-5-0 | £56-10-0 | £56-100 | | |
| W Condon | £11 | £55 | £55 | | |
| Mrs. C Blake | £13 | £65 | £65 | | |
| John Patterson | £12 | £60 | £60 | | |
| Mrs. O | £12 | £60 | £60 | | |

| Shanghassey | | | | | |
|---|---|---|---|---|---|
| **Name** | **One Year Rent** | **Five Year Rent** | **Rent Paid** | **Poor Rate Allowance** | **Income tax Allowance** |
| Mrs. O Shanghassey | £6 | £30 | £30 | | |
| Mrs. M Hastings | £13 | £65 | £65W | | |
| William Todd and co. | £3 | £15 | £15 | £1-13-06 | £0-2-06 |
| Mrs. Leney | £12 | £60 | £60 | | |
| J Casey and Mrs. Whealan | £12 | £59 | £59 | | |
| W Ryan and M Nunan | £12 | £60 | £48 | | |
| D. L Arthur | £8 | £40 | £40 | £5-2-08 | £13-8-0 |
| Henessyand Stuart | £7-4-0 | £35-9-0 | £31-12-04 | | |
| J Mahony and W Enright | £6-10-0 | £31-17-06 | £31-17-06 | | |
| Martin O' Connor | £25 | £125-15-0 | £125-15-0 | | |

As can be seen from the above which are just some of Francis Arthur's properties that had passed on to David Leahy Arthur generated a substantial income for David. They would have generated a more substantial income for Francis as when he owned them they were the best address to have in Limerick. However by the time of these accounts many of these addresses had slipped down the table of desirable locations in which to live and so no longer commanded a premium rent.

In the next table there are details of some of the half yearly incoming and outgoing for David Leahy Arthur for some of his Limerick Properties.

Some of the spaces in the table below were not filled in and I am not sure why.

| Half Year | Head Rants Paid | Boro Rates Paid | Poor Rates Paid | Incom e Tax Paid | Repairs | Fire Insu rance | Agent fees | Remi tances |
|---|---|---|---|---|---|---|---|---|
| Marc h May 1870 | £9-13-03 | £22-13-11 | £40-3-01 | £ | £10-9-04 | £ | £11-2-11 | £151-9-03 |
| Sept Nov 1870 | £5-12-0 | £21-16-5.5 | £31-8-06 | £4-4-06 | £7-12-3.5 | £2-7-05 | £9-6-09 | £73-2-11 |
| Marc h May 1871 | £6-5-07 | £23-11-04 | £ | £0-6-08 | £20-6-01 | £ | £10-3-0 | £138-0-03 |
| Sept May 1871 | £6-8-03 | £23-11-04 | £29-13-07 | £6-14-09 | £9-18-10 | £2-7-05 | £8-10-07 | £81-17-03 |
| Marc h May 1872 | £5-17-09 | £24-8-10 | £ | £ | £29-12-10 | £ | £9-4-04 | £109-19-04 |
| Sept May 1872 | £6-17-05 | £24-8-10 | £33-3-05 | £4-9-10 | £11-17-03 | £2-7-05 | £8-9-0 | £77-6-04 |
| Marc h May 1873 | £115-6-05 | £25-6-03 | £ | £ | £20-5-08 | £ | £9-3-0 | £116-10-02 |
| Sept May 1973 | £6-18-0 | £25-6-03 | £47-2-09 | £3-7-04 | £8-14-03 | £2-7-05 | £8-14-0 | £71-3-09 |
| Marc h May 1874 | £5-8-0 | £24-8-10 | £ | £ | £18-5-09 | £ | £9-4-06 | £120-14-02 |

| Sept May 1874 | £5-18-09 | £26-3-09 | £52-7-06 | £2-4-11 | £5-0-02 | £2-7-05 | £8-14-0 | £70-0-0 |
|---|---|---|---|---|---|---|---|---|
| Total | £64-15-05 | £241-15-9.5 | £233-18-10 | £21-8-0 | £142-2-5.5 | £11-17-01 | £92-12-01 | £1010-3-05 |

Again notice here how much money was still being generated between 1872 and 1874 by what were once Arthur properties, how much it cost to run those properties and taxes etc. they generated.

# Chapter 11

*The wills of Francis Arthur and his daughter Margaret Leahy Arthur.*

You will notice in some places where I am transcribing the will of Francis Arthur that words may not seem correct. This is because the handwriting in the copy of the will I have is terrible and there were a number of words I was not sure of. So in order not to leave big spaces in my transcription I made my best guess at what they were without hopefully changing the meaning of what was on the page. In a couple of places I put question mark beside a word because I was not certain that I had even the intention of the word correct. In his will Francis mentions some family miniatures etc. which went to the Leahy Arthur's. I wonder if they still exist and if so where are they as I have not been able to trace the family to the present day. Also note how Francis had property and business in many different places including Norway of which a small mention will be made later.

The will of Margaret Leahy Arthur was much easier to read as the scribe who wrote it down had much better hand writing than the one who wrote the will of Francis Arthur. Another point to make here is to notice just how wealthy they were compared to ordinary people. It would also be reasonable to assume that as these wills were written when much of the family wealth was gone so they must have been very wealthy indeed. Remember that by the time of this will much of his wealth had been given to various convents as dowries where some of Francis daughters were nuns and where both of his granddaughters were nuns.

***Below is the last will and testament of Francis Arthur of Limerick***

I Francis Arthur late of the City of Limerick in the Kingdom of Ireland merchant but now residing at Dunkirk in France do make and publish this my last will and testament hereby revoking and annulling, and making void all former wills and testaments by me any time heretofore made. Whereas I have by the settlement on my marriage with my present wife Ellen who before our marriage was called Ellen Barrett allotted a certain jointure of one hundred and fifty pounds a year for her support and maintenance during her life in case she should survive me in life. Bar of all I own and have at common law or otherwise and whereas on arranging and settling my affairs with my son in law David Leahy Esquire of the City of Cork I did by subsequent settlement grant and appoint an additional jointure of one hundred and fifty pounds a year payable to my said wife Ellen in like manner during her life in case she should survive me. Now providing the said provision an ample sum for my said wife I do declare that the sum of one hundred pounds which I hereby now bequeath her is in full of all the claims she has or shall have to any part of my personal property whatsoever. I give and bequeath unto my nephew Francis McNamara now residing with me in Dunkirk the sum of one hundred pounds British money to be disposed of as he thinks proper and whereas I have heretofore purchased of John O'Dea of Ennis completely all his right title and in trust in certain houses with their apartments held by his father on lease from the Earl of Edgemont now I do hereby give and bequeath all my estate right and interest in the same houses with their apartments unto my son in law Cornelius Mahoney Esquire of Vauxhall near Limerick his executors administrators and assignees. Whereas my personal effects were sold and disposed of by Daniel Leahy immediately after my quitting Ireland amounted to a very considerable sum. Now in order to give proof of my affection and regard for his (David Leahy) wife Margaret Leahy to make a provision for her independent of her husband , I do hereby give and bequeath the whole produce of such personal effects unto Morgan McNamara merchant of London and to his nephew John McNamara now resident with him my executors, administrators and assign in trust to be paid applied and disposed of for the separate and benefit of my daughter the said Margaret Leahy independent of the influence of her said husband. Whereas the chest containing my plate is now deposited in the vaults of Sir Richard Curtis and Company bankers in London, who have at my request heretofore declared the trust thereof in favour of the said Morgan McNamara but being willing that the same should go with my general inheritance. I give and bequeath all my plate aforesaid unto my grandson the oldest son of the said Daniel Leahy and his sons forever in the nature of a loan and I hope he and they will always be inured to regard the same as old family plate. I will and direct that my furniture and other personal effects which I may have in Dunkirk aforesaid shall be disposed of by my executors and applied so far as they will go in discharge of any claims on me. As to all the rest and residue of my personal estate which shall remain after payment of all my just debts and which residue I believe will be a reasonable sum I give and bequeath the same unto the said Daniel Leahy his executor's administrators and assigns. I appoint the said Morgan McNamara and John McNamara executors of this my last will and testament and I hereby give and bequeath unto them the sum of fifty pounds as acknowledgement of the trouble they may have in the execution of this my will in full. Whereof I the said Francis Arthur have entrusted to the aforementioned hereof all of the same tasks and set my hand and seal this twenty fifth day of September in the year of our lord one thousand eight hundred and twenty three. FRANCIS ARTHUR. THE SEAL WENT HERE, signed sealed published and as well as the other parts hereof by the said FRANCIS ARTHUR. The testator as and for his last will and testament in the presence of us who at his request in his present and in the presence of each other have where into subscribed our executor as Wilfred Alfonso Camus Elirik to Mr. Duval of Dunkirk John Fred Desmadryc Dunkirk..

Note on side of document is in italics below

*Whereas by my last will and testament made declared and published on September last I do order declare and appoint that my silver plate and other valuables in my gift now under the care of Sir William Curtis Bart should at all times hereinafter go and be consider as a lot, soon to be proposed by the person having and enjoying my estate. Whereas a considerable part of my plate and silver articles are now in the care of Mrs Ellen Arthur I now do declare this as the first codicil to my said will and I now advise and swear that all and every said silver articles to be taken soon in like manner as my chest of silver articles now under the care of Sir William Curtis Bart be held by the person actually in possession of my estate. This done my own is mounting given under my hand and seal and declared this to be to be the first codicil to my said will and at all times hereafter to be held as part of my last will and testament I witness whereof I have hereinto put my hand and seal this 17th Day of October 1823. FRANCIS ARTHUR. SEAL HERE.*

Now back to main body.

I Francis Arthur late of the city of Limerick in Ireland merchant now resident in Dunkirk France having made published and declared by my last will and testament bearing the day of September last am now minded to add by way of codicil to my will. Which codicil is all in my own handwriting and I do hereby direct and appoint that the same be at all sums however taken and held as part of my said will. Whereas I have brought with me to France now in the care of my present wife Mrs. Ellen Arthur two portraits in miniature one of myself round with large pearls and one of my dearly beloved Mrs. Ellen Arthur (I think first wife Ellen Sexton) which latter portrait has been burnt and has passed nine times through the fix before it was declared perfect. There are also several other miniatures and engravings on paper which now I do hereby bequeath the whole thereof together with the Bon Dieu which I wear hanging close to my heart to my well beloved daughter Margaret Leahy as the gifts of her own lamented mother. Whereas I have found it necessary to bring with me to France Several articles of silver plate all of which my sister has a particular account

> of all which plate and plates which are in the care of my present wife Mrs. Ellen Arthur (Ellen Barrett) together with opera glasses, reading glasses and three or four pair of spectacles, now I do hereby order will and wish that the whole of the aforesaid articles and every part thereof do pass into the hands of the person looking after my estate David Francis Arthur Leahy. Or such other person as the same shall appoint pursuant to my settlement and as an executor to my said estate in witness thereof I have herein put my hand and affixed my seal this twenty fifth day of November one thousand eight hundred and twenty three at Dunkirk aforesaid Francis Arthur. Seal here.

I Francis Arthur late of the city of Limerick in the Kingdom of Ireland, merchant but now residing at Dunkirk in France do make publish and declare this to be a codicil to my last will and testament bearing date the twenty ninth of day of September one thousand eight hundred and twenty three and do first the same and all other codicils by me made to be derived? Taken as part of my said will whereas by a certain testamentary paper or will all in my own handwriting and signed with my own hand and made at Dunkirk aforesaid and which is intended only to have effect on such property as I may have at Dunkirk after bequeathing same portrait miniatures and the Bon Dieu. I have stated that I found it unnecessary to bring with me to France several articles of silver plate and plates together with an opera glasses a large reading glasses and four pair of spectacles and also by such testamentary paper or will in my own handwriting as aforesaid and which bears date the twenty fifth day of

November last I have ordered willed and directed that all such articles as aforesaid should pass into the hands and possession of David Francis Arthur Leahy or such persons as my estate shall descend to by virtue of my settlement. This will in the nature of things be done soon and I do hereby ratify and reaffirm such bequest and direction contained in the said testamentary paper or will in my own handwriting as aforesaid. Whereas the Reverend Thomas Coll of the parish of St. Michael in the liberties of Limerick aforesaid hath undertaken to move to France and then to proceed to Bremen and Stockholm and to several towns in Norway in order to liquidate and discharge my holdings there (here he mentions that the family had business interests in Norway and these interests were almost certainly managed by family members) . I have given him a list of them and generally to settle my affairs in the whole of Europe and elsewhere. Now in order to inure the said Thomas Coll to execute this troublesome commission I do hereby give and bequeath onto the said Thomas Coll and his assignees during the term of his natural life an annuity or yearly sum of fifty pounds of lawful English money. This money to be paid and payable by half yearly portions on the first day of May and the first day of November the first to be paid whereof on the first of those days which shall first happen after my decease together with a proportional part of such annuity from the last half yearly payment up to and including the day of the death of the said Thomas Coll. Whereas my faithful servant Elizabeth Coulberd the wife of Thomas Coulberd late of the county of South Clare but now residing at Dunkirk aforesaid hath diligently discharged her duty towards me now as a suitable person. I do here by give and bequeath unto the said Elizabeth Coulberd during her natural life an annuity of ten pounds of lawful English money payable on such days and with a proportional part thereof in the event of her death as is herein before specified. With respect to the annuity of the said Thomas Coll I do hereby subject and charge all my chattels real and personal given and bequeathed to my said wife of the twenty ninth day of September last and all other my estate and property which I have any power to subject and charge with the regular payment of the said annual annuities of fifty pounds and ten pounds hereby bequeathed as aforesaid in witness. Whereof I the said Francis Arthur have to this codicil set my hand and seal at Dunkirk aforesaid and also to those other parts this eleventh day of November in the year of our lord one thousand eight hundred and twenty three, Francis Arthur. Seal here. Signed sealed published and declared as well as the other three parts whereof by the said Francis Arthur as a codicil to this will in the presence of us who at his request in his presence and in the presence of others who have subscribed and named as witness Alphonse Canunus of Dunkirk and John Fred Desmadry Dunkirk.

Jeremiah Scully of Twenty Middle Camden Street aged forty years and upwards make oath on the holy evangelists and saith that I know and was intimately acquainted with Francis Arthur formerly of the City of Limerick in Ireland. But late of Dunkirk in France Merchant deceased and with the usual character and manner of handwriting having often seen him write and subscribe his name. Saith he hath lawfully viewed perused and examined a paper writing annexed purporting to be a codicil to the last will and testament of the said deceased beginning whereas my last will and testament and ending this 17th day of October

1823 twenty three and subscribed Francis Arthur. Saith he hath also viewed, perused and examined a paper writing hereunto also annexed purporting to be a codicil to the last will and testament of the said Francis Arthur beginning I Francis Arthur late of the city of Limerick and ending one thousand eight hundred and twenty three at Dunkirk aforesaid and subscribed Francis Arthur. Saith every word setter and figure in said two codicils respectively beginning ending and subscribed responsively as aforesaid are all of the proper handwriting and signature of the said deceased to the best of
my judgment and belief. Jeremiah Scully swore this 8th day of February 1825.

Before us;

I Radcliff on the 30th of March 1825 with the will and three codicils annexed of the goods chattels and credits of Francis Arthur formerly of the city of Limerick in Ireland but late of Dunkirk in France merchant deceased was granted to David Leahy Esq. The residuary executor named in the said will being first sworn by common duly to administer Morgan McNamara and John McNamara the executors having duly renounced the probate and execution of the said will as by act of court approved.

***Below is the last will and testament of Margaret Leahy Arthur daughter of Francis Arthur.***

In the name of God I Margaret J Leahy of Westlawn in the city of Cork widow and relict of Daniel Leahy late of Shanakiel House in the county of Cork deceased. Being of perfect mind, memory and understanding do make publish and declare this my last will and testament hereby revoking all former and other wills by me at any time heretofore made. I give and bequeath unto my executors and executrix herein after named all and singular my real and personal estate monies, securities for money and all such sums as shall be due and owing to me at the time of my decease. Of my real charge or otherwise together with all my furniture, plate, jewelry, carriage, horses and all my goods and chattels of every nature and kind while I may die possessed of or entitled unto upon the trusts and for the purposes concerning the same hereinafter declared.

That is to say I give to my son David Leahy Arthur of Hyde Park my silver chalice, two plated soup tureens the silver salad bowl presented by Lord Cork to my husband, all the plate bearing the crest of a hawk. Five old plated corner dishes one vestment worked by Mrs. Arthur (Ellen Sexton wife of Francis) and the large marble table now in his (David Leahy Arthur) possession.

I give to my son Francis Robert Leahy the paintings of old Rubens and his daughter Saint Cecilia and the “Sybil” all of which are at present in my dining room at Woodlawn (I believe these are now in a gallery in London).

To give to my son Daniel Francis Leahy the following articles one plate chest two silver drinking cups presented by the late Lord Dungarvan to my husband, four silver sauce boats, twelve silver table spoons, twelve silver desert spoons, twelve silver tea spoons, one large silver gravy spoon, one silver soup ladle, one silver fish knife, one small silver salver, twelve silver desert knives, twelve silver desert forks, one butter knife one sugar tongs, two wine labels, two silver meat skewers, one funnel and stand, four salt spoons, all my books and my large desk inlaid with brass. To my daughter in law the wife of said son Daniel Francis Leahy the diamond ring set in dark blue enamel.

I give to my daughter in law the widow of my late son Edward J Leahy deceased one set of vestments, all my house linen and the small diamond ring presented to me by Mary J Arthur (I think this is Margaret Jane Arthur the daughter of Francis Arthur).

I give to my daughter Alice the wife of John Nicolas Murphy all my desks, save that before left to my son Daniel Francis, all my work boxes and their contents, my drawing room clock, the two pale screens and foot stools worked by my said daughter and now in my drawing room at Woodlawn, my silver tea pot, my silver coffee pot and sugar bowl, my large diamond ring and all my jewelry of every nature and kind not otherwise herein before bequeathed.

I leave and bequeath to my grandson Daniel Leahy the younger son of my late son Edward in the event of his attaining the age of twenty one years but not otherwise the following plate that is to say, nine silver table spoons, twelve silver tea spoons, one large gravy spoon, one small silver salver, six silver desert knives, six silver desert forks, one silver butter knife, one old silver sugar tongs, one silver meat skewer, two silver salt spoons All the plated articles not hereinto fore mentioned, I desire that the same shall after my decease be handed to the mother of my said grandson Mrs., Edward J Leahy, to be by her retained in trust for him until he shall attain the age of twenty one years when I desire and it is my will that they be given to him as his absolute property but in the event of his dying before attaining the age of twenty one year's then I desire and it is my will that the said articles of plate and plated goods shall be immediately handed to my son Daniel Francis Leahy to whom in that event I leave and bequeath the same.

I direct my executors and executrix immediately after my decease to sell by public auction all the remainder of my furniture, carriage, horses, harnesses, hay, oats, coal and wine and to pay over the proceeds to my said daughter Alice Murphy to whom I devise and bequeath the same as my real and personal estate, monies, securities for monies and all other my property of every nature and kind not herein before specifically bequeathed subject to the just payment of my just debts, funeral, testamentary and other expenses absolutely free from any restriction or trust at law or in equity or otherwise howsoever as she knows how to dispose of same. I desire that my funeral shall take place at an early hour and that it be perfectly private and conducted inexpensively. I nominate, constitute and appoint my said daughter Alice my residuary legatee. I nominate and appoint my son David Leahy Arthur and my son in law John Nicolas Murphy executors and my said daughter Alice Murphy executrix of this my will. In witness whereof I have hereunto set my hand seal this 8th day of November in the year of our lord one thousand eight hundred and sixty seven. Margaret J Leahy. Signed sealed published and declared by the said testatrix Margaret J Leahy as and for her last will and testament in the presence of us who in her presence and in the presence of each other at her request have hereunder subscribed our names as witnesses D.V. Donegan, John Clarke, J. A. O'Mullane Cork. 8th November 1867.

In her Majesty's court of probate the district registry at Cork in the goods of Margaret J Leahy late of Woodlawn in the city of Cork, widow deceased. I Daniel Valentine Donegan of the South Mall in the city of Cork, Solicitor, make oath that I am one of the subscribing witnesses' to the last will and testament of Margaret J Leahy late of Woodlawn in the city of Cork widow deceased. The said will being now hereunto annexed, bearing date the eight day of November one thousand eight hundred and sixty seven and that the said testatrix executed the said will on the day of the date whereof by subscribing her name at the foot or end thereof the word "estate" on the tenth line of first page having been written on alteration? the written word "and" on the nineteenth line of the same page having been erased and the words "and all" thirteenth line of the third page having been written erasure and all said alterations being marked with my initials as the same now appears hereon in the presence of me and Joseph

O'Mullane the other subscribed witnesses there to both of us being present at the same time and we thereupon attested and subscribed the dais will in the presence of the said testatrix and of each other. D O'Donegan of Nivorual Cook Street in the city of Cork. This fifteenth day of October I pledge by the said Valentine Donegan before the commissionaires of the Court of Chancery in Ireland for administering oaths for administering oaths in the city of Cork and I know the deponent John Marks Chancery law. Be it known that on the twenty eight day of October 1869 the last will and testament hereunto annexed of Margaret Jane Leahy late of Woodlawn in the County and City of Cork widow deceased who died on the eleventh day of August 1869 at Woodlawn aforesaid and who at the time of her death had a fixed place of abode at Woodlawn aforesaid within the district of Cork was approved and registered in the said district Registry attached to her Majesty's Court of Probate of Cork and that the administration of all and singular the personal estate and effects of the said deceased was granted by the aforesaid court to John Nicolas Murphy Esquire of Clifton in said city. One of the executors named in the said will, he having been first sworn will and faithfully administer the same by paying the just debts of the deceased and the legacies contained in her will and he exhibit a true and perfect inventory of all and singular the said estate and effects and to render a just and true account thereof whenever required by law to do so. Power being reserved of making a like grant to David Leahy Arthur and Alice Murphy the remaining executors named in said will when they or rather of them shall apply for the same.

# Chapter 12

*The Arthur's of Kenmare*

Patrick Arthur of Kenmare and family in the 1930's.

This is a branch of our family about whom we do not know as much as we would like. I am in touch with one member of the family who funnily enough is called Patrick Arthur. Some of the information below came from Br. Charles Firmin Arthur some from Gabriel Arthur and some from Patrick Arthur who is one of the Arthur family still living in Kenmare. Other bits came from other members of the Kenmare family whose contributions to the knowledge base I have but I seem to have mislaid the names of the persons who shared the knowledge with me..

Brother Charles (Firmin) Arthur along with my great grandfather Mr. John Arthur who lived in Clonmel County Tipperary were in communication with a Mr. Patrick Arthur of the above family in it is believed in the 1930's, who with great kindness supplied the following account of that branch of the family.

In the late 1880's and early 1890's John Arthur had his photography studio in Kerry for a number of years and it is thought that it was at this time that communication with this branch of the family was established again.

Philip Arthur

After the siege of Limerick with the termination of the Jacobite war a certain Thomas Arthur left Limerick and settled in Cladanure about two miles west of Kenmare. This was in the year 1700 Thomas is supposed to have taken part in the wars between James and William. Later they moved to Derrynacaraugh, Bonane which is approximately six miles south of Kenmare. The history of this Thomas Arthur is lost in the mist of antiquity however we know he had a son named Thomas who in time became a boat-builder. He married and his boys continued in the boat building business. One of them Patrick was employed by the liberator Daniel O'Connell at his home in Derrynane for a time but this Patrick left Ireland around 1847. The other children of this Thomas were Philip, Charles and two others whose names as yet I have not yet been able to trace. Philip & Charles left Ireland for USA and got married in Boston Mass where they died. The two whose names we cannot trace are believed to have settled in west Cork where they worked as boat-builders. It is possible they have descendants who are still living there.

Now Thomas Arthur and Mary Leahy of Cladanure had Patricia in 1819, Mary in 1822 and they were probably the parents of Thomas born before 1819.

Thomas Arthur and Mary Hegarty of Derrynacaraugh had the following children Helen born on the 27th of January 1842, Janet who was born on the 9th of April 1844, Thomas who was born on the 27th of September 1846, James who was born on the 3rd of June 1849, Philip who was born on the 17th of August 1851 and Patrick who was born on the 6th of May 1857.

The children of Philip Arthur and Johanna Connors were Thomas who was born on the 12th of February 1877, Mary who was born on the 9th of April 1878, Abigail who was born on the 19th of December 1879, Patrick who was born on the 19th of March 1881, Philip who was I think born on the 1st of February 1882, Charley who was born on the 31st of December 1883, Anna who was born on the 27th of November 1884, Elizabeth who was born on the 21st of August 1886, James who was born on the 7th of July 1887 (he was 84 in 1971 so it should be him), Ellen was born on the 25th of February 1889 and Philip and Jarlath who were born on the 6th of June 1891 sadly Philip died while still young.

Patrick son of Patrick married Julie Casey Lehr on the 14th of February 1911, Thomas son of Patrick married Catherine O'Shea and they had a daughter called Mary who was born on the 28th of October 1903. Mary daughter of Patrick married Patrick Finnegan on the 3rd of February 2010 and Charlie son of Patrick married Catherine Lovett Gortrooska on the 25th of February 1919. Thomas and Charley were both harness makers in Kenmare in the 1911 census.

Charlie left Kenmare for a midland county possibly Leitrim but what happened him after this is at present unknown. Thomas married twice his second wife being Abbie O'Sullivan of this marriage one boy was born about 1900. Thomas this boy grew up and married Mary Hegarty. Their children were Patrick, Philip, Mary Abbie, Lizzie, Jane, and Annie. Philip lived with his son Patrick in Kenmare. Philip married Joanna O'Connor. Patrick died unmarried in New York in 1931 aged 70 years. Mary Arthur went to Boston and married a Mr. McGuire from Leitrim a builder she was 92 years of age when she died and it is thought that her family is still in Boston.

Abbie Arthur married a Mr. Leary, went to Boston but she returned to Kenmare after 52 years and died there in 1908. Lizzie Arthur married John Quinn near Kenmare; a grand nephew of hers was Fr Dowling who was stationed in New York.

Ellen Arthur married a Mr. Jerry McCarthy a carpenter in Kenmare her son a Mr. McCarthy was a journalist. Annie Arthur married Patrick Brown, a farmer near Kenmare. She died in 1928 aged 72.

Philip Arthur already mentioned living in Kenmare had a family consisting of six daughters and six sons. They were Thomas, a harness maker who went to New York and died there aged 29 in 1906, His family is still in New York Charles Arthur lived in Kenmare, and he married a Kate Lovett and had one child, a girl.

In the old cemetery at Kenmare there is a tomb of the Arthur family of Kenmare inscribed as follows. “Erected by Thomas Arthur, for him and his family 1782” Patrick Arthur had another boy who died aged 5. Here it should be noted that some of the descendants of these Arthur's still live in the area around Kenmare.

Philip and Thomas Arthur.

Abina Arthur from Derrynacaraugh met her husband in the Galtymore in Cricklewood in the 1960's and they moved back to his home in the 1970's.

Abina Arthur is one of the fourteen children of James Arthur who died in the 1970's. About half of their children are still alive at the time of writing but they are very old however last I heard Mary the eldest was still alive in Meath.

Margaret Godfrey nee Arthur (her father was Thomas) Lives in Manchester. Peggy lives in New Jersey and she did a lot of work on her family tree.

Just as with their Limerick cousins the same Christian names have traveled down through the Kenmare Arthur family names like Patrick, Thomas Philip and James there were a lot with these names who were born in the Kenmare area.

While the Arthur family of Kenmare were boat builders for many generations there were also many watch makers in the family especially in the 20th Century.

Wanie O'Brien and Janie Arthur of the Sallyport B & B Kenmare are both daughters of the groom in the wedding photo. The groom's father was Patrick and both he and his brother Charlie are brothers of Peggy O'Connor Hourican's grandfather James and she lives in New Jersey.

Patrick O'Reilly's mother Siobhan also known as Wanie is an Arthur from Sallyport house Kenmare. Her father was Philip Joseph Arthur who married Mai O'Brien and their wedding photo is in in this chapter.

Arthur wedding 9-11-1937 Br. Firmin front far left

## The Arthur's of Norway.

This seems as good a place as any to mention another branch of the Arthur family who went to Norway in the 1600's to act as agents for the Arthur family. Since one of their big business was the timber trade and Irish merchants doing business in foreign countries in those days liked to have family members act as agents for them as they felt that they could trust family to be honest. Apart from the fact that they went to Norway we know little else about them. This information is contained in a document called the Arthur Leger which is in The Limerick City Museum and it was written by Charles William Augustus Arthur about whom more anon. In Francis Arthur's will he mentions property he owned in Norway and as I already said it is likely that even 100 years later there were family members managing the business there. The Norwegian Arthur's even had their own version of the Arthur family crest which is reproduced here. This version was found in Charles William Augustus Arthur's research notes commonly referred to as the Arthur Ledger which is in the Limerick City Museum.

Crest of the Arthur family of Norway from the Arthur ledger

# Chapter 13

*I think this is an interesting piece that was in the glamour of Limerick*

The following is taken from a piece called "the glamour of Limerick" written by A.I. O'Halloran in1928.

It has been said that city families die out in three generations. While this may not be literally true, it is certain that the circumstances of city life do not make for the continuity of race. But what gives the assertion and appearance of actuality is that urban dwellers are much more subject to fluctuations in fortune, owing to the changes in incidents of trade and commerce, than those who are settled on the land, such changes leading to the disappearance of families by migration and emigration. After the third there is a tendency towards a declination in the social scale, with the result that if the slums of any old city were combed out, it would be discovered that many of the submerged tenth are the descendants of one-time wealthy and influential families.

The Arthur's offer a remarkable exception to this rule of urban non-stability, since they were identified with Limerick not for three but for twenty generations and despite the religious and political upheavals of the centuries, seem to have invariably maintained their importance as merchant princes. Nor do they lack memorials in the city. From the early times they were notable benefactors to St. Mary's Cathedral in which there is an Arthur Chapel. Thomas Arthur who was mayor in

1462 built the facade of the choir in "Lofty Marble", and its outer door bears the Arthur's Shield, "Not through a spirit of vainglory".

Daniel Arthur, Mayor in 1552, had the three aisles and the entire choir paved in polished marble, whereas it was called "Leacadaniel". Two hundred and thirty seven years after that, Patrick Arthur donated the ground on which St. Michael's Parish Church was built in 1798 and when he died his body was interred there inside the church a most unusual honor for a layman. It was the same Patrick Arthur who along with his son Francis built Arthur's Quay and the streets adjoining in the early $19^{th}$ Century. So it is that Patrick, Francis and Ellen Street are in honor of him and his immediate family. In the period between 1371 and 1675 the family gave numerous Mayor's and Sheriffs of the name. They also gave two bishops to the Diocese and many other eminent churchmen.

In spite the pressure to convert not many of the Arthur family gave into this pressure. There is a record of a Daniel Arthur in 1609 helping a Scottish missionary. Significantly enough the name disappears from participation in municipal affairs after the year 1695. It would seem that after that they devoted their entire attention to business with what success may be gleaned from how successful Patrick Arthur and his family had become.

I put this in to show how unusual the Arthur family was in remaining at the top of the city for hundreds of years which is very unusual indeed as the influence of most families would wane after a number of generations.

# Chapter 14

This is the Crest of the Arthur family of Glenomera.

*The Arthur's of Glenomera*

The Arthur family of Glenomera originally held lands in Co. Limerick which were lost in the Cromwellian wars and so this is why they moved to Glenomera Co. Clare. It is written in one of the great books on Irish family lineage that this sept of the Arthur family claims to be descended from the "Artureigh" and therefore were an Irish family not related to the other Arthur families (from Burke's landed gentry of Ireland formerly called Burke's commoners) who were of Norman or Scottish descent and it would be true to say that it was their pro-Irish actions that caused them to lose their lands.

*There were two Glenomera houses within a few miles of each other. There was the Glenomera House in Ballyquin*

*Beg, Co. Clare which belonged to the Arthur family and that is the one I am going to be talking about but there was another Glenomera house at Kilokennedy, Broadford Co. Clare. This house never belonged to the Arthur family but rather to the Vaughan family among others even though they were quite close to one another. Glenomera castle was very close to the house in Broadford.*

Below are copies of the only two known photos of the Glenomera house that belonged to the Arthur family. On the right of each photo can be seen the single story part of the house which was the first part of the house to be built in the early 1700's (more info below). Since Charles William Augustus Arthur (The last Arthur to live at Glenomera) was a keen amateur photographer it is likely that the photos of the house and carriage were taken by him (This first photo and the one of the carriage are in the Arthur Ledger in the Limerick City Museum). The other photo of the house which is now in the possession of Veronica Rowe is likely to have been taken by Charles.

Glenomera House. This Photo has been digitally enhanced in order to allow the house in the photo to be seen. The original is in The Limerick City Museum.

This photo of Glenomera house is courtesy of Hugh Weir: Houses of Clare and Veronica Rowe who holds the original

The family moved from county Limerick to Ballyquin, county Clare in 1699 where Thomas Arthur along with

Robert Hannon leased 9807 acres of land from the Earl of Thomond (later they purchased the freehold to this land), Hannon as a Protestant had to be on the lease for Thomas Arthur to be allowed lease the land as a Catholic was not allowed under the penal laws to lease so much land but a Protestant was allowed to. So as a friend of Thomas, Robert cosigned the lease in order that Thomas could take the land. At this stage this part of the Arthur family remained Catholic but that was not to continue as we shall see later. The lease of the 25th March 1699 required that Thomas Arthur should erect and finish a good farmhouse on some convenient piece of land with limestone wall at least 40 feet long and at least 16 feet wide with a loft or second story (Thomas went with a loft) and the house was to be covered with slate and timbered with oak. At the end of the 17th century they intermarried with members of the O'Brien family of Dromoland and the Smith family of Cahirmoyle, county Limerick. At Some point in the 18th Century the leasehold was converted into a freehold on the lands of Glenomera. Griffith's Valuation shows the main part of the Arthur estate was in the parishes of Kilokennedy and O'Briensbridge, barony of Tulla Lower as well as in the parishes of Ruan and Killinaboy, barony of Inchiquin, but they also held land in other parishes Clondagad, Killone, Killaloe, Kiltenanlea and Feakle. As well as all this they acquired an impressive London house along with a house in Dublin and they spent a substantial portion of each year first in Dublin and later after the Act of Union in London. In the 19th century the family also begun spending a portion of each year in France.

The Arthur Carriage. This Photo has been digitally enhanced in order to allow the carriage in the photo to be seen. The original is in The Limerick City Museum.

The Arthur Carriage above along with three others were built around the year 1800 for the Arthur family to be used at their house in Dublin which was at 52 St. Stephens Green. At first they were drawn by eight horses each and later on a mule was substituted for one horse. (I think there was some law or convention restricting eight horses to Royal carriages which could explain the substitution of a mule for a horse) Every year they traveled to France in the four coaches one of which had been adapted especially for carrying children. They had the family coat of arms on the doors of the carriages. The picture above is of what is believed to have been the last remaining coach which was kept at Glenomera house and would as far as we know seem to have been destroyed when Glenomera House burned down around 1905. The last outing for the carriage was on the 28th. December 1902 after Charles William Augustus Arthur had it restored. With a team of six specially trained horses he set out at 10am in the morning and went to Bridgetown, from there they went to O'Brien's bridge where they stopped for lunch. They had intended on going on to Limerick but due to inclement weather they had to return to Glenomera where there was a party that included many notable people as well as about 250 tenants, the party did not conclude until the small hours of the morning.

Thomas at best was considered eccentric and at a house party he created an uproar when he riddled an expensive portrait of his mother with the contents of a revolver and on another occasion he tested different caliber rifled by firing at the windows of Glenomera House. So in the 1860s and early 1870s John Brown and his son Robert L. Brown, acted as receivers for the estate of Thomas Arthur, "a lunatic. This estate was in the baronies of Tulla Upper and Lower and included the mansion house and demesne of Glenomera. In the 1870s Colonel Thomas Arthur of Manor House, Desborough, Market Harborough, and Leicestershire who was a relative, owned 2,622 acres in county Clare and Francis Arthur of Dublin owned 10,534 acres in the same county. This Francis seems to have been related to the Glenomera branch of the family but his lineage is not as yet certain.

When Thomas Arthur moved to Glenomera the area was called Ballyquin and the name was changed to Glenomera at a later date. This Thomas Arthur had no son's only daughters and one of his daughters married a Piers Arthur from Limerick. This Piers may have been an uncle of Patrick Arthur of whom we have already spoken. Piers inherited the Glenomera estate through his wife from Thomas on his death. Piers son Thomas Arthur who died in 1755 then inherited the estate after which he passed it to his son Thomas Arthur C.1740 – 1803. This Thomas is the one who converted to the Protestant religion in 1768. It is believed he was the first member of this family to convert although it was said that the conversion was one of convenience rather than belief. When he went to vote he was challenged that he was a Papist so he converted in order to hold on to the estate and to continue to have a vote. Since he was a papist he could have lost the estate as well as losing the vote, so his conversion as were many others at this time was one of convenience in order to keep what he had. This member of the family may be the one who extended the house to the one you see in the photographs of the house. This Thomas had only two surviving children, his daughter married Richard Henn (D. 1828) of the neighboring Paradise House of Paradise Hill estate and when she died in 1830 without children she bequeathed it to her brother Thomas Arthur (1778 - 1845). Thomas lived on the continent for much of the 1810's and 1820's and later in Cheltenham. He returned to County Clare about this time and he went tolive at Glenomera where he became a model landlord.

Paradise house was burned down in 1970

The aforementioned Thomas Arthur was married to Elizabeth daughter of the Butlers of KILMOYLER IN

THE County of Tipperary. Another Thomas Arthur is mentioned, being born April 1788. He married in 1803 to Harriet, daughter of Edward O'Brien of Dromoland. Their Children were Thomas (born 1809 (evidently ancestor of Capt. Charles) William born 1809
Lucius born 1810, Edward born 1817, Augustus born 1819, Frederick born 1822. There were also 9 daughters.

His relations with at least some of his large brood of children seem to have been less than cordial. His eldest son Thomas Smith Arthur 1806 - 1884 suffered from mental illness and was confined in an institution in Dublin from the 1830's onwards. Before getting Thomas locked up, his father persuaded him to sign a deed that had the effect of disinheriting his second son, William Smith Arthur 1809 - 1839 with whom there were various signs of a family quarrel. When Thomas senior died in 1845, the estate was held in trust for his eldest son and it was his fifth son Augustus Arthur 1819 - 1902 who actually lived at Glenomera. Thomas senior's widow and younger members of the family lived at Paradise House but either in 1855 or 1863 the house was sold back to the Henn family.

Below are some press reports of incidents that happened on the land of Thomas Arthur.

1824

On Saturday night, between the hours of eleven and twelve p.m. six cocks of hay were maliciously set fire to on the lands of Lackareagh, County Clare which is the property of Robert Mc Cutchin, tenant to Thomas Arthur, Esq. and though every exertion was made by Lieutenant Bindon, with the Police from O'Briensbridge, nothing could prevent them from being consumed, notwithstanding the incessant rain. After searching the ground, seven sheep were discovered dead in out-house, apparently killed with sticks and stones, and two of them found hanging across a beam, with their heads much bruised. The houses were then all diligently searched, and in the house of his uncle, John Devitt was apprehended and lodged in the Bridewell of O'Briensbridge, for being found with his clothes wet and not being an inmate and whose father (now herdsman to the ground) was a former tenant and who was ejected by Mr. Arthur, last April. It is hoped some useful information will elicited from him by the Magistrates.

1831

Yesterday three captains of Vessels which are now in the port of Limerick proceeded towards Newcastle, outside the City to witness a horse race. Mistaking the way, they fell in with a party of the "Terry Alts", who were busily at work in turning up some ground at Moreland, which is the property of Thomas Arthur Esq. The 'Terry's' welcomed them and giving each a spade, under the superintendence of mother Alts ordered them to dig, which they did cheerfully. After about two hours hard work they were allowed to walk away unmolested. Mother Alts could with difficulty refrain from laughter all the while the poor Captains were pulling out.

It appears that Mrs. Thomas Arthur had quite a pedigree. "Piers of Grantstow, married Hon. Katherine Le Poer, daughter of 2$^{nd}$ Lord Power of Curraghmore and was ancestor of Butler of Kilmoyler whose representative John

Butler, of Kilmoyler left an only daughter and heiress Elizabeth Butler who married Thomas Arthur of Glenomera (see Burke's Landed Gentry)." from Butler Family Records page.

In 1884 Thomas Smith Arthur died and the estate passed to his brother the Rev. Lucius Arthur 1810 - 1887 who was living in a house in Matlock. The Rev. Lucius Arthur did not relocate to Ireland to live at Glenomera. His son, Thomas Lucius Jervis Arthur 1847 - 1888 probably moved in but he died soon after his father leaving as joint heirs to Glenomera his two young sons, Charles William Augustus Arthur 1882 to 1939 and Desmond Phelps Pery Lucius Studdert Arthur 1884 - 1913. Constance Helen Studdert the widow of Lucius Thomas Jervis Arthur brought the two boys up at Glenomera until 1894 when she married again after which they went to live with her second husband William Paumier Ball in the elegant surroundings of 71 Merrion Square, Dublin. This house later became the home of Sybil Connolly and her couture studio. Both Bell and his wife died in 1902 and the two young men who already had the reputation of being somewhat wild and fearless, were left with plenty of money but no parental guidance to make their way in the world. It would seem that they were not close although both men went into the army however they took different paths in their military service. They both inherited the estate at Glenomera equally from their father as well as receiving a substantial inheritance from their step father William Paumier Ball.

In the 1860s and early 1870s John Brown and his son Robert L. Brown, acted as receivers for the estate of Thomas Arthur, "a lunatic". This estate was in the baronies of Tulla Upper and Lower and included the mansion house and demesne of Glenomera. In the 1870s Colonel Thomas Arthur of Manor House, Desborough, Market Harborough, Leicestershire owned 2,622 acres in county Clare and Francis Arthur of Dublin owned 10,534 acres in the same county Colonel Arthur was a member of the Glenomera Arthur family but we are not sure who Francis Arthur of Dublin was related to it seems certain that he was either a relative of the Arthur family of Glenomera or was related to the Limerick city Arthur family.

The following was reported in the Clare Journal Oct 14 1861, the death at Kingstown, of Charlotte daughter of the late Thomas Arthur, Esq. of Glenomera, County Clare.

Here is the death notice for another member of the Arthur family of Glenomera.
In loving memory of Captain Charles William Augustus Arthur ( he was an uncle of the Charles William Augustus Arthur of whom we talk a lot later in this book) of the York and Lancaster Regiment born April 20th 1851 died in India March 9th 1882 the son of Rev. Lucius Arthur of Glenomera, Co. Clare, Ireland. His father Lucius died Jan 4, 1887, aged 76 years. This inscription is from a graveyard connected with Holy Trinity Church, Matlock Bath, Derbyshire, England, part of the Church of England.

My Great Uncle Charles wrote a little about the history of the Glenomera branch of the family and the following is my edited version of what he wrote.

That a family connection or relationship exists between the Arthur family of Ennistymon and the Arthur’s of

Glenomera there is no good reason to doubt. A tradition to that effect has always existed in the Ennistymon family.

The story of how one of the ancestors of Glenomera House converts to Protestantism was often told at home in Ennistymon when Charles was a boy.

In the old records in the library of the Galway University Charles came access the following entry.
"Thomas Arthur of Glenomera House Co Clare was born 10th.Sept 1806 and succeeded his father in 1845".

This record refers to Thomas Arthur's Son:
***Clare Journal July 12 1838:*** In Dublin, William Smith Arthur Esq. of Lickadoon, Co. Limerick son of Thomas Arthur Esq. of Glenomera, in this county got married to Caroline Francis Sydney, daughter of Frederick S. Parker, Esq. of Saintbury, Dublin.

This records the death of one of Thomas' daughters.
In Memory of CHARLOTTE ARTHUR eldest daughter of the late THOMAS ARTHUR Esq. of Glenomera Co. of Clare died October 9th 1861 aged 57 years.

**Due to the fact that it occurred close to Glenomera it is likely that the Mr. Arthur referred to in the following report involved a member of that family.**

Another sad case of injustice occurred in 1847 in the hills overlooking the little Village of Broadford, Co. Clare. A farmer named O'Keefe fell upon hard times and was unable to meet his rent. He offered two-thirds of it to the landlord's agent a Mr. Watson who refused to accept it.

The Agent then took O’Keefe’s cattle, ten cows and a bull, which were the only source of sustenance to him, his wife and large family. The landlord was one of the well-known Arthur family of Limerick. Some short time afterwards three young men from Co. Limerick William Ryan (Puck); William Ryan (Small) and "Butt" Shea set off to settle the score with the uncompromising Watson. They visited O’Keefe who innocently gave them details of his misfortune but they did not disclose the purpose of their visit. While strolling around the district, they learned from a schoolboy that Watson usually rode on horseback to Arthur's house at a certain time each day. Fortified with this information, they waylaid the agent and murdered him. They then moved off in different directions. Shea and Ryan (Small) were arrested and convicted of the murder and were hanged in Ennis. Ryan (Puck) got clean away, but he was later hanged outside the gaol in Mulgrave Street for the murder of John Kelly of Knocksentry. The most harrowing part of the drama was the arrest of the innocent O’Keefe, who was charged with being an accessory to the murder. He was convicted and hanged in Ennis. It should be noted here that in general the Arthur family of Glenomera were considered to be good and caring landlords who did their best by their tenants however the Arthur running the estate at this time was noted as a bad landlord who had little or no care for his tenants.

Another member of the family a Captain Charles William Augustus Arthur had an unenviable notoriety. In the early 1920’s he was connected with a big lawsuit in England and France which was known as “The Mr. A Case”.

*Marriage Record for Thomas Lucius Jervis Arthur.*

First name(s) Lucius Thomas Jervis

Last name Arthur

Registration year 1881

Registered Quarter/Year April/June 1881

Registration district Limerick

Marriage Lucius Thomas Jervis Arthur married Constance Helen Studdert

Helen Studdert's mother was the daughter of a Protestant minister and her daughter Helen married Thomas Lucius Jervis Arthur who was the father of Captain Charles William Augustus Arthur and it is her marriage record that is above. When Helen's mother became a Catholic her family, in order to placate the Protestant opinion had her confined to a lunatic asylum however she was not long in the asylum when she regained her freedom and she remained a Catholic to the end of her life.

Captain Charles William Augustus Arthur married a Catholic lady a Miss Roche-Kelly who was from a wealthy society family in Limerick. There were two boys of the union the first Charles died soon after his birth but the second Lucius who was born in 1913 went on to live a long and fruitful life. By 1917 Captain Charles no longer lived with his wife nor did he do anything to look after or care for his son Lucius. He did marry again after his first wife died it is said of a broken heart and it is also said that he treated her very shabbily. There will be more to tell about Charles and his brother Desmond anon.

Br. Charles Arthur from the Ennistymon branch of the family received the following letter from Captain Charles William Augustus Arthur. Charles got some of his education in France and so he spoke fluent French he also spent a lot of time there in his early manhood including serving a prison sentence there. It was a tradition in his family to spend part of the year in France.

21 Rue Gudin,
Paris 16 eme,
France.

10 October 1927

Dear Brother Arthur,

I was glad indeed to get your letter.

Until recently I was under the impression that the family was extinct except for myself, (his brother Desmond having died in 1913) having never come across even one of the name.

A couple of days ago I had a letter from a Mr. W.D.H Arthur, who lives in Northumberland and who is a grandson of Colonel Thomas Arthur and is a son of Captain William Arthur RN. He is owner of some property in the neighborhood of Ennis and as he bears the same crest and motto he is undoubtedly one of the family.

This is a subject that has always interested me, as there are few families of such antiquity, and you will find (if you do not already know it) a most interesting account in Lenihan's History of Limerick. This book is rather rare.
I expect to be in Dublin in the near future when I shall certainly give myself the pleasure of going to see you.

Yours very sincerely
Charles Arthur

Sister Cecily Mary Arthur was a sister or a half-sister of Captain Charles the records on this matter are not clear. She was a Protestant and was a member of an Anglican community of nuns called the *Sisters* of *St Mary the Virgin* which at its largest had only nine members in the Convent of St Mary at Clyde Road Dublin. They were a teaching order of nuns at first with a small school on Shelbourne Road. Later they opened two orphanages one for boys and one for girls in two houses near where St, Mary's Home is now on Clyde Road which was also part of their property. They seem to have been set up by the local reverend in the 1890's and it is believed that using his own money as well as some parish money he purchased the properties they used. Br. Charles Firmin Arthur visited her in July 1933, but as she had entered the convent as a novice while little more than a child 24 years earlier having earlier been a student in their school from a very young age so she was not able to give him much of an account of her family history (it would seem that she was sent there when she was little more than a baby and received few if any visits from her family after that). Reverend Sister Cecily Mary

Arthur died aged 85 in 1964 of coronary thrombosis in Clyde Road, Dublin and she is buried in Mount Jerome Cemetery, Harold's Cross, Dublin.

The record on the next page is from the 1911 census seems to refer to Cecily when she was in England. Her Christian name is spelt differently but all the other facts that we know about Cecily are the same as are recorded in this document so it is likely that they were one and the same person. There was an order in England that had the same name as the order she joined in Dublin but they were separate from each other but there does however seem to have been some communication between the two orders of the same name.

**Name:** Cicely Arthur

**Age in 1911:** 29

**Estimated Birth Year:** about 1882

**Relation to Head:** Inmate

**Gender:** Female

**Birth Place:** O'Brien's Bridge, Clare

**Civil parish:** East Grinstead

**County/Island:** Sussex

**Country:** England

**Street Address:** St Margaret's Convent School And Orphanage Moat Road East Grinstead

**Marital Status:** Single

**Occupation:** Sister Of Charity Altar Bread Baker

**Registration district:** East Grinstead

Captain Charles William Augustus Arthur's father was a Lucius Arthur and his mother was Helen Studdert. The latter was the daughter of William Steele Studdert and his wife Constance Massey who was of Scottish descent.

Thomas Lucius Jervis **Arthur** married Constance Helen_ **Studdert**, daughter of William Steele_**Studdert** and Constance_**Massy**, on 28th April 1881. Co Clare where he was a Justice of the Peace (J.P.).Their marriage cert is already on another page above.

Before her marriage Miss Studdert lived at a place called Keeper View and here is a story that was told about Thomas Lucius and how he behaved. He was believed to be a lunatic which is why two men were paid to be with him at all times it can be assumed to keep him out of trouble. Below is a report from the time.

In 1887 while on holidays in Clare Mrs. Arthur arrived quite suddenly to her friend's house. It seems that her husband owing to his intemperate habits was treating her very cruelly. Her husband Lucius had two paid men, who accompanied him everywhere he went. Mrs. Arthur's mother lived on the Arthur estate and was a convert to Catholicism. Here the Grandmother kept the two boys Charlie Charles William Augustus) and Cyril (Desmond). Because of the strained relationship between husband and wife. Mrs. Arthur had been advised to seek a divorce, but her mother, being a Catholic would not hear of the matter.

One day Mrs. Arthur observed a sidecar driving up the avenue in it was her husband Lucius and his two paid attendants, both playing on their whistles. Mrs. Arthur at once rushed to the people of the house exclaiming, "Oh he has come, for God's sake do not pretend you saw me!" The gentleman of the house met Mr. Arthur with great ceremony and commenced by asking after Mrs. Arthur's health. Mr. Arthur said he had come to take his wife home but was informed she was not there, and as proof of the truth the gentleman asked Mr. Arthur to remain that night with them-which he did. It was a hilarious night, the tin whistles had to play Mr. Arthur up the stairs and down the stairs along with everywhere he went after that. Meanwhile the people of the house took Mrs. Arthur to safety at another friend's house where she remained for some days.

Mrs. Arthur was a broken hearted woman and she had a very hard life because of her husband's behavior. She frantically fretted about being separated from her two boys but it was safer for them to not be with her as she could not predict how her husband would behave at any time.

In due course Lucius Arthur died and Mrs. Arthur married a Mr. T.J. Ball in Dublin. Now in 1902 both Mrs. Ball who was 47 in 1902 and her husband also died. The two boys Charles and Desmond were the beneficiaries of Mr. Ball's will which was quite substantial and by now they had also jointly inherited Glenomera from their father Lucius as they had both reached the age of majority to inherit. Charles and Desmond often spent their holidays at the house of a family friend and the house is called Barretstown Castle in Ballymore Eustace, county Kildare. Lady Murray who lived there at that time was their friend. Barretstown is now a holiday camp for children with cancer.

Here is the inscription which is to be found on the grave of a Lucius Arthur "IN LOVING MEMORY OF AUGUSTUS ARTHUR GLENOMERA CO CLARE WHO DEPARTED THIS LIFE MARCH 29TH 1902 IN THE 83RD YEAR OF HIS AGE MAY HE REST IN PEACE I BELIEVE IN THE COMMUNION OF SAINTS" The unusual thing here is the last sentence, does it mean that Lucius was a Catholic as there was a ROMAN CATHOLIC chapel at Glenomera. This Augustus was the brother of Lucius who was the father of Charles and Desmond.

The next time Brother Charles (Firmin) heard of the Arthur's of Glenomera was when Captain Charles got married. Charles was married at Spanish Place its proper name is St James. It got the name Spanish Place because it was attached to the Spanish Embassy and so was exempt from being closed down during the reformation. This church as far as I know was the only Catholic Church to remain continually open in London throughout the reformation. It was used by the Spanish Embassy and was attached to the embassy and so considered part of it which meant it was covered by diplomatic privilege and could not be closed by the British authorities without creating a major diplomatic incident. This church was used by Catholics from the embassy and elsewhere all the time during the English reformation when other Catholic churches were closed. Of course the present church is not the original church but one which replaced it and it is on a different site to the original church. No doubt Charles and Miss Roche Kelly were married in the present Church. There was a big "blow out "at his wedding and a large number of Limerick people were at it.

Charles had a reputation of being quite wild. He used to tear around Limerick at all hours in a motorcar and he received many a summons for speeding.

Desmond Arthur (Cyril) the younger boy was a pioneer pilot. He would seem to have been the pilot of the first plane to fly over Co. Clare. The flight was made in a mono plane which was the exact same plane Desmond learned to fly in and he was known to fly one at that time. (There is a photo of the first flight over Clare which Desmond Arthur is believed to have flown and it is elsewhere in this book) He was killed when his military airplane crashed in 1913 at the Royal Flying Corps (predecessor to the RAF) aerodrome in Montrose in Scotland. At the time he was supposed to be engaged to a Miss Lucas of Newport Co Tipperary however there is no certainty that this was the case. He knew the Lucas family but there is no definitive proof that he was formally engaged to a member of that family. A Ben Lucas was sub-sheriff of Limerick and it is thought that she was a relative of his. However before his death he had made his will in favour of ***Constance Winsome Ropner*** and so she inherited his property. Major George Steel Studdert who lived at Moy Lodge, Lahinch was an uncle of Mrs Lucius Arthur and his son Fred was secretary to the Clare County Council at that time. These people had a part to play in Desmond's will. As you will see his will was surrounded by questions which although legally accepted they are in my opinion of dubious provenance as neither witness to the will remembered signing it although both acknowledged that the signatures looked like their signatures.

The farmers at Glenomera used to tell stories about how adventurous the Arthur boys were. There was a very narrow pathway between two ponds and the two boys had some sort of go-cart with which they would approach the narrow path going down a steep hill. Here it should be noted that it was said that the wheel gauge of the go-cart was wider than the path. The pond is visible in the photos of Glenomera house.

Charles son Lucius was the last of the Glenomera Arthur's to be born in Ireland when he was born on April 6th. 1913 in Lower Baggot Street, Dublin in the family home there.

Desmond Arthur (Cyril) the younger boy was a pioneer pilot. He was killed when his airplane crashed at Montrose in Scotland in 1913 it is thought that Desmond was the first Irishman to die in a military airplane crash. At the time he seems to have been in love with a young lady called Winsome Constance Ropner who was a member of the very wealthy shipping family of that name. He had made his will in her favor and so she inherited his property. His brother Charles was left very little by Desmond and as they had jointly inherited the estate it had to be sold to pay what Desmond had willed to Constance Winsome Ropner. Since Desmond owned half of the Glenomera estate and Charles and Charles owned the other half Charles had to sell the whole estate to pay Desmond's half to Constance as he did not have enough himself to pay the legacy from his own resources. This only happened after Charles had lost his legal challenges in the courts

The next two chapters will tell more about these two brothers.

# Chapter 15.

*Charles William Augustus Arthur*

Charles was born on 24th September1882 and he served as first a Lieutenant and then as a Captain in the Limerick City Artillery. He married Rose the 3rd daughter of John Joseph Roche Kelly in 1904 (She was a Roman Catholic).Violet's grandmother Frances Roche Kelly was the elder sister of 1st Baron Fermoy Edmond Roche. That makes Captain Charles great grandchildren 5th cousins to the future King of England Prince William as because the First Baron Fermoy is his great, great, great grandfather and his sister Frances Roche is their great, great, great grandmother

The only record that I have seen seems to say that Charles Augustus Arthur seems to have died in 1939 in the West Indies it was a newspaper clipping and family lore believed that is where he died however so far no death cert for him has been found.

Charles served with the British army in South Africa during the Boer War and there are a number of letters in the Limerick City Museum written by Charles to his brother Desmond and his grandmother where he talks about his life in South Africa at that time. Charles also served during the First World War in the artillery where he was injured in a shell explosion in 1916. Charles Arthur in the national archive files claims anxiety and mental health issues to get out of military postings so he seems to have looked to be invalided out of the army but instead he was posted to India a posting that was to prove important in his life after the First World War. It was at this time that he and his wife Rose Roche Kelly separated it is believed because of the way he treated her. He had nothing to do with her after this separation neither did he have anything to do with his son Lucius after the separation neither did he help them in any way. Lucius felt this apparent rejection by his father very keenly and he had very few memories of him as they separated when he was quite young.

Charles in a Parisian cafe after his release from prison in France.

Now in 1919 Charles was involved in a very famous legal case, which was known as the Mr. A. case. In 1919 on the morning of Christmas night in the St. James and Albany hotel in Paris, a bedroom door was opened and an Englishman entered where he discovered a Mrs. Robinson (whose real name needless to say was not Robinson) in bed with Mr. A. There were two versions of what Mrs. Robinson said. According to the Englishman Mrs. Robinson jumped out of bed and attacked him "saying my brute of a husband". According to Mrs. Robinson she said that she spoke to Mr. A and said, "I must get back tonight before that brute reaches my husband" Mr. A was not at the trial to straighten out the contradiction. That Mrs. Robinson should so testify was understandable given that the Englishman who entered the bedroom was not Mr. Robinson but a Mr. Newton who was a known confidence trickster, blackmailer, card sharp and forger however it seems that Mr. A believed that Newton was Mr. Robinson.

Now would be a good time to tell you that Mr. A was Prince Sir Hari Singh, the heir presumptive to the throne of his uncle the Maharajah of Kashmir. The India Office asked him to use the pseudonym Mr. A. After this intrusion Prince Hari Singh sought the advice of his Aid-de-camp who just happened to be Captain Charles Arthur who had been recommended to him by the India office as he had served there for a time during World War 1. Charles seems to have advised that Mr. Robinson could sue for divorce in England naming him as co-respondent and that heavy damage could be exacted. This did not worry the Prince as he was very rich and could afford any damages awarded; neither would his people look upon his involvement in this affair in the same way as English people would look upon it. Charles however warned him that the India Office would not look kindly upon him being involved in a divorce and could block him from succeeding to his uncle's throne.

The Prince drew up two cheques for £150,000 each (Worth around £7,000,000 in today's money when, I give approximations in today's money I am referring to how much you would need today to purchase what that that amount would have purchased at that time) which cheques Charles took to London. In London Charles went to see a Mr. Hobbs a man who specialized in the shadier side of the law. Hobbs opened a bank account paid in one cheque, furnished the bank with a specimen signature and proceeded to draw out the whole £150,000. The second cheque was not cashed because when the Prince's solicitors in London learned of the matter they insisted on payment being stopped. Hobbs paid £40,000 (about £900,000) to Newton and Captain Charles. Hobbs told Robinson that Mr. A was prepared to pay him £20,000 (£475,000 approx). Robinson agreed to take £25,000 (£580,000 approx.). He gave Robinson £21,000 (£465,000 approx.) and Hobbs kept £4,000 (£95,000 approx.) as his professional fee as he was pretending to be a solicitor and a solicitor would always deduct his fee. Newton traveled to India in an effort to get more money but he failed.

The scheme came to light when Captain Charles tried without success to get more money from Hobbs. Then Captain Arthur told Mr. Robinson that Mr. A had paid £150,000 and not £25,000. Mr. Robinson then sued the bank in which Hobbs had deposited the cheque for negligently paying to Hobbs what should have been paid to him. This failed because it was adjudged that the money was the proceeds of a theft. To me Mr. Robinson did not think through his actions as by suing the bank for the proceeds of a crime he was just asking the authorities to prosecute. Of course Hobbs greed in not sharing out the money as agreed also played a big part in their downfall.

The exposure of the blackmail resulted in Hobbs being tried and sentenced to a term of imprisonment. Captain Charles who was in France, could not be extradited to England so he was tried there (the offense had occurred in France) was found guilty and served a term of imprisonment in France

Newton had been paid £3,000 (£70,000 approx.) by the bank to appear as a witness in the first trial and turned King's evidence for the second trial. By doing this Newton avoided prosecution and made a profit out of the affair.

## The Captain and the Cocos treasure expeditions

'The lure of buried pirate gold has attracted many treasure seekers throughout the years, but none has proved more enticing than the rumor of hidden wealth of some one hundred million dollars in gold which supposedly lies on Cocos Island, a remote speck of land west of Costa Rica. The tale of this treasure is what inspired Robert Louis Stevenson to write his famous book called Treasure Island which was based on the tales of the treasure that was supposed to be buried on this island.

'Located some five hundred miles off the western coast of Panama, in the tropical seas of the Pacific Ocean, Cocos Island is, an uninhabited land mass of approximately fourteen square miles.

During the age of exploration, the tiny island provided fresh water for passing sailors it also became a perfect treasure hiding place for pirates who looted Spanish galleons along the Latin American coast. Supposedly the pirates Edward Davis, Sir Henry Morgan, Lionel Wafer, and a Scotsman known only as" Thompson," used this "minute dot in the Pacific" as a storage place for their stolen treasures.

The first of these buccaneers to make use of the solitary island as a safekeeping place for his plundered riches was Davis. After filling the hull of his ship with Spanish gold from galleons sailing along the west coast of South America he went to Cocos and, according to a "writing man" on-board the vessel, "beached his ship, cleaned her bottom (necessary to clean off barnacles etc. which would attach themselves to the hull of a ship as these would slow a ship in the water if not cleaned off), re -rigged her and buried his treasure."

In 1671, Sir Henry Morgan, with a force of, 2,200 men and 37 vessels, sacked Panama City. The vast treasures from Peru and Mexico that were awaiting shipment to Europe were loaded aboard Morgan's ships and then the Welsh buccaneer left the city in 'burning ruins. He is alleged to have taken the treasure and buried it in part at least on Cocos.

More treasure was supposedly left there when the English-surgeon- pirate, Lionel Wafer was said to have buried loot on-Cocos in 1710. But over and above any of this wealth was the "Loot of Lima," supposedly hidden on the island by a Scottish pirate known as Captain Thompson. Thompson had put ashore in the harbor of Callo in Peru in

1824 at about the same time that Simon Bolivar was in the process of liberating the Country from Spanish rule. Lima was Spain's wealthiest city in the new world and city officials feared the treasure would fall into the hands of the rebels. So they loaded the most valuable of their riches aboard Thompson's ship the Mary Dear including two gold Madonna's from Lima Cathedral after which they went aboard. The officials assumed that the rebels would not dare attack a "ship under the British flag but the officials did not reckon on the Scot and his crew murdering them in their sleep and putting out to sea to bury the gold on Cocos. Months later the Mary Dear was captured and the crew executed however Thompson escaped and for almost twenty-five years he sailed and pirated the same area with another pirate called Benito who was also known as "Benito of the Bloody sword."

Eventually Thompson became partners with a man named Keating and together they engaged a Captain Bogue and they made plans to recover the Peruvian gold that Thompson had buried on Cocos. However Thompson died before the expedition could get underway and so the treasure map was left in the hands of the other two. After this the crew-mutinied "Bogue was drowned on Cocos and Keating barely escaped with his life before the treasure could be moved. This was the earliest of many unsuccessful attempts to recover the treasure of Cocos Island. One hundred years later a number of' treasure expeditions set out to find the fabled gold. The first of these expeditions was that of the Clayton Metal-Phone Company, Ltd. out of Vancouver, British Columbia, in 1931. One year earlier,, under the name of the "Cocos Island Treasure Company Ltd.," The Clayton Metal-Phone Company was granted all rights to search for treasure on the island by the Costa Rican government, with the concession that the Republic receive a percentage of all finds. The company under the command of Colonel J. E. Leckie felt their chances of discovering treasures buried in past "centuries was extremely good for two reasons one of which was that they possessed maps "with an 'X marked on the spots where pieces of eight, Inca gold and priceless jewels may be awaiting' discovery " and the second was that they carried a device called the Clayton Metal-Phone, which was capable of detecting metals under the earth or in water (it was an early metal detector). Their ship the Silver Wave left Vancouver on February 22nd 1932 with twenty-five men. Under the provisions of the treasure contract of 1930, they could remain on the island until October 1932 although they could then renew the lease if they felt it necessary.

From the outset; the topical growth proved a hindrance to the men as they tried to survey the island. There were marks of previous expedition's empty holes and numerous tunnels in the sides of mountains but the amazing Metal-Phone" only seemed to work near the shore line. Surveys of Cocos proved of little avail and persistent rain made conditions insufferable.

Throughout July, reports of treasure finds and then reports denying these finds were transmitted. In one message after a denial of discovery the expedition's radio operator said "how did anyone ever get the notion we would find anything on this God-forsaken island". Another member Lieutenant Dennis Rooke stated that members of the expedition were nearly starved and were forced to subsist on wild pig meat and coconuts. "Colonel Leckie denied their accusations and explained that Rooke was only on the island a short time. The party was on short rations for a few days while awaiting the arrival of a supply ship, but there was never any hardship or anxiety, nor has there been a single man sick. Any talk of dissension is pure rot. We have an excellent chance of success.

But four months later, on Christmas day, the Vancouver party left Cocos Island after several million dollars had been put into a fruitless expedition. No glittering gold or brilliant jewels were found and the expedition, like so many others before them they returned home a total failure.

Apparently publicity concerning the expedition was an inspiration to other groups. So despite the failure of the Clayton Metal-phone Company, a group of Britons decided to recover the riches of Cocos in 1934. This was promoted by Captain Charles William Augustus Arthur and his company was called the Treasury Recovery Company Ltd. After raising a substantial amount of money they sailed for the island with the same-high hopes as those who had gone before them.

They said that this would be the first scientific treasure hunt. That their experts would tackle it as an engineering problem and that they had definite evidence as to where the treasure is buried. Finally they would be using an airplane for surveying purposes. Unfortunately, the group overlooked an important item in that they failed to obtain proper authorization from Costa Rica. Consequently the republic arranged for the immediate deportation of the treasure hunters. Back in England the Treasury Recovery Company had been told the island was not internationally recognized as Costa Rica territory. Costa-Rica claimed they sent the expedition a message when they were in Panama saying they would be arrested if they landed on the island. However the expedition claimed they never received such a message so the Costa Rican authorities went ahead and sent fifty national policemen to the island with orders to "overcome any resistance."

While the treasure-seekers were being rounded up, Commander Frank Worsley the Captain of the ship they were using radioed an apology to Costa Rican President Jimenez while Mr. Arthur returned to England with the excuse of obtaining a larger vessel for the company. Eventually the entire expedition, with the exception of Mr. Arthur, was arrested and ended up in Costa Rica for trial. Costa Rica confiscated the equipment but released the men in late October after members of the group testified that Mr. Arthur was the sole promoter of the company and "they were only the servants of the promoters." They arrived in England in January two months later Costa Rica renewed its Cocos Island contract with the Clayton Metal-phone Company.

This, however, did not stop the British search for gold. Worsley and the chairman of the Treasury Recovery Company Erik Hankey, made arrangements with Costa Rica for an authorized search of the island in February 1935. On April 5th 1935, Costa Rica gave an official authorization to British Tours Ltd. (This was the old Treasury Recovery Company) who then tried to raise funds in England. Their ship the Veracity again under the command of Worsley reached the Canal Zone in early June. On board was a Belgian called Peter Bergman who had been shipwrecked on Cocos in 1929 and claimed he had discovered the "treasure cache." Bergman had been offered a quarter of any treasure discovered in return for his help. A force of ten Costa Rican policemen was waiting to sail from Puntarenas, Costa Rica with the expedition to protect the Republic's share in the project. Finally, on June 7th 1935 the Veracity sailed from Puntarenas with a ten man police detail and a crew of fifteen under the command of Worsley and his assistant, Commander F. C. Finnis. Their contract provided for the group to stay on Cocos until October. Still the British could not seem to keep themselves out of trouble. Before they even got to Cocos the crew was complaining because they had not been paid a penny for their services since they left England. They were upset over the fact that Mr. Arthur still had control over the operation although he was not with them but was in Balboa and when his cousin Richard Studdert arrived from England and took charge, insult was added to injury.

Charles William Augustus Arthur with his second wife during the Cocos expedition

By September the expedition was near mutiny having not received a penny of their salary and Costa Rica made arrangements with the commanders of the expedition to remove the police force on the island but only if the men abandoned the entire project. Then on October 30th 1935, Costa Rican Congressman Carlos Jimenez (not the president) heatedly accused British Tours Ltd. of selling stock to the English public in the name of Costa Rica. This being for the "unlikely "discovery of treasure on Cocos. He alleged the company's financial operations in London were fraudulent and urged the president to cancel the concession. Mr. Arthur, who was still the main promoter, remained in Balboa fearing arrest if he went to the island. By November 15th the charter for the Veracity (the expedition's ship) was canceled because of the lack of funds to pay the lease. After this things seemed to settle down until February 1936 when Costa Rica ordered the complete evacuation of the isle because of the expedition's failure to come up with "compensation funds" for the government. The order was repealed when at the last minute funds arrived from England to take care of the overdue obligations. But at this time the president declared that "no matter what," the concession would end in April and the expedition must leave the island.

Finally, in March, the hunt came to an end when Bergman disappeared. Most of the expedition left Cocos-to await a return voyage to England and they appealed to the British Foreign Ministry for the salaries they never received. This was after Captain Hardy McMahon the company's representative in Costa Rica announced that of the $200,000 collected in England, only one tenth had been spent on the expedition, the rest going to "administrators in London." Was Captain Charles up to his old tricks defrauding the investors? It seems likely.

In May 1936, the four remaining members of the group on the island were rescued and the "destitute British" started their return journey to England. However perhaps the most bizarre search for the legendary treasure was the one undertaken by Benjamin "Bugsy" Siegel, the notorious gangster sometime in 1937. The racketeer heard there were millions in Spanish treasure buried on the island "from the famous wreck of the Mary Dear" so he and a "Damon Runyon" crew set out after it. Siegel told his "crew they were "gonna grab the stuff, beat it and then we're all gonna go home rich". Siegel was dressed in a "stylish pinstripe suit and pointed two-tone shoes", Siegel's idea of searching for treasure was hurling hand grenades into the jungle. After a few weeks they gave up on their venture and sailed for Europe in an attempt to sell munitions to Mussolini.

So, after one hundred years and more than eighty expeditions, absolutely nothing in the way of treasure has been found and one wonders if there is anything there to be found. When one looks at the various' expeditions of the 1930's is easy to see why they all failed. The Clayton Metal-phone Company had perhaps the best chance but it's doubtful that the detector was very effective, especially when it was reported that it registered metals in an area where digging yielded nothing. (It could just have easily failed to register metals where they really were.) Finally even though Colonel Leckie stated otherwise, the crews were in bad spirits and did not work very effectively. In the case of the British expeditions it would appear that the promoters were not interested in discovering treasure at all. Instead, they wanted to extract as much money as they could from the sale of stock of a company that had already been planned to fail. This hypothesis is strongly supported by the statement of Captain McMahon, and the fact that members of the expedition never received their salaries. Even though Captain Arthur turned out to be a poor treasure hunter, he seems to have been an excellent con man. Siegel's hunt which lasted only a few weeks was an absolute farce and "Bugsy's" idea of treasure hunting by throwing hand grenades about the jungle can hardly be considered a serious search.

The, only remaining question is, was any treasure placed there at all? When Morgan became-governor in Jamaica he may have sent an expedition to recover the loot he stored there although that still leaves the gold from the Spanish ship's that Wafer and Davis preyed upon so it is possible the treasure is on the island yet. This argument is supported by a number of facts. First, neither David nor Wafer died rich men implying that they never retrieved much of the wealth they accumulated over the years. Since they robbed ships on the western coast of Latin America their booty could still be there. They would have had to store it on an island because in that area the Spaniards ruled the coast and the pirates would not land on the mainland and risk capture. The land selected would have had to be uninhabited so the group would not be noticed. The conclusion is that Cocos would be have been the perfect pirate treasure trove. It is difficult to know what chance there is of treasure being buried on the island. However if there is a treasure one wonders if Cocos Island will ever release its fabled wealth to the world. Captain Charles William Augustus Arthur is believed to have died in June 1939 in The West Indies but as mentioned before apart from a press cutting mentioning his death no other documentary evidence of his death has as of yet come to light.

***Telling the above story of the Cocos Expeditions was only possible due to the work and research of Graft Mahon and for that I thank him.***

# Chapter 16

## *Desmond Arthur*

Desmond from photo in Limerick City Museum.

Desmond was the youngest son of Lucius Arthur of Glenomera and in due course he followed his brother into the army when he joined the 5th Battalion Royal Munster Fusiliers. However his past and how he was raised with a father who seems to have been unstable seems to have affected him as I was told that he was prone to mood swings. After some time he was seconded to the 2nd Squadron ROYAL FLYING CORPS in June 1912 (this would seem to have been because Desmond wanted the transfer and he was already a qualified experienced pilot). Sadly he was one of the first members of the Royal Flying Corps (precursor to the R.A.F.) to be killed in a plane crash in 1913 and probably the first Irishman to be killed in an air crash while serving in the R.F.C.

Below is a copy of Desmond's first pilot's license.

233

ARTHUR, Desmond Lucius.

Born 31st March, 1884, at Glanomera, Co.Clare

Nationality British

Rank or Profession Lieut., Army

Certificate taken on Bristol Monoplane

At Brooklands

Date 18th June, 1912

Deceased 27th May, 1913

Desmond's first pilot's license.

The report below shows us that Desmond was an early pioneer of flying before he went on to join the Royal Flying Corps

## A REPORT FROM 1912 ON DESMOND IN AN AIR RACE FROM DUBLIN TO BELFAST

In 1912 an air race was arranged from Leopardstown in Co Dublin to the Royal Ulster Agricultural Society's showgrounds at Balmoral in Belfast, Ireland but had to be abandoned due to bad weather.

However *Mr. Desmond Arthur of Ennis Co Clare* had already tried to depart, but crashed his machine on the Leopardstown field.

A notice in *Flight* magazine of *14th September 1912* read:

## THE DUBLIN TO BELFAST EVENT

Bad weather contrived to spoil the Dublin-Belfast race arranged for last Saturday by the Aero Club of Ireland, and the large crowds which gathered at Belfast to welcome the aviators had to depart disappointed after patiently waiting all day. More fortunate were the spectators at Dublin as they at least saw all the four competitors get away and also witnessed some exhibition flights by Salmet (Henri Salmet was one of the early pioneer French pilots and he was closely associated with Bleriot).

From early morning a continuous stream of people flocked out from Dublin to the Leopardstown racecourse, which had been selected as the starting place and every vantage point in the vicinity soon had its quota of enthusiastic watchers. Soon after 11 a.m. Mr. Astley made a trial trip on his Bleriot plane and the other machines were brought out for engine testing. However in view of the strong westerly wind, the start was delayed for some time. At 1.30 p.m. a message came through from Belfast that the weather was bad there as there was rain and fog in Belfast.

Soon afterwards the proceedings were enlivened with a couple of circuits by Salmet which was followed by a downpour of rain which drove everyone to shelter. This then was succeeded by an unpleasant mist.

At 4.25 p.m. the weather was a little more propitious and Astley started on his Bleriot monoplane, followed by J. Valentine on the 50-h.p. Deperdussin, *Desmond Arthur on the 70-h.p. Bristol,* and Lieut. Porte on the 100-h.p. Deperdussin.

Arthur failed to get clear of the ground, and in landing buckled one of his wheels. Lieut. Porte found the conditions much too trying and after going three miles, he returned to Leopardstown. Astley and Valentine persevered through the vile weather, but conditions got worse rather than better as they went on and to add to their difficulties daylight began to fail. Eventually Valentine came down at Newry while Astley gave up at Drogheda. It was ultimately decided by the authorities that the first prize of £300 should be divided between Messrs. Valentine and Astley, plus £40 each for expenses. The £50 Shell Motor Spirit prize along with £40 for expenses to go to Lieutenant Porte and a special prize of £25along with £40 for expenses to Mr. Arthur.

Desmond was about 5ft 8 tall which meant that he was shorter than big brother Charles. Their mother Constance Ball Studdert (Her first husband was Thomas Arthur) died in 1902 Dublin leaving all her fortune to Desmond but she left nothing to Desmond's elder brother Charles (we do not know why she left nothing to Charles unless she could already see what kind of a person he was going to turn out to be). Her second husband Mr. William Paumier Ball left two thirds of his fortune to Desmond as well and he left the remainder to Mrs Kate Moger for her lifetime and upon her death this would go to Desmond's Brother Charles. Charles paid Mrs Kate Moger £2,500 to buy out her interest in her inheritance from Mr. Ball. At this time we are told that Desmond was knocking about with two young women called Clare and a Nancy however we know nothing more than that about them. It seems that the Nancy used to go and look at aircraft with him remember that female aviators were not uncommon at that time.

The badge of the squadron in which Desmond served.

**Here is a report on the crash at Montrose in Scotland in which Desmond died.**

REPORT ON THE FATAL ACCIDENT TO LIEUT. DESMOND L. ARTHUR, WHEN FLYING AT MONTROSE ON TUESDAY, MAY 27$^{TH}$ 1913, AT ABOUT 7.30 A.M.

*A brief Description of the Accident.* Lieut. Desmond L. Arthur who was flying a B.E. biplane No. 205 which was fitted with a 70h.p. Renault engine on Tuesday May 27$^{th}$ 1913 at about 7 a.m. Lieutenant Arthur left the flying ground at Montrose for an ordinary practice flight and after being in the air for about 30 minutes he was descending in a left-hand spiral at about 2,500 feet he had made one complete turn. Shortly after this the aircraft appeared to change on to the right bank and about this time the outside lip of the top right-hand wing was observed to fail and the planes of the right wing collapsed. At about the same time a puff of smoke was seen to be emitted from the engine and the sound of the acceleration of the engine was subsequently heard. The aircraft then fell comparatively slowly to the ground. The pilot was observed to fall from the aircraft (there is a question did he jump or did he fall out of the plane remember at that time pilots were not allowed to carry parachutes as the top brass were afraid that if they had them they would be less brave as they would have a way to escape a damaged plane or escape rather than fight an enemy) shortly after the acceleration was heard. The pilot struck the ground about 160 yards from the place where the aircraft fell, and was killed instantly. The aircraft was completely smashed.

In the inquiry after the crash it emerged that the wing that had disintegrated in mid-flight had been previously damaged in an unreported incident. A fracture of the main wing close to the wing tip was discovered. This fracture had neither been reported nor repaired, rather someone had glued on a seven and a half inch splice on the wing to disguise the original damage. It was an amateurish job with no intent other than ensuring that whoever had been responsible for the original damage was not identified. As a result the biplane flown by Desmond Arthur was a death trap. The perpetrator of this could not be identified because the biplane had been used at a number of locations including Salisbury Plain, Jersey Brow and Farnborough

Below is the first flight over County Clare and Desmond Arthur is almost certainly the pilot

Desmond's friends at Montrose (The airfield in Scotland where the crash occurred) were appalled at the findings of the committee. They felt that Desmond had not died in a freak accident but rather had been murdered by an irresponsible and unidentified technician. In 1916 Major Cyril Foggin said that he saw the ghost of Desmond walking in the aerodrome. After that there were a number of other reported sightings. Desmond Lucius Arthur now became known as the Montrose Ghost.

Charles and Desmond jointly inherited the Glenomera estate from their father Lucius when he died. They were to inherit their share of the estate when they reached their majority or if you prefer the age of twenty one. On his death Desmond left a personal estate of £9569 (£220,000 approx. 2011). The publication of his will caused a sensation at that time. Desmond left £200 (£4,500 approx. 2011) to each of the executors of his will. The rest of his estate he left to Miss Winsome Constance Ropner, daughter of William Ropner. Miss Ropner was aged 14 when Desmond died and 13 at the time of the signing of the will on 12th July 1912. Miss Ropner was asked to give £1,000 (£23,000 approximately) to his brother Charles and to pay an annuity to his aunt Miss Kate Arthur.

A view of the airbase at Montrose in Scotland at the time of Desmond's crash.

In February 1914 Charles challenged Desmond's will in the High Court he claimed that the will was not duly executed. Lieutenant Hugh Vilmer of the Scots Guards and a Mr. Hyoake who were the witness to Desmond's will testified that while the signatures on the will appeared to be theirs they could not recall ever signing Desmond's will. This was another mysterious circumstance in the life and death of Desmond Arthur. In spite of this the judge ruled in favor of Miss Ropner. It should be noted that the Ropner family were very wealthy indeed and had no need of Desmond's half of the Glenomera estate so why they fought Charles is unknown apart from the fact that perhaps Desmond might not have wanted his half to go to his brother for some reason or another.

The end result of this was that the Glenomera had to be sold to meet the obligations of Desmond's will because as Charles and Desmond had jointly inherited the estate and Charles did not have the resources from his half of the estate to cover the obligations of Desmond's will and still retain the estate at Glenomera.

**This is a newspaper article that was syndicated around the world about the death of Desmond Arthur and his will.**

WILL REVEALS ROMANTIC IRISH AVIATOR LEAVES FORTUNE TO GIRL OF 14 YEARS.

Efforts to annul dead man's expressed wishes came to naught when aired in court in London on March 7$^{th}$ 1914. A romantic attachment to a girl of fourteen is disclosed by the will of the late Lieutenant Desmond Arthur, the Irish Army airman. The will which was proved in the Dublin courts leaves the whole of his fortune of $62,600 to the child Winsome Constance Ropner of Ambleside, "West Hartlepool in Durham. On the dead body of the airman when it was found near Montrose last May after a fall from his biplane at 2000 feet, was a miniature portrait of the girl a photo of which is in this book.

Miss Ropner a pretty child is the daughter of William Ropner ship-owner and granddaughter of Sir Robert Ropner Bart the well-known North Country ship-builder. When the airman was living at Seaton Carew, West Hartlepool some 10 or 11 years ago he became a close friend of Mr. and Mrs. Ropner and their family. Frequently in the later years he spent his holidays at their home and the little girl Winsome was always a great favorite of his. He left Ambleside for the last time only a fortnight before his death flying from there to Montrose. The case came before the courts in the form of an action to establish the will by T. G. Studdert of County Clare, and William Ropner against the lieutenant's brother Charles Arthur of County Clare. The defense was that the will was not duly executed. It was stated that the lieutenant in the will requested that $5000 should be given to his brother if Miss Ropner so wished and Miss Ropner said she intended to carry out that request. After evidence that the will was entirely in the lieutenant's handwriting and the testimony of the two witnesses of the will counsel for the defendant said he did not wish to contest the matter further. Justice Kenny said it was plain that the governing wish in Lieutenant Arthur's mind was to provide for this little child.

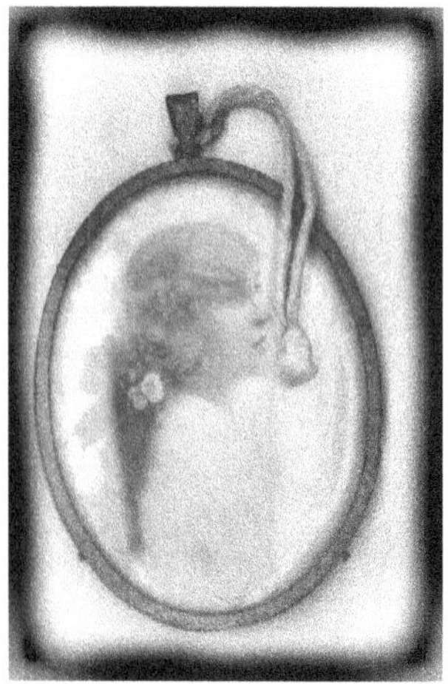

Locket that was around Desmond's neck when he crashed.

Nick Desmond's great grandnephew holding the locket after it was returned to him.

Desmond in same type of plane in which he crashed

Desmond in early biplane

Both the above photos show Desmond in a plane the one on the left is the same type of plane in which he died.

A photo of the crash site taken at the time when Desmond Died

This is a photo of Desmond's funeral cortege in Montrose Scotland

On Saturday 23-03-2013 the grandson of Winsome Constance Winsome Ropner after having been put in contact with Nick Arthur by myself called to Nick Arthur the great grandnephew of Desmond Arthur. Then in a very generous gesture for the 100th anniversary of Desmond's death he returned to Nick the locket that Desmond had next to his heart at the time of his fatal crash. This locket had remained in the possession of Winsome's family since 1913 and it is the one in the photo on another page.

Nick decided to donate the locket along with a number of other items to the squadron museum in Montrose. Below are some photos from the day that Nick went to Montrose to donate the items that had belonged to Desmond. Winsome married another airman called Major George Talbot Wilcox in 1922 and she often spoke about Desmond to her family and how much she had loved him.

On left display case with memorabilia of Desmond Arthur

Replica of Be2 biplane in which Desmond died with Nick Arthur Desmond's

Photo of place where plane came down.

great grandnephew beside it

The miniature of Constance Winsome Ropner is now housed in this display

Desmond's Grave in Montrose

*As Desmond had no children below are the descendants of Lucius Arthur the only child of Charles William Augustus Arthur who was Desmond's brother.*

Lucius Arthur was the only child of Charles William Augustus Arthur's who lived (his other son Charles died as an infant and he had no daughters). Lucius was the last of the Arthur's of Glenomera to be born in Ireland in 1913 and he died in 1991 at the age of 79.

Lucius eldest son was called Brian who was born in 1941 and unfortunately in a sense of Deja Vue he was killed in an air crash in 1974 when he was 32 years old. Brian had two sons the elder one Jules lives in California with his two sons Austin born in 1997 and Alex born in1999. His other son is Nick who was born in 1969 and lives in Suffolk with his daughter Caitlin.

Lucius second son was Ian who was born in 1946. Ian has two boys Tom who was born in 1978 and Charlie who was born in 1979. Ian also has one daughter Lisa who was born in 1986.

Lucius third son was Nick who was born in 1947. Nick has two sons, Chris who was born in 1981 and Julian who was born in 1985.

Lucius third son Nick has lived in the U.S.A. since the 1970's in California and Lucius second son Ian lives in Cornwall.

So far the only grandchildren of Lucius to have children are Nick and Jules the sons of Brian Arthur.

*Below courtesy of Nick Kingsley is a table containing the names of many of the most important members of the Arthur family from Glenomera.*

**Arthur family of Glenomera**

**Thomas Arthur (16??-17??) of Ballyquin.** He married and had the following children:
(1) Margaret Arthur who married Piers Arthur (d. 1752). Robert Hannan and Thomas Arthur leased 9,870 acres in Co. Clare from the Earl of Inchiquin Sir Donagh O'Brien in 1699. The lease was renewed in 1707 to Thomas Arthur alone following the death of Robert Hannan. A condition of the lease was the building of a new house on the estate within nine years of the lease being signed. At his death the estate passed to his daughter Margaret and her husband Piers Arthur as Thomas had no sons and Margaret was his eldest daughter.

His date of death is a present unknown to me.

**Piers Arthur (d. 1752) of Limerick and Ballyquin.** Piers was a merchant from Limerick who was closely related to Thomas Arthur. He married his kinswoman Margaret, daughter of Thomas Arthur (16??-17??) of Ballyquin and they had children.

(1) Thomas Arthur (d. 1755)

(2) A daughter who died on the 17th March 1763.

He and his wife inherited the Ballyquin estate from his father-in-law Thomas Arthur.

Piers died in 1752 and his will was proved at Limerick. His wife's date of death is unknown.

**Thomas Arthur (d. 1755) of Ballyquin**. Son of Piers Arthur (d.1752) of Ballyquin and his wife Margaret, daughter of Thomas Arthur (16??-17??) of Ballyquin. He married Elizabeth, daughter of Capt. John Butler and heiress of the Butlers of Kilmoyler (Tipperary) and had they had children

(1) Thomas Arthur (c.1740-1803)

(2) A daughter.

He inherited the Ballyquin estate from his father in 1752 and he died on the 23rd December 1755. His widow got married a second time in 1760 to a Luke Wall (d. 1781) of Springmount (Clare). Springmount was ransacked and burned by a mob in 1780 her date of death is unknown at present.

**Thomas Arthur (c.1740-1803) of Ballyquin.** Son of Thomas Arthur of Ballyquin and his wife Elizabeth Butler who was the daughter of Capt. John Butler, Thomas was born about 1740. It is Probable that the person of this name who was an Ensign in Kennedy's Regiment in1756 is this Thomas Arthur. He was Justice of the Peace for Co. Clare in 1766. He became a freeman of Ennis (Clare) in 1773 and he was the High Provost of Ennis in 1789.On the 1st October or November 1766 he married Lucy (d. 1815) fourth daughter of Sir Edward O'Brien of Dromoland. They had children some of whom died young.

(1) Mary Arthur (d. 1830) She married Richard Henn (c.1764-1828) of Paradise House (Clare) in August/September 1793 but their three children all predeceased him. Mary who was his heir bequeathed the Paradise estate to her brother Thomas Arthur. She lived her later years at Claines (Worcester) and died at Worcester in August 1830; her will was proved in the PCC on the 30 November 1830.

(2) Thomas Arthur (1778-1845).

He inherited the Ballyquin estate from his father.

He died in 1803. His widow died in April 1815.

**Thomas Arthur (1778-1845) of Ballyquin/Glenomera**.

Only son of Thomas Arthur (c.1740-1803) of Ballyquin and his wife Lucy who was the daughter of Sir Edward O'Brien of Dromoland (Clare). Thomas was born on the 6th April 1778 and he was educated at Magdalene College, Oxford where he matriculated in1795. He was the High Provost of Ennis County Clare in 1809. It was said that he was "An excellent landlord, kind and indulgent to his tenants, truly charitable and humane. He kept a dispensary near [Glenomera] for the benefit of the poor people of the neighborhood. His principles as a politician were very liberal, and he was a strenuous advocate and supporter of Catholic Emancipation." However, his relations with his children seem to have been more strained. He was responsible for committing his eldest son and heir to a lunatic asylum in the 1830s and he cut off his second son who lived abroad from 1833-36 from any chance of inheriting his estate one of the reasons being that he was not able to discover where he resided. He married Harriet the second daughter and co-heiress of William Smith of Cahirmoyle (Limerick) on the 10th April 1803 at Dromoland, and they had children.

Thomas inherited the Ballyquin estate from his father in 1803, and changed the name to Glenomera. He also inherited the Paradise estate (Clare) through his sister in 1830. He lived on the Continent for much of the 1810s and 1820s, and thereafter at Cheltenham, before finally returning to and settling at Glenomera in the 1830s. After his death his widow lived at Paradise House and then their younger children sold Paradise House back to the Henn family (the Henn family who were barristers had owned Paradise house before the Arthur family had inherited it) in 1855 or 1863.Thomas died on the 6th May 1845 from an attack of paralysis after two days illness at Leamington (Warks). His wife's date of death is unknown.

Below are the children of Thomas and there seems to have been another three children for whom we have no record so it can be assumed that they died young, one internet source gives their names as Lucy, Harriet Grace or perhaps Frances.

(1) Thomas Smith Arthur (1806-84) of Glenomera. Eldest son of Thomas Arthur (1778-1845) and his wife Harriet, daughter of William Smith of Cahirmoyle (Limerick), born 10th September 1806. He was educated at Eton and

Magdalene College, Oxford where he matriculated in 1827. From 1826 onward he began to suffer periods of mental illness. After spending one year at Oxford, he returned home but from 1831 he needed a 'keeper' to look after him. He fell out with his father over his mental state, and was eventually detained in Swift's Hospital, Dublin as a lunatic at his father's request. In 1837 he sought a writ of habeas corpus for his release from the hospital, but he seems to have remained confined for the rest of his life. In the 1860s and early 1870s John and Robert L. Brown acted as receivers for his brother Lucius estate. They also acted as minders for Thomas Lucius son who also seemed to have mental problems. During all this time Thomas brother (Richard) Augustus Arthur seems to have lived at Glenomera. He was unmarried and had no children.
He inherited the Glenomera estate from his father in 1845. At his death it passed to his next surviving brother, Rev. Lucius Arthur. Lucius died on the 12th September 1884.

(2) William Smith Arthur (1809-39). He was born on the 13th June 1809and he lived on the Continent during the years 1833-36. In 1837 he was in dispute with his father about a document executed by his father and his elder brother which had the effect of excluding him from succession to the estate. He was married but it is not certain to whom he was married.

(3) Rev. Lucius Arthur (1810-87). He inherited the estate and only held it for a few years before his death. Lucius never visited the estate after he inherited it. His son Thomas inherited the estate from his father but again he only held it for a few years.

(4) Charlotte Arthur (c.1811-61). She died unmarried on the 9th October 1861.

(5)Maria Arthur (c.1812-54). She died unmarried at Leamington on the 22nd July 1854 aged 42.

(6)Anne Arthur (c.1813-85). While not certain it is possible that she is the person of this name who died at Limerick in Jul-Sep 1885.

(7) Edward Arthur (1817-53). Was born on the 7th January 1817. He was educated at Rugby and Trinity College, Dublin (he was admitted in 1835, he got his BA in 1839 he got his MA in 1840 and he was called to bar in 1852. He was a barrister-at-law who died unmarried and without children at Bray in Wicklow on the 6th August 1853.

The next two children were twins.

(8) *Twin,* Florence Theodosia Arthur (c.1819-1866). She was born in Florence in Italy in 1819 and she was living with her brother Lucius in 1851. She died unmarried on the 30th September 1866when she was 48 years old. She was buried at Malvern Wells (Worcs).

(9) *Twin,* (Richard) Augustus Arthur (1819-1902). He was also born in Florence in Italy on the 27th August 1819. He was educated at Shrewsbury and Trinity College, Dublin. He was admitted in 1836 to a B.A course and he received

his BA in 1840 and in 1843 he got his MA. He was a Justice of the Peace for Co. Clare and was appointed a Governor of the Limerick District Lunatic Asylum in1848. He lived at Glenomera in 1840s and 1850s and in contrast to his father had a reputation as an oppressive landlord who evicted tenants in 1848 in the middle of the famine. He married Augusta (b 1847), eldest daughter of Lt-General George Dean-Pitt CB, Keeper of the Crown Jewels on the 13th August 1885. Later they lived in London and Rome where he died on the 29th March 1902. He was buried in the Campo Cestio Cemetery in Rome. His will was proved in Dublin on the 4th August 1902 and his effects totaled £2,106.

(10) Canon Henry Arthur (1820-95). He born in Paris on the 12th November 1820 and he was baptized there on the 26th November 1820. Henry was educated at Winchester and Trinity College, Dublin. He was admitted to a B.A. course in 1838 which he received in 1842. He received his MA in1845. He was the Canon of Ferns Cathedral and he married Ellen the second daughter of Henry Joy Tombe on the13th April 1847 at St Peter's, Dublin. He died without having any children in Dublin on the 30th March 1895. His will was proved on the 21st June 1895 in which he left effects with a total value of £5,114.

(11) Rev. Frederick Brian Ború Arthur (1822-70). He was born in Paris on the 12th September 1822 and he was baptized there on the 1st October 1822. Frederick was educated at Rugby and Trinity College, Cambridge. He was admitted in 1841to a BA course from which he qualified in 1846. He obtained his MA in 1851 when he

was ordained a deacon and then in 1846 he was ordained to the priesthood of the Anglican Church. In 1855 he became curate of Oddingley and later at St Mary Leeds and then in Langstaffe (York's). He remained unbeneficed and died unmarried at Brislington in Somerset on the 19th January 1870. His will was proved on the 10th August 1870 leaving effects valued under £9,000).

(12) Julia Isabelle Adelaide Arthur (1826-53). She was born on the 21st November 1826 and she was baptized at Cheltenham on the 28th December 1826. She died unmarried at Thornhill, Bray (Wicklow) on the 3rd October 1853.

(13) Augusta Catherine Arthur (c.1829-42). She died at Torquay on the 11th June 1842 when she was 13years of age.

**Arthur, Rev. Lucius (1810-87) of Glenomera**. He was the third son of Thomas Arthur (1778-1845) and his wife Harriet who was the daughter of William Smith of Cahirmoyle (Limerick). He was born on the 31st July 1810. He was educated at Harrow and Trinity College, Cambridge. He was admitted to trinity in 1828 to study for a BA which he received in1836. He received his MA in1839. He was ordained a deacon in 1839 and was ordained a priest in 1840. In 1841 he was appointed curate of Henley (Suffolk) at Bishop Ryder Church, Birmingham. He went to Donaghmore, Dromore (Down) in 1846. During the years 1853-54 he was at Oddingley (Worcs) and he was at Quarry Hill, Leeds (York's) from 1854 to 1861. He was a strong and outspoken churchman, apparently of too advanced a type for the north of Ireland. Three parishioners at Donaghmore laid a complaint as to his teaching before the Bishop of Down and Connor, "who however, showed it to be groundless". He married Caroline Elizabeth (1812-69) a daughter and co-heiress of John Heycock Jervis of Moseley (then in Kings Norton (Worcs) on the 21st April 1840 at Kings Norton (Worcs), and they had children.

(1) Harriet Elizabeth Augusta Arthur (1841-1923). She was born between Jan-Mar 1841 at Wilmington (Sussex). She married Richard Percival Fry (d. 1892) of HM Indian Navy on the 26th April 1871 but they had no children. She died on the 6th August 1923. Her will was proved on the 18th October 1923 and the value of her effects was £623.

(2) Ellen Lucy Julia Arthur (b. 1842- 1893), She was baptized on the 4th August 1842 at Henley in Suffolk. She married George Stevenson of Birkdale (Lancs) who was the son of William Stevenson a paper-maker on the 2nd February 1893 at St Luke’s, Paddington (Middx), but they had no children.

(3) Maria Anne Florence Arthur (c.1843-1878), She was born about 1843 and she died unmarried on the 31st July 1878. She was buried at Wirksworth (Derbys).

(4) Charlotte Katherine Susan (Kate) Arthur (1845-1932). She was baptized at Perranarworthal (Cornwall) on the 5th June 1845. Evidently she was a 'character as she entered her occupation in the 1911 census as 'Trying to bear the burden for others' and 'Acting as mistress of my own house'. She died unmarried at Tunbridge Wells on the 11th December 1932.

(5) Thomas Lucius Jervis Arthur (1847-88). He inherited the Glenomera estate from his elder brother in 1884 but he lived at Tor House, Matlock (Derbys). He died on the 4th January 1887 and was buried at Wirksworth (Derbys). His will was proved on the 31st March 1887 in which he left effects £2,084. His wife died on the 1st April 1869 and was buried at Wirksworth.

(6) Edward Henry Frederick Arthur (1848-49). He was born sometime between Jul-Sep 1848 but he died in infancy sometime between Oct-Dec 1849.

(7) Grace Caroline Frances Arthur (1849-1925). She was baptized at Oddingley on the 11th November 1849. She married Rev. Frederick James Johnston-Smith LLD (c.1852-1928) of London on the 6th November 1889 at Matlock, Derbys. She died at South Acton on the 19th November 1925. Her will was proved on the 31st December 1925 and she left an estate valued at £648).

(8) Charles William Augustus Arthur (1851-82). He was born on the 20th April 1851 and he was baptized on the 27th April 1851. He was an officer in Derbyshire Rifle Volunteers. He was an Ensign from 1869 to 1870 and he was a Lieutenant from 1870 to 1871). He was then posted to the Edinburgh Artillery Regiment of Militia where he was a Lieutenant from 1871 to 1874). After his service there he was transferred to the 84th Regt. of Foot where again he was a lieutenant from 1874 to 1880). From 1880 to 1882 he was a Captain in the 65th Regiment. He died unmarried at Morar, Bengal (India) on the 9th March 1882.

**Thomas Lucius Jervis Arthur (1847-88) of Glenomera.** He was the eldest son of Rev. Lucius Arthur of Glenomera and his wife Caroline Elizabeth who was the daughter of John Heycock Jervis of Moseley, Birmingham (Warks). He was born 30th June 1847. Thomas was a Lieutenant in the Durham Fusiliers and a Captain in 6th Rifle Volunteers. He was a Justice of the peace for County Clare. He married Constance Helen Studdert (c.1859-1902) a daughter of William Steele Studdert of Clonboy (Clare) on the 28th April 1881. They had the following children.

(1) Charles William Augustus Arthur (1882-c.1937). His life is dealt with earlier in this book.

(2) Desmond Phelps Pery Lucius Studdert Arthur (1884-1913). ). His life is dealt with earlier in this book.

(3) Cecily Mary Arthur (b 1882 to 1964). Family believe she was a sister of Charles and Desmond but not sure if she was a half-sister or a full sister.

*Thomas inherited the Glenomera estate from his father in 1887 but died the following year.*
He died on the 19th February 1888. His will was proved in Dublin on the 18th April 1888 which left effects valued at £2,848. His widow married William Paumier Ball (1857-1902) of 71 Merrion Square, Dublin on the 2nd October 1894 at St Cuthbert, Kensington (Middx). William was a barrister-at-law and the son of Rt. Hon. John Thomas Ball who had been a Lord Chancellor of Ireland. William died on the 17th June 1902. The will of Constance was proved in Dublin on the 20th October 1902. She left an estate which was valued at £2,570. Her second husband's will was proved on the 13th November 1902 and his estate was valued at £21,081.

**Charles William Augustus Arthur (1882-1939).** Charles was the eldest son of Thomas Lucius Jervis Arthur (1847-88) and his wife Constance Helen Studdert the daughter of William Steele Studdert of Clonboy (Clare). Charles was born on the 24th September 1882. Charles and his younger brother jointly inherited the Glenomera estate from their father in 1888 but he did not gain control of his half of the estate until he came of age in 1903. Glenomera house was destroyed by fire in 1905 (there was a question of Charles having set the fire in order to get the insurance money but this has never been proved). He was said to have an income of £7,000 a year in 1909 before he was forced to sell the estate. After his brother's death in 1913 the estate was sold to pay his brother's legacies. Charles is believed to have died in the Barbados or Trinidad in about 1939. He served as a Captain in the City of Limerick Artillery and Royal Munster Fusiliers. In the First World War he again held a temporary commission as a captain in the artillery. After being injured on the western front in 1916 Charles was posted to India with his first wife Rose Roche Kelly and it seems that it was at this time that their marriage finally broke down completely. After he returned to Europe he was appointed as Aid-DE-Camp to Prince Hari Singh the nephew and heir presumptive of the Maharajah of Kashmir. While in that employment he was involved in a notorious fraud case (known as the Robinson case or 'Mr. A' case), but he was not charged with any offense at that time. Later he spent time in the United States and France, before he was arrested in Paris in 1924 on charges of fraud relating to the 1919 case. Extradition proceedings against him by Great Britain failed but he was tried and imprisoned for 13 months in France as that was where the original offense had taken place. In 1926 he was dismissed from the army with a dishonorable discharge because of what he had done. By 1934 he was promoting an expedition to recover a reputed pirate treasure from an island off the coast of Costa Rica. This may have been developed more as an investment scam than with any serious expectations of success. Although the reports of buried treasure on the island were legion and many other adventurers had tried and failed to locate it. Bankruptcy proceedings were initiated against him in 1939, when he was believed still to be living in the Caribbean, but he was probably already dead by then. He married his first wife Violet Rose Roche- Kelly (1881-1927) in 1904.She was the third daughter of John Joseph Roche-Kelly of Rockstown Castle and Islandmore (Limerick). His second wife was Alice M.S. Aitken alias Rodwell whom he married in 1930, and they had no children. He had children with his first wife Violet Rose Roche-Kelly.

(1) Charles Augustus Arthur who was born on the 11th July and died on the 5th August 1905.

(2) Lucius Charles Algernon Arthur (1913-92). Lucius was born in Dublin on the 6th April 1913. He worked for the British Sugar Corporation and lived at Tostock (Suffolk). He obtained a pilot's license in 1938 and he married, Lucius served as a pilot in the Second World War and was shot down. He spent time in a prisoner of war camp after being shot down. Phyllis B. Lewis in 1940. They had three sons. Lucius died in Jun 1992, aged 79.

**Desmond Phelps Pery Lucius Studdert Arthur (1884-1913).**He was the second son of Thomas Lucius Jervis Arthur (1847-88) and his wife Constance Helen Studdert who was a daughter of William Steele Studdert of Clonboy (Clare). Desmond was born on the 31st March 1884. Desmond was a pioneer Irish aviator and he served as a Lieutenant in the 5th Battalion, Royal Munster Fusiliers. He was seconded to 2nd Squadron, Royal Flying Corps in 1912 but was killed as a result of a wing failure during a training flight which seems to have been caused by the collapse of one wing of his plane which was the result of previous damage having been covered up rather than repaired, The incident was subject to two different official War Office inquiries with the first seeming to whitewash anyone of responsibility for Desmond's death but after many complaints about the findings of the inquiry a second one was held. It was said that Montrose was being haunted by Desmond because he was unhappy at being blamed for the crash in the first inquiry however after the second inquiry cleared him of all responsibility for the crash his ghost was seen no more. Desmond was unmarried and without children. He and his elder brother jointly inherited the Glenomera estate from their father in 1888 and Desmond came of age in 1905, the year the house was destroyed by fire. He was killed on the 27th May 1913 at Montrose in Scotland where his plane crashed. His will was proved at Dublin on the 9th June 1913 and he left an estate which was valued at £9,569. He bequeathed the majority of his estate to Winsome Constance Ropner of West Hartlepool (Durham), a 14-year old girl with whom he had formed a romantic attachment having been friendly with her and her family for many years. The will was challenged by his brother but it was upheld in 1914 so in order to fulfill the bequest the Glenomera estate had to be sold.

# Chapter 17

*Here is a little about some of the ordinary people who lived on the Arthur estate at Glenomera*

*I would like to express my thanks to* ***Kerri Ferguson*** *from* ***Australia*** *and* ***David Ballesty*** *also originally from* ***Australia*** *whose great great grandfather worked as coachman and groom to the* ***Arthur*** *family of* ***Glenomera.***

This chapter may jump around a little bit and that is because there is a lot to be learned about these people the people who lived on the estate yet so there is not as much continuity between them in their stories as one would like

**Some records from the "*John Temperley*" in 1863 and from whose records we get the names of some people who definitely came from the estate.**

The Parish of Broadford at one time comprised the old Civil Parishes of Kilokennedy and Kilseily. Blackhill which is mentioned is not a townland in its own right but rather a sub-division of the bigger townland of Ballyquin Beg. Ballyquin Beg (where the Arthur Glenomera house was situated) is a townland. A townland being the smallest rural division to be found in a Parish in this case in this case Ballyquin Beg was approximately 270 acres situated in the old Civil Parish of Kilokennedy. Ballyquin Beg is situated about 3 miles south east of the village of Broadford. Here it would be a good idea to mention that there was a second Glenomera house which had the address of Broadford (it was close to the Arthur Glenomera House) and this house did not and never did belong to the Arthur family whose house Glenomera was at Ballyquin Beg. So when researching we must be careful not to mix up the two houses even though both were called Glenomera and were quite close to each other. One was in Broadford and the Arthur house was in Ballyquin Beg. Sadly neither house is standing now. The Arthur house burned down in 1905 and the Broadford house was demolished around 1920.

John Hogan was coachman and groom to the Arthur family of Glenomera, Ballyquin Beg in the middle of the 1800's and his children were Ann (Australia), Margaret, Thomas (Australia), John (Australia), Michael (Ireland), Mary (Australia), Patrick (Australia) and Brigid (Australia). As you can see most went to Australia but some stayed in Ireland and they have descendants living in the area still.

Thomas Hogan who was 20 and James his brother who was16 although they said their native place was "Blackhill" it must be remembered that townland was on the Glenomera estate. I have looked at these boys before and suspect that they must have been cousins of Kerri Ferguson. Winifred Hogan (a widow and mother of the boys) was also on the voyage of the *"John Temperley"* in 1863 but she appears on a different sheet titled "Widows". She does not name Glenomera as her native place but there are other documents which place her there and I suspect she is the Winifred Hogan named on the Griffith's Valuations as living in Ballyquin Beg possibly a sister in law of John Hogan the coachman and groom to the Arthur family of Glenomera.

Winifred Hogan and her son Thomas died within six months of each other in 1883. She and Patrick had five sons John, Michael, Thomas, Patrick, James and a daughter who died. When Thomas died aged just 41 his wife named Glenomera, County Clare as his place of origin on his headstone so he and his mother must have spoken of it. James and Michael died in Sydney in 1900; Patrick was in Sydney as well but we have not yet discovered when he died unfortunately. We still have no idea what happened to John or the daughter. Thomas married Margaret Hickey from County Tipperary in 1871. He was a publican in Sydney and they had one son (also Thomas) and five daughters. After his death his wife Margaret remarried John Ryan and they had one daughter together and she continued as a publican for many years.

Aileen and Peter Hogan are descendants of Thomas Hogan son of John the coachman and are farming in Australia today continuing the Hogan affinity with horses as they keep horses on their farm.

Kerri Ferguson is descended from John Hogan who was coachman and groom to the Arthur family of Glenomera, Ballyquin Beg and the name Ferguson came into the family with a Ferguson from Benvoran.

David Ballesty is descended from Patrick Hogan and Winifred Hogan through their son Thomas and his wife Margaret Hickey and at present he is living outside Australia.

Michael Hogan who was Thomas and Patrick's brother and John Hogan's son stayed in Ireland and was married twice. First he got married to Mary Bolton and they had 6 children together. Michael's second wife was Mary Hogan (possibly a relative?) and they had 9 children together.

A Bridget Bolton (18) states her native place as Glenomera and also states her occupation as "Housemaid". I suspect that would place her at the big house rather than working for some other local family. Note that Bridget also names her parents, John and Mary Bolton as still living and on the Glenomera estate as well.

Catherine Daly (21) states she is a servant and that her native place is Glenomera. She also names her parents as living and still on the Glenomera estate.

Margaret Maroney (18) states that she is a servant and names her native place as Glenomera. She names her parents and states that they are still living at Glenomera.

Bridget Donnellan (21) states that she is a servant and her native place is Glenomera. She also names her parents as still living on the estate.

Bridget Donnellan (25) states that she is a servant and her native place is Glenomera. She also names her parents and says that they are still living on the Glenomera estate.

A Jim McNamara mentioned a person named Gunning from Glenomera and Kerri Ferguson came across a newspaper clipping regarding a marriage in New South Wales which mentions a Gunning from Glenomera. These two people would seem to be connected.

With regard to one record containing the names of two women called Bridget Donnellon. The first Bridget claims that she has a relative John Donnellan, a cousin in the colony. The second Bridget claims that she has a relative

John Donnellan in the colony and that he is her brother so it seems likely that they were cousins.

DEATHS BY DROWNING—LOSS OF THREE HUMAN BEINGS.

We regret to state that between the hours of eight and nine o'clock this morning three human beings, (two men and a woman) were drowned at the Long Pavement, near Capt. Kane's residence, in the north liberties of this city. What makes it more melancholy is, the two men were brothers. Their name was Danaher, of Ballyfinan—that of the woman we have not been able to learn. It happened in the following manner:—The men, accompanied by another woman whose name was Margaret Lynch, of Glenomera were coming on a common car to this city. On their way they met the deceased female coming to market with a bag of potatoes on her back, and out of compassion they allowed her to get on the car. When they came to the Long Pavement, the road was flooded over to an alarming height, and the wind being very boisterous at the time, the horse lost the direct track, and falling into the deep water, the three of them were drowned. —Their bodies were since found, and an inquest was held upon them at the Exchange The woman, Lynch, was saved—so also was the horse, but not before he was two hours in the water.—*Limerick Standard.*

A newspaper article involving another resident of Glenomera.

**Now here is another note from a newspaper of nearly 150 years ago.**

Monday night a large stack of oats, the property of John Vaughan a Farmer at Glenomera, Co. Clare, was maliciously set on fire and entirely destroyed. This surname is often associated with the other Glenomera but there were Vaughan's on the Arthur estate also.

This piece is about a Catherine McMahon of 21 years of age and a servant.

Her name can first be found in the Immigration Deposit Journal of 1863 where her address is named as

"Glenomera" Broadford, County Clare (this may be the other Glenomera which is close to the Arthur estate but never belonged to the Arthur family. It seems likely that the people on the Broadford Glenomera would have known many of the people on the Ballyquin Glenomera estate). Her contact is named as the parish Priest at Glenomera. She can be seen arriving on the sailing ship "Sirocco" with two other McMahon's. On this document you can see that under the column "Relations in the Colony" she names a Bridget Hogan as a "2nd cousin living in Surry Hills". It is very_unusual to see a "numbered cousin" such as a"2nd cousin". Catherine could read but not write. Her parents are named as "Pat McMahon & Nancy McMahon" both of whom were dead.

This is the Immigration arrival record of one Patrick Hogan.

He appears to be the son of Winifred Hogan from Blackhill. Arrived in Sydney on the "Tudor" on the 17th August 1860.The record clearly states that his parents are Patrick and Winifred Hogan and that Winifred is still living at Glenomera (in 1860).This would make him a brother to the boys Thomas and James who were already in Australia and who have been mentioned already. (Note that the record states that there is already a brother, Thomas, living in Sydney).

Stephen Crowe:

Townland name entered as: Glenomera, County Clare

Date of birth: c.1833

Marriage(s): 1863. Mary McNamara, Melbourne, Victoria

Date of emigration: Unknown.

Port of Departure: Unknown.

Name of Ship: Unknown.

Place of Arrival: Unknown

Residence in Australasia: Melbourne, Mandurang, Sandhurst, Victoria

Researcher: Margaret O'Callaghan 39 Graham Avenue, McKinnon, Victoria, Australia 3204

Victorian Birth Transcription.

Parents: Mary McNamara who was born c 1847, Glenomera, Co. Clare. She got married in 1863 to Stephen Crowe in Melbourne who was born c 1833 in Glenomera, Co. Clare and he seems to have worked as a carter. Their children were John born c1864 and Mary Ann born 10 30pm 1.11.1867 146 High Street Carlton, Victoria.

**Name:** Patrick Crowe

**Spouse Name:** Mary McNamara

| | |
|---|---|
| **Marriage Place:** | Victoria |
| **Registration Place:** | Victoria |
| **Registration Year:** | 1883 |
| **Registration number:** | 3906 |

Since the experienced researcher Margaret O'Callaghan got the information about "Glenomera" from the records, we can rely on the authenticity.

The Record below is from the Victorian archives rather than the New South Wales Archive.

This would seem to be Stephen Crowe's arrival details

| | |
|---|---|
| **Name:** | Stephen Crow |
| **Estimated Birth Year:** | about 1835 |
| **Age:** | 19 |

| | |
|---|---|
| **Arrival Date:** | Aug 1854 |
| **Arrival Port:** | Melbourne, Australia |
| **Departure Port:** | Liverpool |
| **Ship:** | William Money |
| **Nationality:** | Irish |

As of yet we do not know the ship on which Mary McNamara arrived as there were so many Irish migrants with the same name and about the same age.

**THE JAMES**

On the 8th April 1834 an emigrant vessel named *"James"*, sailed from Limerick bound for Quebec but did not complete the journey. 241 people on the voyage lost their lives when the vessel sank. Some of those passengers were from Glenomera two of them appearing to be young boys between the ages of 7-14. There was a John Hayes and James Hayes on board who were farmers from Glenomera and a John Collins as well as a William Terry.

# Chapter 18

*The Arthur's of Ennistymon*

Patrick Arthur ancestor of the Arthur' of Ennistymon:

It has been difficult to get much information about this Patrick Arthur who spent his last years in Ennistymon around the beginning of the 19th century. From him have descended the Arthur's of Ennistymon, families in New York, Galway, Dr. Charles Arthur's family in Brighton, the Bennan's of London, the Cassidy's near Ennistymon, McCarthy's of Fermoy, the O'Dea and the Flatleys of Kinvara, the McDonough's of Ennistymon, the Kelly's of Clonmel, the Bourke's of Clonmel & the Johnson family of Kinvara. This Patrick is recorded as dying at the age of 98 in 1841 which means that he would have been born in 1743. It seems possible to me that Patrick was the son of a first marriage of Patrick Arthur of Limerick which I have discussed in an earlier chapter. His son William always refused to discuss family history except to say that he was directly related to Patrick Arthur of Limerick. My great uncle Br. Charles Firmin told me this and he said that his father Joseph William who was Williams's son could never get him to talk about how close the connection was except that it was very close. I think the reason could be that as William's father Patrick was disinherited by his father Patrick of Limerick in favor of the children of his second marriage (which would have been a common event at that time as many men married at least twice during their lifetime due to a wife getting ill or dying in child birth etc.) and the new wife of course would want to protect the inheritance of her children over the rights of the children of the previous marriage. At that time the husband decided who would inherit as there were no laws restricting his right to decide. As a result of Patrick of Ennistymon being disinherited there may have been a level of bitterness there certainly this was the impression my great uncle Charles had. He said that his father (Joseph William Arthur)said that there seemed to be bitterness in his father's (William Arthur) voice whenever he asked him about the family history but he did not know why that bitterness was there and I think that perhaps this may be the reason. As said earlier two daughters of Patrick of Limerick have turned up (in the Ryan family records) who were much older than any than any of Patrick's recorded children this could be indication of an earlier family. I will say more about this shortly.

In the marriage agreement between William Arthur and John Considine in 1813 there is the mention of a Joseph Arthur a merchant in the city of Limerick. This Joseph may have been the son of Joseph Arthur who was a Merchant or possibly even Joseph himself. Joseph senior had his business in Denmark Street. It would seem that Joseph was the younger brother of Patrick Arthur (Patt) of Limerick as their businesses were running beside each other in 1769 in Limerick's Denmark Street. Patrick Arthur of Limerick, Ennis and Ennistymon was the father of William Arthur of Limerick and Ennistymon. Therefore it is possible that the Patrick Arthur of Ennis and Ennistymon was the first son of the Patrick Arthur of Limerick as I discussed in an earlier chapter. But I will reprise it below.

The oral history of the family states that Patrick of Ennistymon was a direct descendent of Patrick of Limerick so how could this be. It seems probable that Patrick of Limerick was married twice and that Patrick of Ennistymon (I call him Patrick of Ennistymon even though he only had houses in Ennistymon and possibly a farm there as his main business interests were in Limerick and Ennis) was a son of a first marriage. Patrick of Ennistymon died in 1841 at the age of 98 ( death notice in local newspaper)which would mean he was born 1743 when his possible father Patrick of Limerick (who was born around 1717) would have been about 26. Now Francis the son we know about was born in 1758 when Patrick Arthur of Limerick would have been about 41. To me the huge gap between the two births suggests that Patrick of Limerick had two wives and that as was common at that time. The second wife would have defended the inheritance rights of her children by having the children of the first marriage removed from all rights of succession to their father's estate (again this was a common practice at that time). In the registry of deeds there is a reference to a Patrick Fitz Patrick Arthur which of course means Patrick the son of Patrick Arthur and this could be a reference to Patrick the son of Patrick of Limerick. Charles William Augustus Arthur in the Arthur ledger refers to Francis Arthur as Francis Fitz Patrick which of course is Francis son of Patrick I find it unusual that both possible half-brothers are referred to as being the son of Patrick. This was a way of naming that had almost died out by this time however it seems to have survived in the great families of the city of Limerick so it would seem that as both are referred to with the Fitz Patrick they could be related. Finally another unusual fact to me is that both

Patrick's in documents of the time were often referred to as Patt rather than the more usual Pat this to me indicates a possible relationship as that spelling seems to have been used within the family. He may well have set Patrick of Ennistymon in business before cutting him off and if there were other children he may have set them up in business also or encouraged then into the Priesthood, to become nuns or the Military as was common for children of first marriages at that time. The Joseph of whom we spoke earlier could also have been Patrick of Ennistymon's brother rather than his Uncle as it is possible that he was a younger brother of Patrick of Ennistymon. This could explain why he is on the marriage contract of Patrick of Ennistymon's son William as a witness. This theory is a good one and fits the facts as we know them but finding documentary proof from that time will be difficult if not impossible. It was very common at that time for men to marry multiple times as many women died in childbirth or from illness and for other reasons at a young age (The same was true for women whose husbands died young which was also common). It was usual for any children of previous marriages not to be mentioned in wills or other documents so it was normal for any record of their relationship to their father to have been forgotten and lost over time as all documentary evidence would likely have come from and referred to the family that inherited the father's estate. I was told that there was a huge anger in the Ennistymon (as mentioned already) Arthur's among the older generation (in 1800's) about discussing the relationship to Patrick of Limerick in fact as I already said all they would say was that the family was directly related to Patrick of Limerick. This could be explained by this theory and the fact that Patrick of Ennistymon was cut off from his family would explain this anger and the unwillingness of Patrick of Ennistymon and his son William to talk to their family about their Limerick relatives could be explained by anger at being cut off. Finally the name Patrick seems to have gone through the family as being the name given to every first son of the family for generations. Patrick of Limerick's grandfather was a Patrick Arthur who was an aide de camp to Patrick Sarsfield (this Patrick seems to have been the son or a grandson of a Patrick Arthur of Cloonlara who died about 1675). We know from his will that this Patrick had a son in Limerick at the time of his death and at a later time his land appears recorded as being in the possession of Francis (known) son of Patrick of Limerick. Patrick of Limerick's son Francis had a son called Patrick Edmund who was his only son and therefore his first born Now in this entire story where was Patrick of Limerick's son Patrick as it seems unlikely that Patrick of Limerick would break with family tradition and not name his first son Patrick so perhaps his first son was the man I call Patrick of Ennistymon. A funny fact here is that while every first born male child up to Patrick of Ennistymon was called Patrick he did not continue the tradition as his first son was called William who was the son of Patrick's second marriage. Here however it is possible that Patrick of Ennistymon had a son called Patrick with his first wife but so far I have not been able to trace any children of his first marriage. At that time if a first son died in infancy the name was sometimes given to the next son to be born but not always. By that theory if Patrick of Limerick had a son called Patrick who died his next son would be called Patrick instead he was called Francis so it is possible that that Patrick of Limerick had a son called Patrick who lived. Patrick of Ennistymon seems to have had had at least two sisters from the possible first marriage of Patrick of Limerick and they are listed below. I have no doubt that they are definitely lost daughters of Patrick Arthur of Limerick and this information comes from records belonging to the Ryan family of Limerick who were related to the Howley's and other Limerick families.

## Margaret Arthur:

She was born 1744 and she died in 1775. She married John Howley about 1769. The proof that she was a daughter of Patrick Arthur is that her daughter Helen Howley Ryan refers to Patrick of Limerick as her grandfather in correspondence in possession of the Ryan family and to the fact that her grandfather Patrick died in 1799. As far as I can find out there was only one Patrick Arthur who died in 1799 in Limerick and that was the man I call Patrick of Limerick.

## Ursula Mary Arthur:

She seems to have been a sister of Margaret which would make her a daughter of Patrick of Limerick and was living in the palatinate in Germany where she seems to have been a nun. A letter from her in the possession of the Ryan Family of Limerick written by Ursula Mary talks about all this and gives us the clues as to who Margaret and Ursula Mary may be. While I am certain that they were daughters of Patrick of Limerick (previously unknown) I suspect that they could be the sisters of Patrick Arthur of Ennistymon from a first marriage of Patrick of Limerick.

Walter Arthur of Ennis seems to have been a brother of Patrick of Limerick. This Walter is mentioned in a number of documents and I have the text of the documents below.

**Walter is mentioned below in this registry of deeds in 1752**

**Reg. of Deeds 158-156-108323**

Registered 11th November 1752 by Richard Studdert Lease & Release dated 18th and 19th August 1750 between Richard Brew of Ennis, Co. Clare gent of the one part and Richard Studdert of Clonderlaw, Co. Clare, of the other part. Reciting that Francis Gore of Clounroad, Co. Clare, Esq. did by indenture dated 5th April 1740 demise to said Richard Brew the Abby Meadow and the Abby Garden situate in the town of Ennis for the lives of said Richard Brew the lessee, Richard Brew the younger, his eldest son, and of Francis Dixon gent, at £7 yearly rent. That Francis Gore did by same indenture of same date demise to said Richard Brew the two tenements in the town of Ennis called Trisey's these tenements come with two stables & back garden thereto, which stables said Richard Brew has since converted into a Malthouse, for the term of three lives at £19 yearly rent. That by indenture dated 25th Oct. 1726 William Westby of Ennis Esq. demised to said Richard. Brew the meadow then and ever since in occupation of said Richard. Brew running on south with the Causeway leading from Ennis to Clonroad, for 3 lives with a covenant for renewal forever, which lease was then in the hands of said Richard. Brew and once renewed that said Richard. Brew was seized in fee simple of part of the garden backwards of said two tenements and adjoining said Richard Brew's garden. That Richard Brew did by lease & release for cons 'on therein mentioned convey said freehold interests to Anthony Casey of Mount Scott, Co. Clare., Esq. subject to proviso of redemption. That said Anthony Casey did by lease & release dated as therein mentioned assign the mortgage to Maurice Studdert of Ennisconch, Co. Limerick gent. That said Richard Brew for cons 'on therein mentioned agreed to convey the equity of redemption of said mortgaged premises to said Richard Studdert & his heirs. Witnesseth Richard Brew for cons 'on therein mentioned [illegible] to Richard Studdert said Abby Meadow & said Abby Garden and tenements with house & back garden thereto belonging & said meadow & garden backwards of said two new tenements & all his right of renewal thereto. To hold to Richard Studdert and his heirs forever.

*Witnesses to deeds: Thomas Stitt of Kilkishen, Co. Clare, gent and Walter Arthur of Ennis, Co. Clare, merchant.*

*Witnesses to memorial: Thomas Stitt & Thomas Kean of City of Limerick, gent.*
*Thomas Stitt sworn at Ennis 12th August 1752 before B. Whitney on circuit.*
*Here again is our Walter leasing Birchfield Estate and then leasing it to James O'Brien of Limerick.*

*1796:- Lawrence Comyn* leased Birchfield to Walter Arthur of Ennis and Walter Arthur to James O'Brien of Limerick.

Below Walter is welcoming the act of Union in 1800 along with other important people from Clare.

From the Ennis Chronicle 26 September 1799:

We whose Names are hereunto subscribed, deeply interested in the peace and prosperity of the Co. of Clare and Kingdom at large, APPROVE of the Measure of a LEGISLATIVE UNION with Great Britain on equal and liberal principles, and on a sense of mutual interests and affection, as the only means of tranquilizing this County, and abolishing those religious distinctions which have unhappily distracted this Kingdom.

Walter Arthur

It is probable that the Walter and William Arthur mentioned below are sons of Walter Arthur of Ennis mentioned in the last piece.

Registry of Freeholds 1828 for the Baronies of Bunratty, Inchiquin and Tulla:
Surname Index

Title: Registry of Freeholds 1828
Type: Freeholders registry
Dates: 1828
Place: Baronies of Bunratty, Inchiquin & Tulla
Source: *Clare Journal & Ennis Advertiser* -
December 1828

Registry of Freeholds.

County of Clare.

The following are two of the Notices of Applications to Register Freeholds, delivered to the Clerk of the Peace, for the County of Clare, which were heard at Ennis Sessions, on the 14th day of January 1828, at 10 o'clock in the morning.

| **Surname** | **Forename** | **Address** | **Holding** | **Barony** | **Amount** |
|---|---|---|---|---|---|
| Arthur | Walter | Ennis | Rent charge on land at Dromeavan | Inchiquin barony | Ten pounds |
| Arthur | William | Ennis | Rent charge on land at Cloncolman | Inchiquin barony | Twenty pounds |

Below William Arthur (almost certainly the son of Walter Arthur) appears along with others offering a reward for the capture of some thieves. The amount each donated is also mentioned. I think the single numbers refer to the number of pounds being donated by that person and some of the donations are in shillings and pence and even in guineas

Clare Journal, Thursday, 5th May, 1803

Whereas on the night of Wednesday 27th Day of April last in the absence of Michael Canny of Ennis, Notary Public, when he was at the Sessions at Milltown. Some villains attempted to break into and plunder his house and on the night preceding the shop of Mrs. Gorman of Mill Street in said town was broke open and plundered of several articles of value. The shop of Mrs. McNamara of Church Street was also attempted in like manner and on the night of the 1st inst. the shop of Mrs. White in Church Street was also broke open as were several other houses and shops in the town of Ennis within these few nights past. We, the inhabitants of the said town of Ennis, do hereby offer the several sums to our names respectively annexed as a reward to any persons who shall within three calendar months from the date hereof apprehend and prosecute to conviction any of the persons concerned, given under our hands this 5th day of May 1803.

Charles Mahon, 5 Gs; James Kinnane, 1, Luke McGrath, 1; William Arthur, 1; James Hickey, 1; James Gallery, 1; Francis Swyny, 1; Rich. England,1; Michael McNamara, 1; Wm. Fitzgerald, 2; Michael Hickey, 1; John Leary, 1; Francis Daly, 2; John Tierney, 1; Edward Mallon, 1; Robert Kean, Chas, 2; Anne White, 1; John England,1; William Greene, 2; John O'Neill, 1; James O'Connor, 1; John Carroll, 1; Michael Hilliard, 1; Luke Thomas, 1; William Emerson, 2; James O'Neill,1; George Lardner, 1; Mat. Williams, 2; James Sexton, 1; Dan. McMahon, 1; Hugh M'Loughlin, 2; James O'Brien, 1; Thomas Roughan, 1; Thomas Butler, 2; Pat. Kean, 1; Daniel Roughan, 1; Michael Canny, 2; Wm. McGrath, 1; Edm. Donnellan, 1; James McLaughlin, 2; Michael Danaher, 1; George Edwards, 1; Thomas Darcy, 2; John R M'Grath, 1; James P Crowe, 1; Catherine Gorman, 2; J. O'Neill, tobacconist, 1; John O'Donnell, 2; Richard Floyd, 2; William Kenny, 1; Daniel Finucane, 2; Anthony Horahan, 2; John E Kenny, 1; J. M'Cullen, 11s. 4 1/2d.; Edw. Haire, 1; Mich. Walsh, 1; M. O'Dea, 11s.4 1/2d.; Richard Baker, 1; Sylvester O'Gorman, 1; Ellen Hogan, 11s. 4 1/2d.; Joseph Haire, 1;

Edmond Lynch, 1; Walter Nevian, 1; Andrew Joynt, 1; Daniel O'Keeffe, 1

Below is a letter was signed by Walter Arthur along with others showing that they were loyal servants of the King of England.

Clare Journal, Monday, 13th February 1797

To Maurice O'Connor Esq, Vice Provost of Ennis. Sir, We the Inhabitants of this town, take this opportunity of expressing our most perfect approbation of the great zeal, unwearied diligence and strict impartiality you exerted in billeting the soldiery in the late marches through it. Being entirely convinced that in the discharge of that duty your conduct was governed by the most unbiased wishes for the public good. The period was awful and alarming, far beyond any example of our time: It was not a time for languor or parsimony and here thank heaven there did not appear a symptom of either, as if but one animated by the same spirit of loyalty and diligence to the best of Kings, cherished the weary soldier with liberality, doubly comfortable because administered with cheerfulness.

James Kenny, Edward Mallon, James Kinnane, Walter Arthur, John Ed. Kenny, Matts. Brennan, Jhn Chartres, Basil Lukey, P. Butler, Robert Weldon, Terence McMahon, John Lyons, Thomas Dulhunty, J. Gregg, Matt. Power, Laurence Comyn, Hugh McCloskey, James Stuart, James O'Gorman, John Speilesy M.D., Thomas Butler, Richard Griffin, Neptune Blood, Patrick Davoren, Henry Hewitt, Joseph Cox, Robert Kean, Michael Hicky, Richard Janns, Michael Walsh, John Whitestone, Thomas Crowe, Wm. Fitzgerald, Patt. Sitred, Jonas Studdert, Wm. Brampton,

John O'Donnell, Thomas Hewitt, Percival Banks jun., Michael Dwyer, D. Barrett, John R McGrath, William McGrath, Daniel Finucane, Hugh Brigdale, Hugh McLaughlin,

Although it is possible in light of the above showing Walter to be a man of some importance as he was important enough to be requested to sign such documents I do not believe he is the most likely person to be the father of our Patrick Arthur of Ennis and Ennistymon even though said Patrick did have a wine and spirits business in Ennis. It should however be noted that many of the names associated with Walter Arthur are also associated with the Arthur family of Glenomera and therefore at this time the families must still have been close. Perhaps Walter and Patrick Arthur of Limerick's father was a nephew of the man who founded the Glenomera line.

An important point to note is that Walter Arthur of Ennis and Patrick Arthur of Limerick were conferred with the freedom of Limerick on the same day and I believe this suggests that they were very closely related probably brothers.

There is a record in Maynooth College that tells us that Patrick of Ennistymon came from an illustrious family, the Arthur's of Limerick City. Patrick of Ennistymon was married twice the first time in Ennis on the 3rd September 1770. Unfortunately have not yet found her name but he is recorded as a Limerick Merchant. His second wife a Mulqueeny was an Ennistymon woman, for the name was common at that time in the district. His son Francis (a priest) was of the second marriage and it seems probable that James and William was of the second marriage, as most probably were the girls who became Mrs Cassidy, Mrs O'Donnell, Mrs Craig and Mrs Mc Donagh.

In 1813 William Arthur (Patrick Arthur of Limerick, Ennis and Ennistymon's son) was a young merchant living in Limerick, and by 1824 he was recorded as having a tobacconist at no 1 Georges street with another establishment at 16 Patrick Street where he carried on the business of grocery and wine merchant. William is recorded on 15th September 1818 as having houses and a business at Bridge Street with a valuation of £50. In 1813 a connection of Williams lived in Ennis, he was a Patrick Arthur, a publican (which seems to have been one of the businesses that he had in Ennis as well as Limerick). He was of course his father Patrick of Ennistymon. It would seem so as there are two records to show that Patrick had a connection with Ennistymon one is inscribed on the tomb of his second wife in the old cemetery at Churchill Ennistymon. The second is that he is also recorded as owning at least two houses in Ennistymon one where he died (now called the Hill house) where he died in 1841 at the age of 98 and the other called Deerpark where his son William lived some of the time and where his grandson Joseph William was to spend most of his life.

The inscription on Patrick's grave reads.

> In spem beatae ressurectionis
> The mortal remains of Mrs. Patrick Arthur alias Mulqueeny lies beneath this tomb, which was erected by her son the Rev Francis Arthur in grateful remembrance of a beloved parent. She departed this life July 10th. 1845 aged 62 years.

May the lord have mercy on her soul?

The house Patrick of Ennistymon lived in.

Patrick also owned this house in Ennistymon it is known as Deerpark.

Francis Arthur (Patt. Arthur's) son had one son. The source of this information along with Patrick's birth record is a letter written by Rev Mother Prioress Maurus O.S.B. of the Benedictine Convent Princethorpe to Brother Charles Arthur about Catherine Helen Arthur. In this letter she speaks about Francis Arthur's son Patrick Edmund dying. In the transcript of Francis trial it mentions that he was the father of a large family. Further information from the above letter reveals that Mother Mary Jane Arthur was the granddaughter of Francis Arthur and her father was Patrick Edmund Arthur the only son of Francis Arthur.

The piece below seems to refer to Patrick Arthur of Ennistymon and how he along with two others was to repair the road from Ennistymon to old Deerpark.

From the Spring Assizes of Co. Clare' Grand Jury 1807. The work to be done in 1808

Ennistymon to Ennis, between Ennistymon and the old Deerpark which is where one of Patrick Arthur's houses in Ennistymon was situated
To Edward O'Brien, Andrew Stacpoole esqrs. and Patrick Arthur, to repair thirty two perches from Ennistymon to Ennis, between the Seffions house of Ennistymon and Millmount Bridge for which he was allowed £7 - 11shillings and 2 pence

Below is the registration of freehold by Patrick Arthur of the property now called the Hill House.

**The Clare Journal, and Ennis Advertiser**
**Ennis, Monday, May 18, 1829**

The following is one of the Applications made to the Clerk of the Peace, for the County of Clare, for Registry of Freeholders, at Ennis, on the 3rd day of June, 1829 Patrick Arthur of Ennistymon House and out-offices with land annexed, in Ennistymon, barony of Corcomroe. This seems to have been what I call the Hill house because one of Patrick's descendants who married a man called hill. Deerpark seems to have been built by Patrick for his children

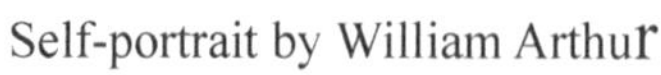
Self-portrait by William Arthur

Margaret Considine c1850 taken by her son Joseph William Arthur.

Note with relevance to the following passage £1,000 in 1812 would be worth approx. €42,000 in today's money, £500 is worth approx. €21000 and £250 is worth approx. €10,500.

These are inflation values the purchasing power of the amount in 1813 would be much greater that the straight inflationary value.

**Here is an exact copy of the marriage agreement (the language could be seen as a little arcane, legalistic and difficult to at times understand but I thought the original should be preserved rather than interpreted) solemnized between William Arthur, Merchant of The City of Limerick and of Margaret Considine of Ennis 1813.**

"This indenture made the first day of September in the year of Our Lord 1813, between William Arthur of the City of Limerick, merchant of the first part, John Considine of Ennis in the county of Clare, Tobacconist and Margaret Considine of Ennis, spinster, second daughter of said John Considine, of the second part, and Joseph Arthur of the City of Limerick, merchant and Patrick Arthur of Ennis in the County of Clare, publican of the third part. Whereas a marriage is shortly to be solemnized between the said William Arthur and the said Margaret Considine for and in consequence of the said intended marriage and of the covenants, proviso's and agreements herein after particularly mentioned And on the said William Arthur's part to be made, done and performed hath on the said intended marriage taking effect paid to the said William Arthur the sum of £1,000 sterling, as the marriage portion with the said Margaret Considine, at and before the sealing and delivery of these presents;

the receipt whereof the said William Arthur doth hereby acknowledge and from every part doth hereby exonerate, acquit and discharge the said John Considine his exors, assors and assigns on this proviso and it is the true intent and meaning of these presents and of the parties hereto to permit and suffer the said William Arthur to have receive and take the said sum of £1,000 to his own proper use and benefit. In the case of the said Margaret Considine shall happen to die within the term of six years, leaving no issue of the said intended marriage, lawfully to be begotten, that then and in that case, he, the said William Arthur his exors, assors, admors and assigns shall well and truly pay to the said John Considine, his exors, heirs, assors and assigns the sum of £250 sterling being one fourth of the marriage portion of the said Margaret Considine and upon this further proviso, that if the said Margaret Considine shall happen to survive the said William Arthur, her said intended husband, leaving no issue of the said intended marriage lawfully be begotten, or in the case of the said William Arthur's failure in his trade, that then and in that case, he the said William Arthur for the purpose of securing a provision for the said Margaret Considine , his said intended wife hath executed this bond, with the warrant of attorney for confessing judgment, thereon bearing equal date with these presents to the said Joseph Arthur and Patrick Arthur, and in trust to be paid to the said Margaret Considine, her exors, assors and assigns and to no other use intent and purpose , whatsoever in the Penal sum of £1,000 sterling conditioned for the payment of the sum of £500 sterling and for the performance of all and every, the covenants and agreements herein before mentioned, the said William Arthur doth hereby, exors, assors and assigns covenants , promise and agree to and with the said Joseph Arthur and Patrick Arthur, exors and their assigns that he the said William Arthur, exors, assors and assigns shall and will from time to time and at all times hereafter at the reasonable request but at the proper cost and charges of the said John Considine or Margaret Considine, exors, assors and assigns, make, do and execute all and every such further and lawful and necessary act or acts deed or deeds, devices, conveyances and assurances in the law for the further, better and more perfect carrying the true intent and meaning of these presents and of the parties hereto into effect as their council, learned in the law shall reasonably advise, devise or require, in witness whereof the said parties have here unto put their hands and affixed their seal the day and year first in these presents written.

Signed, sealed and delivered in the presence of:

Michael Lynch, Pat Daly, William Arthur, John Considine, Margaret Considine, Joseph Arthur, Patt Arthur.

Received from the above named John Considine and the sum of £1,000 sterling being the consideration money in the written deed mentioned in the day and the year within mentioned. A memorial of the within deed was entered into the Registry Office in the city of Dublin 5th November 1812 (20'c in B 659 n22, no. 459210) and the execution of said deed memorial was duly proven pursuant to an act of parliament in that case made and provided.

Note in this document how Williams father Patrick is referred to as Patt just as Patrick of Limerick often was.

John Griffin Dep. Reg.

The Next piece is about Mary Considine who seems to have been a sister of Margaret Considine who married William Arthur.

It would appear that Margaret Considine's sister Mary married another man called Arthur. The man she married was called Patrick Arthur and from research it appears that he was a member of the Arthur families that came over with Strongbow. Although he was from Clare his ancestors were from the Limerick Tipperary border and had been dispossessed by Cromwell and transplanted to Clare. Some of his descendants are now in America.

As said before William was in business in Limerick where he owned a number of shops and here is an advertisement from the Limerick Chronicle for his business in 1819.

Mentioned in the advertisement are two of the shops William had but along with the shops I have discovered a number of other properties he owned which would explain why it was said that Joseph William was brought up as the son of a wealthy family. I do not know how he acquired his wealth but it seems likely that his father gave him a good start in life and his natural Arthur business sense allowed him to build up his own wealth.

Now here are some more properties William had an interest in , in Collooney Street he had a house and yard at number 26,a house at number 35 and another house at number 36, In Moylish he had a house and office at 2A and he had the land at 2B. There may be other properties but as yet I have not traced them.

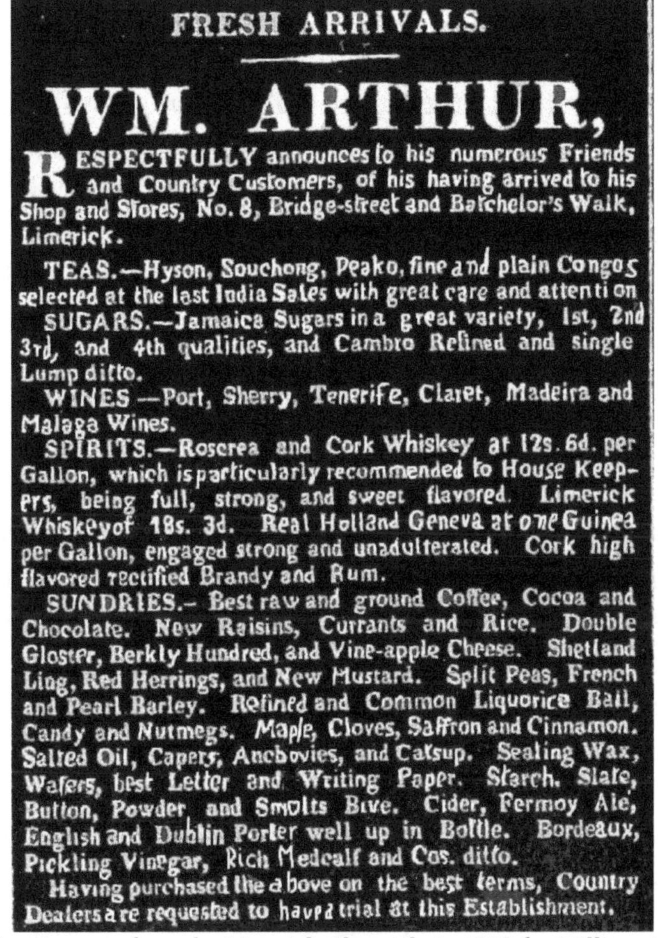

FRESH ARRIVALS.

WM. ARTHUR,

RESPECTFULLY announces to his numerous Friends and Country Customers, of his having arrived to his Shop and Stores, No. 8, Bridge-street and Batchelor's Walk, Limerick.

TEAS.—Hyson, Souchong, Peako, fine and plain Congos selected at the last India Sales with great care and attenti on

SUGARS.—Jamaica Sugars in a great variety, 1st, 2nd 3rd, and 4th qualities, and Cambro Refined and single Lump ditto.

WINES —Port, Sherry, Tenerife, Claret, Madeira and Malaga Wines.

SPIRITS.—Roscrea and Cork Whiskey at 12s. 6d. per Gallon, which is particularly recommended to House Keepers, being full, strong, and sweet flavored. Limerick Whiskey of 18s. 3d. Real Holland Geneva at one Guinea per Gallon, engaged strong and unadulterated. Cork high flavored rectified Brandy and Rum.

SUNDRIES.- Best raw and ground Coffee, Cocoa and Chocolate. New Raisins, Currants and Rice. Double Gloster, Berkly Hundred, and Vine-apple Cheese. Shetland Ling, Red Herrings, and New Mustard. Split Peas, French and Pearl Barley. Refined and Common Liquorice Ball, Candy and Nutmegs. Maple, Cloves, Saffron and Cinnamon. Salted Oil, Capers, Anchovies, and Catsup. Sealing Wax, Wafers, best Letter and Writing Paper. Starch. Slate, Button, Powder and Smolts Bive. Cider, Fermoy Ale, English and Dublin Porter well up in Bottle. Bordeaux, Pickling Vinegar, Rich Medcalf and Cos. ditto.

Having purchased the above on the best terms, Country Dealers are requested to have a trial at this Establishment.

An advertisement from the Limerick Chronicle in 1819 for William Arthurs shops.

There is a reference in an 1848 document to a Patrick Arthur owning two houses and land in the parish of St. Patrick's in the townland of Reboge. If this is Williams father it would have at this time have passed down to Joseph William and could be some of the remaining property in Limerick that Joseph William is referred to as going to Limerick to sell after his father Williams death.

During the building of the Christian Brothers Monastery in Ennistymon about 1824 the annals of the monastery record that the brothers resided temporarily in a house entered by a bow-way and owned by a Mr. Arthur, this man was of course Patrick Arthur of Ennistymon and the house was called Deerpark where William lived at times but where his son Joseph William was to take up full time residence.

On the rent-roll of Colonel McNamara from 1863 we find the name James Arthur (he was a brother of William Arthur) as being a tenant in New Street (now Main Street) James does not seem to have been married and had no children but he lived in Patrick Arthur's house with his sister in a house today known as the Hill House as one of Patrick's descendants called Hill now owns the house. Under the same date we find the "Representatives of Patt Arthur" living at the Cottage (Deerpark House). These representatives of Patt Arthur of course were Joseph William Arthur and his young wife. Again note the spelling of his name as Patt.

Three of the sons of Patrick Arthur (of Ennistymon) went to Limerick where they took up the grocery business and in time became very wealthy. One of these sons was William Arthur who married Margaret Considine.

The following are some notes about members of the Arthur family that may be of some interest.

These come from official records in Limerick.

1811 Martin Arthur left money to build an orphanage.
1824 William Arthur was a grocer and wine merchant in 16 Patrick Street and a tobacconist at 1 Georges Street.
1831 Martin dies intestate.
1853 Peter Arthur lives in Patrick Street.

The following information came from Records Office in Dublin. The following wills were proved.

*Thomas Arthur* – Glenomera, Co. Clare. 1811.
*James Arthur* – Dunquin, Co. Clare 1814.
*Rebecca Arthur* – Ennis 1825.
*Thomas Arthur* – Worlds End Cottage, Killaloe 1828.He was buried on an island on the river Shannon and as he seems to have been a Catholic as the grave yard used was only for Catholic's. He may be related to the Arthur's of Limerick or possibly the Arthurs of Glenomera (he may have been descended from an ancestor who did not convert). The name Thomas would indicate a possible connection to Glenomera as this name was very common in that line.

*Michael Arthur* – Beanpark, Killaloe.

The following information was giver to Brother Charles Arthur by the protestant rector of Ennis in 1832.

December 2$^{nd}$ 1786 – Miss Jane Arthur, married Mr. John Sexton. Jane Arthur was the daughter of John Arthur Esq. Ennis.

January 26th 1790 – Anne Arthur married Cornelius O'Callaghan.
July 7th 1799 – William Arthur married Miss Anne Crowe
May 17th 18?? (Difficult to read the year) baptized John Arthur, son of William Arthur and Anne Crowe.
September 10th 1803 – Baptized Walter the son of William Arthur and Anne Crowe.
September 2nd 1806 – William the son of William Arthur and Anne Crowe.

There is no information on whether these people were Catholics or Protestants although it seems probable that they were protestant as this information was provided by a protestant clergyman.

This member of the Arthur family was Mayor of Galway.

1546 Stephen Lynch Fitz Arthur.
1560 Stephen Lynch Fitz Arthur.

# Chapter 19

*Here is a short biography of Catherine (Kate) Cooney who was the wife of Joseph William Arthur. This piece was written by her son Br. Charles (Firmin) Arthur in 1965.*

Kate Cooney taken 1900

Kate Cooney, the daughter of John Cooney and Alice Lahiff was born at Kilshanney, Co. Clare about the year 1838. In the family there were five boys and three girls. The boys were called John, James, Patrick, Martin and Austin. The names of the girls were Kate, Mary who became a Mrs. Callinan and Brigid who went to Australia to enter a convent. The Cooney family had a small farm with the usual thatched cottage of those days. By 1965 the house had been rebuilt and Austin Cooney and his family occupied the farm. Kate's brother James was a shopkeeper in Ennistymon when Kate was in her teens. He dealt a good deal in tobacco and for this reason he used to go to Limerick regularly to replenish his stock. It was while on such business that he came to know Joseph William Arthur who was also in the tobacco trade at that time and thus a friendship was formed between the two young men. Joseph at this time was about 36 and not yet married. His mother Mrs. Margaret (Considine) Arthur was living in the cottage in Ennistymon and by the year 1858 Joseph was lining there with her. Evidently he seems to have given up whatever business he had in Limerick by this time. Through his friend James Cooney he had come to know James sister Kate at Kilshanney. She was a young innocent country girl who knew very little about the world. She got a primary education at the local school and she certainly never traveled more than a few miles from her native home. So it came to pass that she married the young Limerick city businessman, now living with his mother in Ennistymon and she came to live there in 1858 ( I believe that she lived with her brother in the town until she got married). Her brother James had a shop and his own property in the town. It seems likely that Joseph Arthur her husband had taken up the profession of photography by that time.

In 1859 Joseph William Arthur was married to Kate Cooney in the kitchen of the farmhouse in Kilshanney, the officiating priest being the Very Reverend Fr. Verrilly P.P. Many years ago a Br. Leo Nestor an old Christian Brother told Charles that he had danced at the wedding. He was a distant cousin of Kate and in subsequent years he always called to see her whenever he visited Ennistymon. Some years Charles requested Rev. Fr. O'Donoghue P.P. of Kilshanney to inspect the marriage register in the period we are talking about for details of the ceremony but Fr. O'Donoghue informed Charles that immediately after Fr. Verrilly's death a "vagabond" of a housekeeper whom he had burned the book. From conversations Charles had with his brother William (there were 24 years between them) the eldest of the family Charles came to believe that periodically at any rate the marriage was not a happy one. This may have been due to the disparity of age between husband and wife.

Joseph was a good living man, faithful and straight he never drank but he lacked anything of a business capacity to make a comfortable home for his family. He was city born and well educated while Kate was a simple country girl with a sharp temper which was explosive at times. With all that she was most affectionate and forgiving. A big family of nine came along in due course and there was an interval of twenty-four years between the oldest and the youngest, William being the oldest and Charles being the youngest. From her marriage in 1858 to her death in 1901 there was a period of much poverty and diversity in Ireland. She experienced very little of the wealth and standard of living which we know today. She was ten or eleven years of age when the terrible famine of 1848 broke out all over Ireland followed by the terrible epidemic of the cholera. Kate used to speak sometimes about the bread they used to make from potatoes.

Charles never remembered his mother speaking of her girlhood days at home and stranger still he never heard her speak of her brothers, sisters, father or mother. Charles was only a child when his father died in 1890 yet he was deeply impressed by the deep sadness and melancholy by which she was surrounded in the years that intervened until Charles left for college in Baldoyle in 1900. She dressed in deep mourning for the rest of her life. There were only five of the children left at the old home and then after three or four years Frank left for Dublin and later for London. Joseph used to leave home for months at a time traveling on photographic business so that for the last six or seven years of his life at the cottage the family consisted of Kate, Catherine, Madeline and Charles.

Kate was of a very religious turn of mind. Except during the severe cold of winter she rose for daily mass saying her morning prayers devoutly before she set out. Daily communion was an unknown practice in those days but she never missed monthly confession and communion. One day in the year she had a mass said in the house by one of the curates. The mass was said in the parlor on the left as you enter the hall. That parlor was later used as a bedroom.

Kate's greatest cross in her life was her youngest daughter Madeline. Madeline became a permanent invalid about the age of five, her trouble started with epileptic fits. These came at intervals every few months. Evidently no doctor was called and even if one were called there was at that time no remedy for this terrible disease which there is today. The disease dulled Madeline's mental faculties and her brain had ceased to work. By the age of nine she had lost all control over the use of her feet and hands. There was no deformity whatever but she had lost all power of observation of temper or affection. Her position at the age of twelve and indeed to the end was that of an infant a week old. Every necessity had to be done for her and to her sister Catherine fell the duty of attending to her day and night. To Catherine's great credit she took on the duty of attending to Madeline and she did it with great devotion for twenty-nine long years. Kate's constant prayer was that God would take Madeline before her own death but Madeline lived for about eight years after Kate died. Madeline never lost her innocence and she was about twenty-nine when she died at Nazareth House Belfast. She was interred in the cemetery of that home in 1909.

Kate had no pleasure outside her own home. She cooked well whatever there was to be cooked Charles was certain that there were no luxuries. She baked almost all of the bread that they ate. She made all of the underclothes that Charles wore as well as knitting all of his socks. Charles never wore long pants until he went to college. She did all the laundry and kept the house in good order. Since Charles had to be in school every morning at 8 o'clock they had an early breakfast. There was always a bit of lunch ready for him when he blew in at 12.30 and his dinner was ready when he came home at 3.00 p.m.

During his childhood and teenage years he never heard her say an unedifying word not to mention a bad word. He was sharp enough to notice that when married women of her acquaintance came into the house for a chat she broke into the Irish language when she had something not suitable for his ears to hear. The subjects that we hear about and read about today in the public press were a closed book as far as she was concerned in those days.

Kate allowed herself one very small luxury, which was an occasional pinch of snuff. Cigarette smoking among women was virtually unknown but not a few of them kept a snuff box. Charles invariably did the purchasing for her rarely exceeding a pennyworth a week and it should be remembered that a penny was worth considerably more than it is now. She always used Hignett's Snuff and in a curious coincidence when Charles went to Liverpool the brother's residence where he lived had formerly been the home of the Hignett family of snuff fame.

Kate liked to have some of the old occupations she had as a girl in her old home of Kilshanney and so she always kept a little Kerry cow, some fowl, as well as a flock of geese and ducks. She found her recreation in these possessions. Before the winter set in she always secured a store of turf and a ton of coal against the cold of the coming months. She loved all her children without exception but she was not too demonstrative in the way she felt that affection. She could raise her voice and her tongue when the occasion demanded it but that was rare and only a passing phase and never did she harbor the smallest dislike for any member of her family.

Kate was rather small in physique and remained rather slight all her life. On the whole she was blessed with good health in mind and body, but occasionally although not often she got fits of retching and vomiting. On these occasions she was quite upset and the trouble used to continue for a day or two. Charles was of the opinion that this trouble proceeded from eating some food, which did not agree with her.

As far as Charles knew his mother never traveled much beyond her home. He believed that she was never in Ennis the home of her mother in law Mrs. Margaret Arthur and he was fairly certain that she was never in Limerick the hometown of her husband. When her son John and his family came to live in Kilkee about 1894 she and Charles used to go down once in a while to visit them for a day. Charles never knew her to be absent even one full day from the home.

The people of Ennistymon regarded her as an excellent woman who brought up a big family, kept them in order and always gave them good example. She was thoroughly honest in her dealings with all who had business dealings with her and she devoted all of her care and attention to the welfare and care of her family, never interfering with the affairs of anyone outside her family. She had her share of the cross but she bore it patiently. Very often her finances were at a very low ebb and there was the constant cross of the physical condition of poor little Madeline. There was never any serious family trouble except in the case of Madeline, sickness was unknown. There was never an accident, never a lawsuit, and none of the family ever had any trouble with the civil authorities. They were all fervent in religion and the crowning happiness was that two of her daughters became Sisters of Mercy and two of her sons became Christian Brothers.

That was the Kate Cooney that Charles knew for the years before he left to join the Christian Brothers. He was never able to do anything financially to help her but she gave him every care in sickness and in health. She supplied all his wants and he well remembered the day in May 1900 when he said goodbye to her little realising at the moment what the parting meant and so he did not feel their separation. That goodbye meant that he would never again see her in this world for she died only ten months later of pneumonia. Her close friend Fr. John Connelly C.C attended her at her deathbed.

Taken after Kate Cooney's funeral in 1910.

*Occasional words and phrases have been edited in the above in order to bring the text up to date and hopefully make it a little easier to read. This editing has been as minimal as possible.*

# Chapter 20

*A little information about some of the children of Patrick Arthur of Ennistymon and their respective families*

Apart from William who is dealt with in other chapters not a lot is known about the other children of Patrick Arthur of Ennistymon. Those we know of seem to be the children of Patrick's second marriage to Miss Mulqueeny who was an Ennistymon woman.

## Margaret

Margaret Arthur married a Mr. McDonough of Ennistymon. They had three boys, Francis, Edward, and Patrick. Francis inherited his father's property. His first wife died and then he married Margaret Walshe a daughter of Roderick Walshe of Ennistymon. This was not a happy marriage so Francis left for Australia and he was never heard from again. He left one son, Edward from the second marriage. Edward lived in his father's house in Ennistymon and he married Elizabeth Cooney who was the daughter of Patrick Cooney of Kilshanney these Cooney's were cousins of the Arthur's. There were three children of this marriage Frank who died in 1946, May and Tessie. Tessie married a man called Hill which is how Patrick's house became known as the Hill house. Sadly Tessie passed away shortly before this book was written. Edward son of Margaret Arthur immigrated to Australia and Patrick another son of Margaret Arthur entered the church.

## Father Patrick McDonough:

Father Pat McDonough

Father Patt as he was familiarly called was the son of Margaret Arthur and a grandson of Patrick Arthur of Ennistymon. He was born in Ennistymon in 1827 and very probably got his education from the Christian Brothers in the town. He went to Maynooth in 1845 where he excelled in his studies. He was noted for his knowledge of Irish history and antiquities. Father Patrick was ordained about 1852 and he was immediately appointed to a professorship in the Chair of Rhetoric at the Irish College in Paris, where he spent a few years.

Later he was appointed curate to his Uncle Francis Arthur (who was a son of Patrick Arthur of Ennistymon) in Kinvara, Co. Galway and in 1873 he was made parish priest of Clarenbridge. While father Patrick was a professor in Paris his health gave way necessitating a change to his own native land. He died on December 30$^{th}$

1903 aged 76. He was buried at Rovenheagh outside Clarenbridge.

### Mrs. O'Donnell:

Mrs. O'Donnell was another daughter of Patrick Arthur of Ennistymon. She married a well to do hardware merchant in Corofin, Co. Clare where they carried out a very extensive and lucrative trade. She had four children who were called Patrick, Francis, Brigid and Margaret Jane. Both Patrick and Francis died unmarried. Jane was educated at the Dominican College, Taylor's Hill in Galway but sadly she died when she was 18.

Brigid married Mr. John O'Dea, a brother of Dr. O'Dea who died in Ennistymon about 1894. Their first child was called Arthur. Brigid died giving birth to her second child and both mother and child are buried beneath the altar in the wing of the Carmailite Abbey in Loughrea, Co. Galway. Arthur O'Dea then married Mary Mahon. The children of that marriage were Daniel Alphonsus, Patrick, John Joseph, May Francis who became a nun, Brigid and Jenny both of whom became nurses in England.

## Fr. Francis Arthur:

Fr. Francis Arthur

1815 – 1876 on the right hand side of Patrick's house (the Hill house) in Ennistymon there is a single story annex that was built to house Fr. Francis when he came to visit his relations in Ennistymon. Elsewhere in the book there is a photo of the house and on the right hand side of the photo as you look at it you can see the single story addition to the house that was built for Father Francis to stay in when visiting. He went to Maynooth to study for the priesthood on August 26th 1836 on his 19th Birthday and he was ordained on the 21st May 1842. In 1847 became he became administrator of the Parish of Kinvara in Galway where by all accounts he was a very good priest. He was instrumental in helping John Blake Dillon one of the leaders of the Young Ireland movement to escape from Ireland first sheltering him in his house. When he was told he had been informed on he managed to spirit Dillon to the Arran Islands disguised as Fr. Kelly who was Fr. Arthur's curate. From the Arran Islands John Blake Dillon completed his escape first to France and then to the U.S.A. When Fr. Francis went to Kinvara before the famine there were 1800 families in the parish but when he left Kinvara in 1867 for Croughwell there were less than 700 families left in the parish which is a testament to the devastation wreaked on large areas of Ireland by the famine.

Below I have the will of Fr. Francis Arthur which you can compare to the wills of other family members earlier in the book specifically I am speaking of how little he had to leave after spending his life in the priesthood.

*Reverend Francis Arthur P.P. late of Croughwell County Galway testator deceased.*

In the name of God I Father Francis Arthur of Croughwell in the district of Kilmucduagh in the county of Galway being of sound mind and intellect do make this my last will and testament revoking any and all wills previously made by me.
I will and bequeath that all my lawful and just debts be paid. I will and bequeath to my nephew Rev. Patrick Mc Donough all the rest and residue of my real and personal property after payment of my just and lawful debts. I hereby appoint my nephew the above named Rev. Patrick

Mc Donough my executor to carry out the true intent and meaning of this my last will.

Signed: Fr. Francis Arthur P.P

Signed sealed and declared in the presence of us and we have hereunto attached our signatures in the presence of each other and in the presence of the testator the 15th day of March in the year of our lord 1869.
Timothy Shannon P.P.
Michael O'Flanagan C.C.

Another daughter whose name is not in my records married a **Mr. O'Donnell** from Corofin. Co. Clare who was a hardware merchant there.

There was a **Mrs. Cassidy** who was a daughter of Patrick Arthur and that is all I know about her.

The last one I know of was a **Mrs. Carrig** who was also a daughter of Patrick Arthur and again that is all I know about her.

# Chapter 21

*The children of William Arthur son of Patrick Arthur of Ennistymon*

William had one daughter.

## Mary Arthur

She was baptized 7th may 1832 in St. John's Co. Limerick. Mary is believed to have died young as there are no records of her. She died on 17th February 1836 as I have seen a record of a child of that name dying on that day and that child was from the right place to be her and her father is named as William Arthur. In Brother Charles (Firmin's) notes he referrers to her as an interesting child.

*The sons of William Arthur son of Patrick Arthur of Ennistymon possible first son of Patrick Arthur of Limerick*

William had nine sons.

## Francis Arthur

Francis was born in Limerick in about 1814.He was the eldest of a large family consisting of 9 boys and one girl. William Arthur was his father and Margaret Considine was his mother as well as this he was a brother of Joseph William Arthur of Ennistymon. Francis was a manager in the large firm of Quinn LTD Limerick. Quins begun trading as wine, tea and spirit wholesaler's in1822 and Quins remained in the Stephen's family for almost two centuries until it closed in 2006. Francis also owned property in Limerick, where he had a house at number 35 in the parish of St. Michaels; in Edward Street he owned a house and office at number 56. He has another house and yard at number 50 in the parish of St. Michael's.

Two photos of Quins in 2006, note how little it must have changged since the time of Francis being manager there.

Francis married a Limerick lady whose name seems to have been Mary but we have no record of her surname. Of this marriage there was a large family but as far as we know none of these children were born in Limerick they were all born in New York. Francis and his wife arrived in New York on the 28th July 1847 when he was 25 years of age aboard a ship called Eagle (we do not know why he left Ireland but we can assume that it probably had something to do with the great famine that was raging at that time in Ireland). In 1855 he was living in Kings County, Brooklyn and in 1856 on the 18th September Francis became a naturalized citizen of the United States. When 1865 came around he was still living in Brooklyn,

Ward 4, District 2, King , New York however his wife Mary had died in on 27-04-1865 and he was left to raise 7 children on his own and their ages ranged from one to fourteen. They were called Mary A. Arthur 14 years old, Kate Arthur 13 years old, Anna Arthur 11 years old, Frank A. Arthur 9 years old, William Arthur 7 years old, Emma Arthur 5 years old and lastly John Arthur 1 year old. James Walter another son died on 19-05-1852 when he was 14 months of age. In 1865 the property where he lived was valued at $3,000 and as this was after the civil war the value of his property had gone down from the $4,500 it had been worth before the Civil War in 1855.On 23rd April 1866 there was a piece in The Brooklyn Daily Eagle asking anyone who had a claim against Mary Arthur his late wife to bring them forward. In 1870 he is recorded as having brought a case against a Gideon Gates for defamation of character. By 1880 Francis had married another Irish lady called Mary (again we do not know her surname) but all the children of the first marriage had moved out by now and they were on their own until their children arrived. By 1930 there were two sisters living together in ward 16 in New York working as seamstresses who may have been two of the daughters of Francis Arthur. Their names were Mary A Herring and Margaret Arthur.

HARDWARE DEALER.

EDWARD D. WHITE & CO.,

208 FULTON, CORNER OF PINEAPPLE ST.,

BROOKLYN,

Dealers in Hardware, Iron, Steel, Plated,

BRITANNIA & HOUSE FURNISHING GOODS.

EDWARD D. WHITE. ELIJAH W. NICHOLS, Jr.

This is an advertisement Edward D. White's store in New York in which Francis Arthur was a partner.

Along with being a property developer Francis was in business as a dry goods merchant in company with his son-in-law, a Mr. White. This Mr. White carried on a drapery business or as New Yorkers termed it, a "dry goods store" it seems to have been at 208 Fulton, corner of Pineapple Street, Brooklyn. h. 170 Livingston. In 1879 Francis was living in Butler St, Brooklyn. Francis Arthur's first wife had died when his children were young. So as already mentioned after a short time he married again and they 2 children, Francis a boy and a girl who later became a Mrs. White. In 1887 on the $28^{th}$ of September Amy/Emma his daughter from his first marriage got married to a Mr. Frank J McHale. Francis was short and stout in appearance. He is said to have dressed in typical Yankee style, wearing a mustache. He seems to have died on the sixth of November 1891 and is buried in the Holy Cross Cemetery Kings County Brooklyn New York. We knew little more of this Francis Arthur as he communicated little with his brothers Joseph William in

Ennistymon or William in Brighton. He must have been well off as he is recorded in several places as having servants.

## Edmund Arthur

Edmund was baptized on 7th October 1823 in St. Mary's, Limerick. He also is believed to have died fairly young.

## Jem (James) Arthur

James it seems never married and lived at number 1 old town Ennistymon which had a stable and workshop and this seems which may be the house I refer to as the Hill House. James lived there with his aunt and her family. She inherited the house when he died. James was in business in Ennistymon and had a shop there. I have not yet found any record of when he died.

## Joseph William Arthur

Joseph William Arthur (son of William Arthur and Margaret Considine):

Joseph William Arthur was one of the many sons of William Arthur, merchant, Limerick. He was born in Limerick in the year 1820. Very little has come down to us of his boyhood years. Along with his brothers he must have attended a private school in Limerick because unless Catholic children of his day attended a Protestant school there was no education for them. Here the parents had to step in and either employ a private teacher or send the children to a private school.

*Joseph William Arthur and family outsude Deerpark in the 1870's.*

Of the latter class of academy it is certain that there were quite a few when Joseph was a lad. He was an intelligent man and wrote English with grace and ease. Their parents, not content with educating them obtained for them the service of a skilled musician who instructed them in the art of playing different instruments. Joseph became an accomplished musician in theory and practice. He grew to be a young man of much culture and taste. He loved painting and had a great love of flowers as well as having a poetic turn of mind and he known to have composed some beautiful verses.

Belonging as he did to an aristocratic family in the city he ever regarded and kept himself as a young gentleman. He smoked cigars but rarely if ever drank alcohol. In fact he displayed a horror of drink.

An oil painting of him painted when he was about 30 is still in the possession of a member of the Arthur family and there is a story that Joseph William painted this portrait himself. (A photo of that portrait along with a photo of his wife Margaret Considine in later life are the two people in the pictures a few pages back) In it he wears a well cut coat of superfine black cloth, cut after the fashion of the day, a white cravat circles the neck above a linen shirt ornamented with frills and a gold chain hangs gracefully from his neck into his vest pocket. A gold ring clasping some precious stone is on the ring finger of left hand. His hair is parted on the side, curls over his head, and side whiskers-fashionable at the time- appear of a brown tinge.

His parents, having at the very outset of their lives an abundance of wealth in money, property and lands took life easily. To some extent this was not altogether in favor of Joseph's future. His training as a level headed business man seems to have been sadly neglected as a number of different business ventures he was involved in failed.

He was about 25 years old when an awful famine was sweeping throughout Ireland and this did a lot of damage to his parents businesses. One by one he had stood at the open graves of brothers whom he loved dearly. They were Walter, Edward, Harry and Paddy.

His brother William was at this time a medical student in Dublin and Frank was working in Quinn's large wholesale store in Limerick. Frank emigrated to the U.S.A. in 1847 and William ended his days as a doctor in England.

By the year 1846 his mother & father had lost almost all they possessed in Limerick and had retired to Ennistymon. This was the last vestige of property that had once belonged to the once powerful and opulent Arthur family of Limerick.

It was in 1847 pestilence and famine struck the land. Joseph's father had gone on a short errand from Ennistymon to Limerick caught cholera and was laid in his grave that night. It is very likely that Joseph attended his father's funeral. With tears in his eyes many years later he pointed out the grave to his eldest boy William but the location of that grave has not come down to us.

For some time Joseph had been in business as a tobacconist. His mother was living in Ennistymon where he supported her, and at the same time he was helping his brother William the medical student financially. William received his medical License in 1847 and from then on was able to make a living for himself.

It was probably because of having to support his mother that Joseph deferred his marrying until he was much older than was usual at that time. He was about 37 years of age when in 1859 he married Katie Cooney the daughter of John Cooney of Kilshanney, which is about 3 miles north of Ennistymon.

That a city man of the type of Joseph William should be joined with a simple country girl seems at first strange. However the explanation behind this match is in my opinion very interesting.

Her brother James, much older than Kate was a hardware merchant in Ennistymon and he was married to Margaret Quinn. During the year at regular intervals James Cooney went to Limerick in order to transact business with the firm of Messer John Quinn. The manager of the firm at the time was Francis Arthur, Joseph's brother. On one of these visits James Cooney who was partial to a drink of whiskey fell in with some "sharper" who relieved him of a bundle of bank notes for which he gave him in return some counterfeit gold coins. In good faith James passed this gold coin on to other people with the result that in a short space of time he found himself in custody. It is likely that Joseph and Francis often met James Cooney in Ennistymon and now that he required friends the two brothers attended the court and went bail for him. From that day forward their friendship was sealed. Sometime later another incident happened that sealed their friendship more firmly.

Joseph was buying smuggled tobacco to sell in his shop, this was tobacco which had been smuggled and so was illegal and on which no duty had been paid. The penalty was drastic; it would have meant a long term of imprisonment, with confiscation of the accused properties.

These were the days when the stealing of a sheep was punishable by death. James Cooney came to the rescue by giving a guarantee of his good behavior so saved the situation for his friend.

Sometime after this Joseph must have failed in business. His brother Francis had married a Limerick lady and had gone to the States. His mother was growing old and living alone in Ennistymon. He sold whatever property was left in Limerick and came to live at Deerpark.

He first opened a spirit store in a small shop belonging to the family in the market place but after a short time this venture also failed. Joseph William was never intended by providence to serve customers behind a bar.

At this period a new art had made its appearance in Ireland, the art of photography. Few people in the western parts had ever seen a photograph except maybe an odd one sent from friends abroad. Very few knew how these were produced.

Joseph was a man of artistic inclinations and found that this was a profession that would suit him. He understood that it was an art not very difficult to acquire and he knew that in an easy and congenial way there was money to be made from it. He accordingly journeyed to Clonmel, in order to learn the photographic arts from a Mr. Collins who in those far off days was known as a photographic artist. Mr. Collins as well as having a studio in Clonmel had a studio in Kilkee not too far from Ennistymon where Joseph was now living and it seems likely that Joseph William met Mister Collins in Kilkee and arranged to go to Clonmel to learn the photographic arts from him. In due course he had learned all he could about the profession and purchased for himself a camera, the appliances and chemicals needed in the producing of photographs.

This is a photo of the last of the old Arthur cameras taken at Deerpark circa 1950 it was destroyed by Catherine after this photo was taken.

We cannot now understand the wonder that the camera aroused in those who saw it in those far off days and now for the first time Joseph had found something that he was good at and money poured in to him as fast as he could produce photographs.

Now we know how Joseph William and James Cooney had become fast friends. James had 2 sisters, one being married to a Darly Callinan at Kilshanney. The other sister Katie was still living at home. She was much younger than Joseph being then only 24 or 25 years old.

One day Joseph turned to his old mother who was now 73 years of age. “Mother” he said “I am going to be married to Katie Cooney”. His mother made no objection, so the marriage took place in the kitchen of the old farmhouse in Coolin near Kilshanney.

They lived at Deerpark Cottage and one by one little visitor after another appeared starting in 1860. First William who became Brother Canice, Minnie who became Sister Augustine, Margaret who became sister Aquin, John, Catherine, Joseph, Francis, Madeleine and Charles who became Br. Firmin.

Joseph Arthur and his wife brought up a Christian family. They had their trials and sufferings and a very large share of the cross. Though living in a country town for many years Joseph William Arthur always behaved as a gentleman and as a person who believed himself superior to others who were not of the same class as himself. To the end of his life he attended mass on Sundays attired in a frock coat and silk top hat. He loved to wear a flower in his buttonhole and one of his eyes being of defective vision an eyeglass was always suspended at this breast.

Joseph William Arthur had ever enjoyed perfect health until his final illness attacked him about May 1890. He was placed under the care of a Dr Ferris in the county infirmary, Ennis and was treated there but he returned to Deerpark a dying man. He lived until 29th November 1890 when, after receiving all the rites of the holy Catholic Church he peacefully passed away. He expressed a wish to be buried beside the old Cistercian monastery in Kilshanney. Later the remains of his dear wife were laid beside him.

Taken outside Deerpark after the funeral of Joseph William in 1890.

## William Arthur

William was baptized on the 26th June 1822 St. Mary's, Limerick. William went on to be a doctor. He qualified as a doctor in Dublin in 1847 and he served as a house surgeon in a Dublin Hospital during the famine. After a short time in Dublin, William moved to London and in 1850 he became a member of the Royal College of Surgeons. He appears to have been a very intelligent man, this can be deduced from the fact that in 1855 he got his Doctorate of Medicine in the University of Glasgow and in 1856 he was awarded his LSA in London. About 1858 William married Ada Anderson but it is believed that this was not a happy marriage. To the best of my knowledge there were 9 children of this marriage most of whom died young. The 3 who lived were, Charles, Verena and Cecelia (usually called Minnie).

Cannon Charles Arthur son of William Arthur

Charles was educated in Valladolid in Spain and in due time he was ordained to the priesthood. At the beginning of 1946 Charles had a short illness and died on the 29th Jan at the Ursuline Convent in Brentwood, Essex where his sister Cecelia was Mother Superior at this time. At the time of his death he was a Cannon. William's other surviving daughter Verina married a Mister Workman and immigrated to Australia with her family.

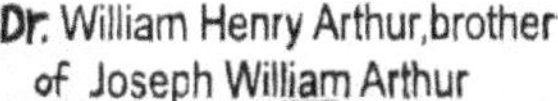

Only known photo of Dr. William Arthur.

Dr Arthur's first wife died in 1882 when he was 57. He met Miss Lucy Duke who was a Protestant and she converted in order to marry him. Her conversion and marriage were against her family's wishes. There were 2 children of this marriage, a girl Poppy and a boy Edward Albert however Edward Albert died in infancy. Poppy married an American actor but she died a short time into this marriage and as far as we know she did not have any children. William himself died in 1892 shortly after his brother Joseph William.

## Walter Arthur

As far as we know Walter died fairly young.

## Harry Arthur

Harry too is believed to have died fairly young.

## Edward Arthur

Edward is also thought to have died fairly young

The young men above may have been the victims of one of the many outbreaks of cholera and other epidemics that occurred around that time.

## Patrick Arthur

He was baptized on the 8th May 1828 at St. Michael's, Limerick. He is believed to have died fairly young. His Grandfather Patrick Arthur was a sponsor at his baptism.

A Sundial that used to be in the Garden of Deerpark house.

# Chapter 22

*The children of Joseph William Arthur*

## William Arthur

William was born in Ennistymon on September 24th 1860 and he was the eldest child of his family. At the age of six he went to school where his first master was Br. Vincent Culkin and after Br. Vincent he was taught by a Br. Raymond Ring. By the time he was 16 years old he had developed all the characteristics of a carefree, self-willed, hot-tempered youth.

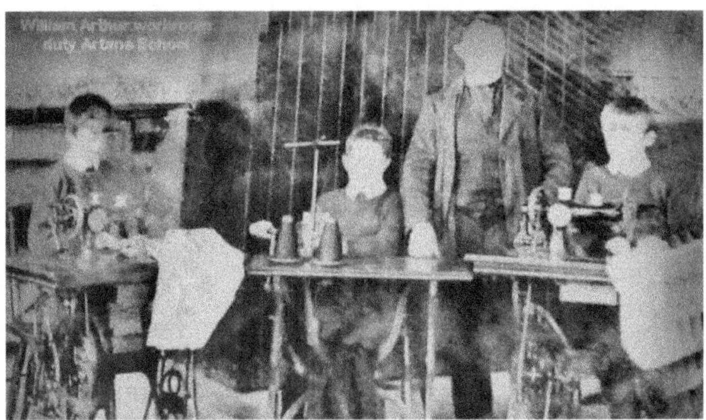

Brother Canice (William) Arthur at work with the boys in the work room at Artane.

He followed in his father's footsteps and become a professional photographer. It should be remembered that at that time taking and developing photos was something only a small number of professional photographers and very keen amateurs could do. So the young William was able to earn a very good income for such a young man, as everyone wanted to have his or her photo taken. However this excess of money led him to him having a gay and spendthrift life when he was not working.

A photo taken by the Anderson Studio of a young lady who was either an actress or a school teacher. This may have been taken by William Arthur.

His parents were not happy with the way he was leading his life and so his father arranged that he should go to his uncle (Francis Arthur) who was a well to do man in New York. William was delighted at the prospect of going to the United States because there he would be out of the reach of parental observation and virtually on his own. When William reached Ellis Island in New York he was met by his uncle and cousins who were able to speed his exit from Ellis Island compared to most of the others who had been on the ship. They took him to their home and the following week he was working in the studio of the Anderson Bros, Photographic Artists at Broadway They were especially well known for photographing theatre people).

After a few months at home he left Ennistymon for other parts of Ireland for his work as a photographer and then after long intervals used to return to visit his family. This went on for some years and all the time large sums of money were earned and spent as fast as they were earned on clothes, socials, dances and every worldly entertainment that came his way. By now he was 28 years old. In mid-summer 1888 a telegram was handed in to William's father's house in Ennistymon saying that William was seriously ill and could someone come and see him.

Deerpark the Arthur family house in Ennistymon.

One of his brothers went and found him in a critical semi-conscious state. A doctor said his condition was very serious and was due either to drugs or to some potion to which he had been introduced. That night he was heard to shout out “I want that grace! I want that grace!” and by dawn he was exhausted and fell asleep. He was taken to hospital the next day and a few days later he was well enough to travel home. His mother slowly nursed him back to health. He was advised that that he should go away to complete his recovery so he went to Cobh and after a few months his health was completely restored. It should be noted that it was at this time that William begun to return to the church.

He returned to photography only now he put aside most of the money he earned which after a few months he sent it to the parish priest of Ennistymon to purchase a silver sanctuary lamp which is now in the parish church of Cloona a few miles east of Ennistymon. William was now a daily attendee at mass etc. After about a year William decided that he wanted to become a Christian Brother so he returned to Ennistymon and went to Br. Gall Stephens who was not yet convinced of his vocation and told him to go away and talk to his parents, which he did. His mother was delighted but his father wanted him to forget the idea however he was determined and so his father relented. At the end of July 1889 he went to St. Joseph's, Marino where he came under the wing of Br. Raymond Ring his old teacher. Br. Evangelist McKeown taught him how to cook, to lay a table, to bake bread, to shine brasses and to do all that is down in the twentieth chapter of the constitutions.

He was sent to Westland Row to complete his training under Br. Paul Moran who had for many years been a valet to a gentleman in Co. Kildare. Then he went to Richmond Street where he was both cook and nurse to all the brothers there. Br. Canice as he was now known made his first profession on Christmas Day 1890 and his final profession on the same day 1896. In 1902 he was transferred to Mount Sion in Waterford where he no longer had to cook as they employed a cook however he was in charge of everything connected with the kitchen, refectory and grounds. He was next posted to Sexton Street and then Enniscorthy. After Enniscorthy he went to Salthill Industrial School, Galway and then he was transferred in 1910 to Glin Co. Limerick to manage the farm attached to St. Josephs School there where they shared the campus with the Sisters of Mercy. The girls did the cooking and Canice suspected that the sisters were giving the lion's share of the food to the girls. He spoke to Sister Catherine who expressed surprise that anyone would think that she would treat the boys differently to the girls. So Canice asked Sr. Catherine if she had heard what the Bishop said in the Church on the day of the Confirmation. Sister Catherine asked what had he said and Canice replied that he said that “the girls at this school are like turkeys fattened for Christmas and the boys are like greyhounds, they are so thin and miserable looking”. The sister laughed and after that there was no need for further complaints. Next he returned to Salthill to take charge of the workshops as he had made a very favorable impression during his first session there and he was there for the epidemic of 1918 swept through the school fortunately he was one of the 25% who did not get ill.

His next move was to Carriglea in Co. Dublin. However he was only there six weeks when the brother in charge of the juvenile workroom in Artane died. Br Otteran Ryan who was superior in Artane did not know Canice but his sub-superior Br. Cyprian Carroll did and it was through his recommendation that Canice was posted to Artane. He was to remain in Artane for the next twenty years. When the boys were not working Canice was well known for entertaining them with his many magic tricks he also taught the boys how to dance and knit. Canice remained in charge of the workroom for 24 years with one very short interlude when he worked in the kitchen. At the beginning of 1941 he fell and broke his arm, which as he was now over 80 years of age was slow to mend. A short while later a doctor after examining him noticed that his hearing was failing. Towards the end of 1941 he was transferred to St. Patrick’s Baldoyle from Artane and it was here that he died on the 25th of April 1942.

## Minnie Arthur

Minnie Arthur was the eldest daughter of Joseph William of Ennistymon, born in 1862. She grew up a very beautiful girl and was educated in the local convent of Mercy. Although a good and devout girl she never displayed any predisposition for the religious life in her early years.

At the age of 18 she was sent by her parents to Limerick to learn about the confectionery trade at the establishment of Mrs. Kent. Upon the completion of her training in this business she obtained a post in Clonmel at another confectionery establishment owned by a Mrs. Kiely.

Photo of Minnie, Margaret and William 1883

She kept this position for 5 or 6 years where she became a favorite with all her acquaintances.

About the year 1888 she left Ireland rather suddenly for the United States for some reason or other. Perhaps to save her parents grief or for some other motive she never made reference to. She left without telling her parents and this was a great blow to them. It is believed that she obtained a post in a hospital in that great city. She must have felt very unhappy in a strange land among strangers without a friend.

At her first opportunity she went to Meriden to visit her sister Margaret, then a young professed nun in the Mercy Convent there. We can visualize how this must have been after a 4-5 year separation. They must have shared their innermost thoughts with each other; they spoke of the old home in Ennistymon, of their parents and of their younger brothers and sisters. The visit came to an end and the sisters said goodbye. Minnie took the train back to New York. The visit seems to have made a very deep impression on her. She contrasted her life in New York with that of her sister in the peaceful convent. She now saw the world as she had never seen it before, an inward voice surely urging her to leave all things and follow him.

Before long Minnie Arthur was in communication with the Rev Mother of the Sisters of Mercy in Brooklyn New York and when arrangements were completed, she entered the community of that Convent as a novice. She made her perpetual profession 3-4 years after her entrance. After a short time her superiors sent her to take up position among the orphan children of the Guardian Angel House in Brooklyn. In this institute Sr. Mary Augustine as she was now called spent her time working with the orphan children.

She had always enjoyed robust health but in the beginning of Jan 1911 she contracted a severe cold. Her life was drawing to a close and she died at an early age on Jan 6th 1911.

A few years after her death a gentleman entered the establishment of John Arthur her brother in Clonmel. He approached one of the boys in the house saying "pardon me sir I have been attracted by the name Arthur at the front of your shop. John asked him his business and the man said that he was wondering if he knew a Minnie and in a few moments the man produced a photograph of Sister M Augustine as a young professed nun. There she stood arrayed in the immaculate habit of the Sisters of Mercy." It is indeed Minnie," John said with great emotion. "Where is she now?" "In heaven I hope" replied the man. The stranger drew his hand across his face, lent over the counter and wept like a child. He left as abruptly as he had entered the establishment giving neither name nor address.

Sister Mary Augustine is buried with her sisters in Religion in the Sisters of Mercy Plot in the public Cemetery, Brooklyn, New York.

## John J Arthur

John my great grandfather was born in 1867 in Ennistymon and he died in Clonmel in 1951. He married twice, his first wife Margaret O'Donnell died on the 29th September 1926. Margaret was the mother of all his children as he had no children with his second wife Margaret Leonard who died on the 31st August 1976. John had eight children four of whom were born in Clare one in Kerry, the youngest Charles was born in Clonmel, County Tipperary while two died in childhood. John was a professional photographer like his father before him but he seems to have been an itinerant photographer until he finally settled in Clonmel sometime between 1905 and 1911. His first shop was in O'Connell Street where now there is a dry cleaning shop and then he moved to 18 Parnell Street where he remained for the rest of his life. I was told that in earlier times when he was an itinerant photographer he was known to do midnight flits from places to avoid paying his bills.

Three advertisements for John Arthurs shop in Clonmel the third one was placed after his death. Note shop called John J Arthur in first two and just called Arthur's in third one

## Margaret Arthur (Sister Mary Aquin)

Margaret was the third child of Joseph William and Catherine Cooney. She was born in Ennistymon in 1869. She was a very beautiful child and if any character was outstanding it was that of her generosity. As a child and girl it was her delight to share whatever she possessed with her brothers and sisters. When she was only five or six years old when as a result of the carelessness of a servant a vessel of boiling water fell on her head. It was thought that she would be disfigured for life however a local woman knowledgeable in herbal cures made a remedy, one of the ingredients being laurel leaves. The result was that in a very short space of time little Margaret was cured. Not a trace or the slightest mark was left.

Margaret was sent to school to the local Convent of Mercy. She grew up a most virtuous girl, and after passing through the usual curriculum of that school, she became an assistant teacher to the nuns. For a short time Margaret acted as governess to the daughter of Dr. William Arthur of Brighton who was her Uncle. Margaret returned briefly to Ennistymon to say goodbye to her beloved ones there. At the beginning of 1886 she made arrangements to enter the Meridian convent in the diocese of Hartford, Connecticut USA.

She had only been a few days at sea when a terrible storm swept the Atlantic from Ireland to America. Tempestuous weather and mountainous seas prevailed. Huge waves broke over the ship and even old sailors on board thought they were in imminent danger of floundering. Margaret was very frightened, but a De La Sale brother on board acted as the Good Samaritan and helped to allay her fears. She entered the convent on 15th December 1886 when she was seventeen years old. She did all that a postulant had to do and after the allotted time she received the religious habit with the White veil and she took the name Sister Mary Aquin. The life of a white novice in religion is a very uneventful one. She rose at the first strike of the bell in the morning, made her prayer and meditation, heard holy Mass, taught the children to love God, took part in daily recreations, read spiritual books, examined her conscience, did some study and said her rosary. This was one day in the life of a Sister of Mercy.

Sister Mary Aquin was appointed to teach in St Roses School, Meridian in the Primary grade. She was enthusiastic for hard work in St Rose's and her efforts were crowned with success. Her zealous labors were continued in Derby, New London, Rockville and Torrington. With her pupils and ex pupils she was an exceedingly great favorite. Some of her ex pupils would travel hundreds of miles to see her. Letters she received from her sisters in religion breathed sentiments of the most cordial affection.

Sr. Mary Aquin marked with an X with her sisters in Religion.

She was only 4 years in the States when news of her father's death reached her. It was a fearful trial to the young nun, but she bore it bravely. She provided spiritual help to her family by the beautiful letters of condolence she sent them. Her mother's sudden death eleven years later was a stunning blow, but perhaps the greatest trial was the death of her beloved sister Minnie, Sister Augustine in Brooklyn. Minnie was her only known brother or sister in America and great was their joy at their occasional meetings.

On 1930 Margaret was re-appointed to Torrington after an absence of twelve years In September that year an offer made by her brother to send some photographs from Ireland she responded “I think better not to send the album, not but I’d be glad to see it, but life is so uncertain, if I died it would be lost." She was in perfect health when she wrote that sentence, but 3 weeks later she had died.

## Francis Arthur

Francis married Mary Walsh of Gorey. Their children were Charles and Marie. They lived at "Sancta Maria" Taylor's Hill Galway. It was used as a boarding house for students during the winter and a holiday home for the Christian Brothers during the summer Brother Charles (Firmin) or Brother William (Canice) possibly had something to do with this.

Charles was a doctor, and he married Fionnuala Monaghan of White Hall, Dublin. They had 3 children, one of whom was called Jonathan. Charles eventually went to England where he practised as a doctor where he died and was buried in Watford, Hearts.

Frank Arthur

Marie married Donie Donovan from Limerick, a lieutenant in the Army and they had 2 children, Francis & Helen. Both children lived with their mother and grandparents after Donie went to New York where he died around 1990 on Montauk Island. To the best of my knowledge Marie obtained a Church annulment of her marriage to Donny Donovan so she then married Paul Keenan a New Yorker and Vietnam veteran. They lived at Rockaway Point on Queens NY for five or six years. Gabriel Arthur met Paul in Dublin on one occasion. When Paul passed away Marie returned to Galway and had nice flat on Nuns Island in Galway City. She sold the Arthur home, Sancta Maria on Taylor's Hill before she re-married. Marie's son Frank now lives in Cork with his wife Fionnuala and they have three grown children Fiona, Jonathan and Simon. Sadly Fiona died a number of years ago and Jonathan's daughter got married in 2017 in Dorset. Helen is now called Helen Chambers but she was married to Des McInerney first. She lives in Blackrock in Dublin and she had three children from her first marriage Carol, Adrian and Dave as well as having grandchildren.

## Catherine Arthur

Aunt Kit Arthur
Deerpark.

Catherine in later life.

She was born in 1871 I think and lived at Deerpark house in Ennistymon all her life. It is believed that she entered a convent for a while but she found that the life was not for her. She remained living at Deerpark House for the rest of her life and she even took up the family business of photography and worked as a professional photographer for a while. She had a reputation for being quite straight laced but with a very roughish sense of humour at the same time. She was the one her brothers and sisters came home to visit along with her brother Joseph who lived with her a lot of the time. She used to go to Clonmel from time to time to visit her brother John there.

## Joseph Arthur

Joseph was born on 17th May 1872.

Joseph Arthur in his band uniform 1912.

Like his father Joseph worked as a professional photographer and he used Ennistymon as his base while he travelled all over for work including going abroad.

Joseph had nine children William, Mary, Charles, Augustine, Joseph, John, Frank, Aquin Margaret and Gabriel. Of these at the time of writing Gabriel is the only one still alive. Gabriel worked as a music teacher thereby carrying on a long tradition of members of the Arthur family being musically talented. Mary or Catherine Mary also known as Aquin had one child Anne Marie who lives in London where she works as a practice nurse although she is coming close to retirement. Aquin (Anne Marie's mother) was also a nurse who had served in the British army during World War II. Gabriel also has one daughter Fiona who lives in Lewis Sussex and works and as head archivist the University of Sussex. John had two daughters Danielle who used to work at Heathrow airport in charge of the information desk at terminal 4 and Michelle who is an actress and she lives in Los Angeles. Michelle regularly turns up in American made T.V. dramas and movies. The only member of Joseph's family left in Co. Clare is Miriam who is Augustine's daughter. She lives with her mother in Lisdoonvarna. Frank joined the priesthood where he served as a chaplain in the U.S. army and later as a parish priest in Fishguard and Caerleon in Wales. He retired to Lisdoonvarna in the 1990's and he used to stand in for priests who were on holiday until he died in 2010.

## Madeleine Arthur

Madeline was the youngest daughter of Joseph William Arthur of Ennistymon. Born in the year 1880 she was a strong built child up until her 7$^{th}$ or 8$^{th}$ year, when she contracted a serious disease that increased as the years went on. In her 13$^{th}$ or 14$^{th}$ year she fell and broke a hipbone an accident from which she never recovered. She now became completely bed-ridden and it is to the eternal honor of her sister Catherine that she remained at Madeleine's bedside as a faithful and constant nurse. It was thus that one sister sacrificed her future wellbeing and happiness for the comfort of her afflicted sister. Madeleine's life was martyrdom. She suffered intensely at times. In 1909 she died in a hospice in the charge of the Sisters of Nazareth in Belfast.

## Charles Arthur

Charles was born on 20th January 1883 and died 25th September 1969. He was one of four children of Joseph and Kate who became Christian Brothers or Nuns, as well as being their youngest child. Charles started school in the Christian Brothers Ennistymon in September 1887 where he was only an average student and he left school in the spring of 1900. After leaving school he entered Baldoyle on 5th May 1900. On 1st November 1900 Charles was accepted as a novice and adopted the name Br. Firmin. A few weeks after the completion of his novitiate Br. Firmin was posted to Derry where he spent five happy years. When he was finished in Derry Firmin was posted to Carrick on Suir and then to New Ross within the space of one year. After this he went to Artane where he spent three years and there he worked from dawn to dusk with the boys as well as teaching them and on Sundays taking them for long walks (Br. Firmin loved to walk). From Artane he went to Clonmel for one year and from there to Glin where he spent three years doing much the same kind of work he had done in Artane. From Glin he went to Westport for one year. These constant changes were not a reflection on Firmin's abilities but were rather the norm at the time it was only later that brothers were changed less frequently.

Brother Charles Arthur

In 1916 Firmin returned to Artane. There were about 800 boys in Artane at this time and there were 20 Brothers and a number of lay teachers to take care of all these boys. Firmin on this occasion was given charge of the world famous Artane Boys Band with a bandmaster to help him. During the 1920's he often walked around Croke Park with the boys. Firmin spent a total of thirty seven years in Christian Brothers Residential Schools but he preferred to call them residential Colleges. During these 37 years he spent two periods in Artane, Glin and Tralee as well as one in Galway, Letterfrack and Carriglea. It should be noted that at this time the authorities were paying the brothers in Artane only 7 shillings per week per boy to maintain the boys in the school. It seems likely that it would have been roughly the same amount for each boy in all the other schools. It should be noted that Firmin abhorred violence as was clear from his attitude to the Great War 1914-1918, The War of Independence, The Civil War and The Second World War 1939-1945 which contrasted with the attitudes of many of the other brothers. Although Br. Firmin served in many of the schools where later there were accusations against some brothers of mistreating the boys at no time did Br. Firmin's name come up as being one of those brothers who mistreated their charges. If fact he seems to have been in trouble with the provincial of the order for complaining about how the boys were treated in some institutions.

In 1930 Firmin was transferred to St. Joseph's Tralee for a short time and after that to Galway where he spent five happy years as it reminded him of his home in Clare. Subsequently he taught in Carriglea, Co. Dublin and Letterfrack Co. Galway. In January 1939 he was transferred to Saint Edward's College, Liverpool, this was his first time out of Ireland and he remained there until August 1944. He was there when the Germans were bombing Liverpool and he must have been terrified. In August 1944 he was sent to Brentwood and here he was even more exposed to the flying bombs that the Germans were now using. They were always passing over and from time to time one exploded near the school. In 1949 Firmin requested that he return to the Irish Province. This request was granted and he returned to St. Joseph's Tralee where he spent two years and he was then transferred to Saint Joseph's Industrial School Glin where he spent ten years. It is worth noting at this time that along with music the main subjects that Firmin taught were woodwork and drawing. After he finished teaching class he continued to provide supervision during the long periods of supervision.

Firmin loved to read, particularly the newspapers and it was he who kept all the other brothers informed about the outside world. He was also known to have very strong opinions on how the Industrial Schools were run (he was inclined to exaggerate the value and importance of these institutions). Firmin wrote in the Brothers Educational Records that neither the Government nor the Brothers did all they could to run these schools efficiently. For that time he was a rarity as a Christian Brother who criticized how the institutions were being run but as we now know he was not listened to by his superiors. He loved to walk and he walked three to three and a half miles a day using a pedometer to measure how far he had traveled. Another love of his was photography, which he must have inherited from his father who as we know was a professional photographer. In those days most photographs were black and white however Firmin was known to add color to his photographs although not always successfully.

He was transferred to St. Theresa's in Limerick from Glin in the early 1960's when he retired from active work. He liked St. Theresa's as there were a good number of interesting walks that could be taken from there and when out walking he wore gloves and carried an umbrella on his left arm and a pedometer on his right leg. Happily he enjoyed good health, had a zest for his meals and rarely visited a doctor. In 1965 he told another brother that he had diabetes and as far as anyone knows this was the only time he ever mentioned that he had it. Finally at about 6.45 a.m. on the 29$^{th}$ Of March 1969 Firmin died having been ill for three days. His nephew Fr. Frank Arthur celebrated his Requiem mass and after the mass the funeral took place to St. Lawrence Cemetery where the prayers at the graveside were recited by Fr. Frank Arthur.

# Chapter 23.

*The children of the children of Joseph William Arthur*

John Arthur in front with family in early 1920's

## John J Arthur, Clonmel

John married Margaret O'Donnell of Kilrush whose father was a doctor there. Margaret died on 29th September 1926 in Clonmel aged approx. 60 years and John died on 30th June 1951 aged approx. 84 years. Their children were John, Joseph, William who died in childhood, Charles, May, Francis, Adelaide and Kathleen who also died as a child.

John Arthur Senior got married for a second time to a Margaret Leonard of Navan but there were no children from this union. They lived at 18 Parnell Street Clonmel. Margaret died on the 31st August 1976

18 Parnell Street Clonmel

The sign above on the right is all that is now left of John Arthur's shop and you can see an arrow on the photo of the shop showing where it was.

## Family of John Arthur son of Joseph William Arthur:

### John Arthur

John was the first to go to America. He went in 1915 and by 1920 he was married to Mary Franklin and living at 201 East 92nd Street New York where he worked as a carpenter in a shipyard. Alice their first daughter was born on 20th December 1920 and she got married to Joseph Anthony Falson in 1946, their daughter Joanne is now living in North Carolina. Joanne got married in 1968 and she has a son called Kenneth Michael Patrick Falson, a daughter, one granddaughter Alexandria (called Allie) and a grandson. John senior also had a son called John Falson and a daughter called Margaret (10-6-1931) known as Peggy. Peggy married a man called Landy and they had a daughter called Donna May whose married name is Jacobellis. Joseph Falson died in 1997 and Alice died in 2014 and they are both buried in the Calverton National Cemetery. By 1930 John was an inspector with a Board of

Education. There is a record of John and family sailing from Cobh to New York in 1924. Mary and Alice sailed second class on board the White Star Ship, Baltic from New York to Ireland in 1923 arriving on the 7th May and they seem to have stayed at Wellington Street, Cahir which is where the family of his wife Mary Franklin were form.

## Joseph Arthur

Joe was born in Listowel Co. Kerry on the 10th June 1893. While in Ireland Joseph worked as a photographer like his father and had his own shop in two different locations in Clonmel. One of these which is no longer in existence was in Mitchell Street but it was knocked down when the Main Guard in Clonmel was being restored to how it originally had looked when it was built. The shop he had in Mitchell Street was a later addition to the side of the fabric of the Main Guard building and so was demolished during the refurbishment of the Main Guard.

Joe Arthur's shop in O'Connell Street Clonmel.

The other shop (photo on previous page) was at number 4 O'Connell Street Clonmel. Joseph married Edith Louise Chapman (she had worked as a teacher) on the 30th January 1922 in Clonmel (Edith was a member of the Church of Ireland while Joseph was a Catholic she did convert but it may have caused a problem for them). They immigrated first to Toronto Canada where Edith had a brother and then they went to the U.S. in 1926 where they had two 2 girls, Alice and Margaret. Joseph lived at 2804 Wellman Avenue, Bronx, New York. Joseph died on Mary.12th March 1967 aged approximately 74 years and his wife died on 8th August 1969. Like his father Joseph worked as a photographer when in Ireland but he did other things in New York to earn a living. When Joseph retired he returned to Ireland and he went to live in Cork. Mary who was the wife of his brother John was one of the two people who signed Joseph's petition for naturalization as a witness in December 1930 and at this time Joseph was working as a stockman. Joe and his wife are both buried in Clonmel near where his father and mother are buried.

## Mary (Mai) Arthur

Mary also known as Mai was born in Kilrush, Co. Clare in 1890. May married Patrick Keogh of Clonmel in 1922. They had two children one child Helen was born in 1924. May died on 1st May 1928 giving birth to Helen's brother who unfortunately also died and I believe his name was Arthur. Patrick died on 18th June 1940.

Mai Arthur.

Helen as she was known or Ellen as she was on official forms was born on 13th November 1924 at 47 Upper Gladstone Street, Clonmel. Ellen Mary Margaret Keogh (Kelly) married Mick Kelly on the 29th August 1949 in Cahir County Tipperary a few miles from Clonmel. Michael Kelly was born on November 20th 1922 in Clonasalee, County Laois. Michael worked for the Department of Agriculture all his working life and lived in Clonmel, County Tipperary from about 1945 on. Mick and Helen had four sons James, Paul, Michael and Joseph. James, Michael and Helens first son has one daughter Niamh and two sons Conall and Daire. At the time of writing one of James children Conall has a son who was born in Jamaica where he used to live but he is now back in Ireland and working as a lecturer in theoretical mathematics in the University in Cork. Niamh has her own business and she works as a consultant to various businesses. Daire works in information technology as a corporate problem solver in England. Paul, Michael and Helens second son worked in the University of Limerick in the I.T. department but he retired in 2018. Paul did not get married and has no children. Michael, Mick and Helens third son was a Primary school teacher and principal and is now retired. He has one son Cormac who is married to Yhan and Cormac works as a CGI artist in Dublin specializing in being a 3d model maker. Michael junior also had twins Michael and Jack who sadly died in infancy. Joseph, Michael and Helens fourth and last son has two sons Colm who went to Trinity College where he studied law and then to England for further study and is now qualified as a barrister who is working in London and Brian who has returned college to do another degree in digital journalism. Helen died on 19th March 2007, Mick died on the 21st April 2013 and they are buried together in St. Patrick's Cemetery, Clonmel.

## Adelaide (Addie) Arthur

Addie was born in Co. Clare and Addie married William (Billy) Waldron of Clonmel in 1926 (William's family had been members of the R.I.C.) but they were never blessed with any children. William died on 27th July 1974 and Addie

William Waldron and Addie Arthur
in early 1920's.

died on 1st February 1991. William had a shop and bar in O'Connell Street Clonmel until he retired when he moved to Silversprings in Clonmel. Here is Item that may be of interest as it has to do with another member of Williams's family. There is or was a chemist shop in Limerick belonging the Widdess family, Nelly Purcell, William Waldron's sister, worked there as a book keeper. The shop was it is thought originally in Nenagh before it moved to Limerick. I do not know if the shop it is still in the possession of the Widdess family. One thing Nelly told my brother Paul is that they had fierce trouble getting paid by farmers for the drugs they got, on tick, for their animals. Even when they owed a big bill, they could ring on a Sunday (shop obviously being closed) and they would turn up expecting to collect what they had ordered on tick, whatever they needed for their animals This would happen in spite of the bills not being paid still Mt. Widdess would give the farmers what they needed, so the animals would not suffer needlessly. A general rule of thumb (but not absolute rule) was, the bigger the farmer, the bigger the bill on tick, and the harder it was to get paid.

## Frances Arthur

Frances was born in Co. Clare. Frances married Edward V White in 1930 and they had 2 children, Gabrielle who was born in 1932 and sadly died aged 12. Frances was born in 1934and she married Tom Bourke. They have fourteen children all of whom happily are alive at the time of writing along with many grandchildren. Edward White has the distinction of being the only person to be elected Mayor of Clonmel for five years in succession sadly he was to die during his fifth term in office.

## Charles Arthur

Charles Gabriel Arthur was the last of John's sons to go to New York. He sailed from Cobh on board the ship SS Republic which departed on the 22$^{nd}$ September 1929.

There was a story told about Charlie and that is that when he was 18 he decided to go to the U.S. to join his brothers. He knew that his father would not approve so he and three friends decided to go to Cobh get on a ship and go to New York, however they only had enough money to pay for the passage on a ship so they walked all the way to Cobh. When the four of them reached Cobh the other three begun to have second thoughts and decided to return to Clonmel but Charlie got on board the ship and went to New York where he spent the rest of his life apart from a few visits home to Clonmel in later life. He seems to have worked as a rent collector for a while there. In 1935 Charles petitioned for naturalization and one of his witnesses was John's wife Mary. At this time he is recorded as living at 2804 Willman Avenue, Bronx New York. Charles married a lady called Mary Love. By 1940 Charles was working as a handyman in an apartment complex and had three daughters called Margaret born 1936, Bernadette and Patricia. In another place his occupation is listed as porter. Charles came home to visit on a number of occasions in his later years with a granddaughter called Donna. While not certain it is thought that Charles died in New York on January 1984. Charles was a larger than life character and I had the good fortune to meet him in Clonmel on two occasions.

There was no contact with the Americans for years and we had no knowledge of what has happened to them. Lately contact has been reestablished with a granddaughter of John Arthur son of John Arthur senior of Clonmel who is a retired nurse in North Carolina (she worked in New York but retired to North Carolina) and she is called Joanne Falson.

## Family of Francis Arthur son of Joseph William Arthur

Francis married Mary Walsh of Gorey and they had two children whose names were Charles and Marie.

Marie and Donny on their wedding day

Marie married Donny Donovan from Limerick, a lieutenant in the Army and they had 2 children, Francis and Helen. Donnie went to New York where he died in 1990 at Montauk Island. His children stayed in Ireland and lived with their mother and grandparents in Galway. To the best of my knowledge Marie obtained a Church annulment of her marriage to Donny Donovan and after she got the annulment she married Paul Keenan a New Yorker and Vietnam veteran. He was I believe a good bit older than she was. They lived at Rockaway Point on Queens NY for five or six years. Gabriel Arthur met with

Paul on one occasion when he was visiting Dublin. When Paul passed away Marie returned to Galway and she had nice flat on Nuns Island in Galway City. She sold the old Arthur home called Sancta Maria on Taylor's Hill before she re-married. Marie's son Frank now lives in Cork with his wife Fionnuala and they have three grown children Fiona, Jonathan and Simon. Sadly Fiona died about 15 years ago and Jonathan's daughter got married in 2017 in Dorset. Helen is now called Helen Chambers but she was married to Des McInerney first and now she lives in Blackrock in Dublin. She had three children from her first marriage Carol, Adrian and Dave as well as having grandchildren.

Dr. Charles Arthur.

Charles was a doctor, and he married Fionnuala Monaghan of White Hall Dublin. They have 2 children, one called Jonathan the other was called Fiona. Fiona had two sons one called Jonathan not sure of the name of the other sadly while still quite young Fiona got cancer and died. Charles eventually went to Brighton in England where he practiced as a doctor. Charles died in 1970 and was buried in Watford, Hearts.

**Family of Joseph Arthur son of Joseph William Arthur:**

*Here I must thank Gabriel Arthur here for the following pen pictures of his brothers and sisters.*

## Mary Margaret Arthur

Mary Margaret was known as Minnie. She was born in 1913 and she died in 2008 aged 94. Minnie was a music teacher and at age 17 was the pianist for the well-known West Clare band called Madigan's Band. She had a great touch for dancing rhythms and she was well known. She married a well-known Welsh rugby player called Vernon Phillips at the London oratory and lived near the Lickey Hills just outside Birmingham. After her marriage she completely gave up music. In later life she was often treated as a rich lady and never bothered to contradict the illusion God bless her. Although she was born in London, she was treated as an Irish lady.

## William Arthur

William was born in 1916 and he died in 1971. William was the tough guy of the family who had a degree in coarse language. He also swore like a trooper notwithstanding the fact that he was a great hero to his younger brothers. William was very was popular with the town lads and although he could be quite sensitive he was a manly type of person. He tried for the Garda Siochana and lighthouse keeping. He even tried the priesthood but absconded in midterm from one of the Dublin seminaries which one we never heard of on account of the silentium magnum on the subject (in those days a son leaving a seminary was considered a great disgrace on a family and the family whose son left would do their best to keep the fact quiet). By the way his father Joseph also absconded from St. Flannans College in Ennis. William Henry footed the fee wishing his father Joseph to become a doctor too. William ended up as an honest farm worker in Lancashire and passed away at a young 55.

## Joseph Arthur

Joseph was born in 1916 and he died in 1983. His brother William inherited Deerpark but around 1950 William signed it over to his younger brother Joseph who had served his apprenticeship to a master builder in Dublin called Jennings. There is a story that the master once asked Joe to hammer a nail into a large plank. The pupil very confidently started hammering but the nail simply refused to go in. Seemingly the master had spat on the hammer's head and prevented the hammer doing its duty. In Deerpark Joe renewed all the floors and installed electricity and a bathroom but the lovely original Georgian windows were replaced. When in his early forties, he had a serious nervous breakdown but happily he recovered his health again. He married a girl called Bridget Phelan. Her relatives ran the Cliften Bay Hotel where many years ago Gabriel visited them. They poured out two Guinness and charged him the net price! Joe was artistic and painted a few pictures. As a lad he was cycling with a friend to Kilkee one summer when a horse a few yards ahead of them was struck with lightening. He died while tending the garden at Deerpark aged 68

**Margaret Mary also known as Aquin**

Margaret Mary was born in 1918 and she died in 2004. She could ignore the sillier social conventions when the humor of the situation would suit. Wherever she was the laughter would spread. When quite young she visited the 1925 World Exhibition with her father at Wembley. She did her nurse training at Charing Cross during WW2 and joined the Countess of Antrim's Corps. This took her to the concentration camps and she was at the Belsen when it was liberated but she would never speak of her experiences there. In her capacity as matron she was tea hostess to the old queen Elizabeth the Queen Mother. She married Frank Brennan they had a daughter who is also nurse and her name is Anna Maria. I was told that for all the excellent qualities she had cooking was not one of those qualities.

## Charles Arthur

Charles was born in 1920 and he died in 1998. Charles was considered by some to have too much character. He was intelligent, observant a bit of a satirist and had a way of indulging in snide humor towards people whom Gabriel often noticed deserved it. As a kid he was often accused of mixing with bad companions by the unthinking few, whereas Gabriel thought he liked colorful characters. He spoke with quite an English accent as did his brother Frank. He spent some years in the Isle of Wight and the Channel Isles. He returned to Ireland in early 1960's and sculptured crosses and tombstones and helped to install a small hydroelectric scheme at the waterfalls for the Falls Hotel. He had a decent knowledge of engineering plant. Later he assisted in Irish Forestry Commission in their work. Charlie was liked by many people and the immense number at his funeral would indicate this with some kissing the coffin.

## Frank Arthur

Frank was born in 1924 and he died in 2010. Frank was nice looking always with a mischievous smile and loved adventure. At about 14 years of age he built a stone house at Deerpark and it measured 6 by 12 feet on the inside. It had three niches in the wall in which he hoped hens would lay eggs. On another occasion he collected a great heap of scrap metal much of it left by circuses that came to the Deerpark field annually. So although he had signs of becoming man of enterprise he felt the priestly calling. The war had just started and he went to a house in Balbriggan to prepare for matriculation.

World War II was still on when he moved to Chester Salvadorian College (now a great law school) He did higher studies there and then went to Freiburg for more cramming, having received an MA at Reading, Berks. He worked in South Wales, London, East Anglia and Michigan USA and finally at Lisdoonvarna Clare. He was always a devoted but conservative pastor and he died and is interred at the Kilshanny Cistercian Abbey or more correctly Cist Cell where many of the Arthur family are buried.

Frank Arthur and the late Brother C. F. Arthur (Ennistymon)

## John Arthur

John was born in 1926 and he died in 2009. John had an enormous amount of life's gifts, he was tolerant, and his wit at times was delightfully risque. With those God given gifts he could always make those people who were around him happy. A favourite with all at home and abroad he always seemed to be happy enough. He worked for an exclusive London men's clothing store and before that he worked on the buses in Birmingham. But for most of his working life he was with Global Tours so he was well travelled. He married Antonina Cameleri from Cairo. They had two daughters Danielle (Mrs. Tyreman and Michelle an actress in California.). John himself was a fair enough actor playing a part in a period play about Lord Edward Fitzgerald. He also did a mob character with the great actor manager Andrew Mc Master in a Tale of Two Cities. One of Gabriel's greatest memories of his brother John was that in June for many summers, their father would take both John and himself to Kilkee for the season. They were both were left to themselves (because their father was there to do his work which of course was as a photographer) and they became experts on maritime life, exploring cliffs, caves and rocks. Gabriel said thank goodness for that childhood experience and both he John and their father had a daily swim every day in Kilkee.

## Gabriel Arthur

Gabriel was born in 1930 and happily he is still with us although now in a nursing home. At 14 after the Christian Brothers in Ennistymon, Gabriel went to the Jesuits at Mungret College. He played the piano much less than he would have liked to but used the great library and listened to classical music on a good old wind up gramophone that was there. Immediately World War II finished he crossed the Irish Sea and joined his brother Frank at Chester where he completed a three year course in philosophy. When finished at Chester he went down to London and worked for Burns Oates near Westminster Cathedral. At this time he took up music and became associate member after attending London College of Music. As a result of having this little qualification he was easily accepted by private fee paying schools. He had the privilege of teaching the children of the rich to whom he taught Latin and Scripture. Health problems put an end to the daily toil so then he had to do private tuition to pay the state pension stamps. A while after this he had a bladder operation and then he had to have a quadruple heart bypass. In his last school after 13 years he was co-head! Now as old as the hills he still feels fair enough although in a nursing home since he had a bad fall. Gabriel has one daughter Fiona Courage who is head archivist at the University in Brighton.

Gabriel with Mary his wife and Fiona his daughter

## Augustine Arthur

Augustine was born is 1932 and he died in 1999. Augustine (better known as Gus) and Gabriel his older brother were babies together. He was sought after both as a musician and a drinking companion. He played the piano like an orchestra, using all ten fingers and engaging correct and good systems of harmony. He played piano for Madigan's Dance Band, for the Four Courts and several other Ceilidh Bands. Gus was tough, slightly nervy and with a truly electrical sense of humour. He assisted with rural electrification for difficult to get at houses and did some work at the Shannon Precinct. He was received into the Irish Navy as a cook but after trying things out he knew that the marine profession wasn't for him. Gus lived at Lisdoonvarna and died aged 58 years. _He had one daughter Miriam who with her mother is the only member of the Arthur family who still live in Co. Clare.

Where Charles William Augustus Arthur and his brother Desmond grew up after their mother remarried.

# Chapter 24.

Roy O'Connor, Nuala O'Connor, Kate O'Connor, Patrick Wynne, Michael O'Connor, Dwayne O'Connor, Patrick Hilliard at the wedding of Michael O'Connor's daughter Kate. They are related to the Kenmare Arthurs through the maternal line.

Thomas, Marten and Patrick Arthur. members of the Arthur family of Kenmare

# Chapter 25.

The photos on the following pages were taken in 2019 by my brother Paul and they are of places that either were built by the Arthur Family in Limerick and how they look now or places that were associated with the Arthur family and how they look now.

The first set of photos come from Arthurs Quay shopping centre which was built where the old Arthurs Quay built by Patrick Arthur was. Of course he needed his own quay to cater for his import export business which had grown too large to be accommodated by the quays that were already there.

Front Arthurs Quay shopping centre along with a view of Patrick street

This is on the inside wall of the Arthurs Quay shopping centre.

Arthurs Quay 1955 before it was redeveloped.

This is on the wall inside Arthur's Quay Shopping Center.

Side view of Arthurs Quay shopping centre

ARTHUR'S QUAY CENTRE
THIS FOUNDATION STONE
WAS LAID BY
CHARLES J. HAUGHEY T.D.
TAOISEACH
In the presence of
ALDERMAN TIM LEDDIN P. C.
MAYOR OF LIMERICK
ON THE 30TH of MAY 1988
A COMMERCIAL RETAIL DEVELOPMENT
BY
TIERNAN-O'CALLAGHAN (PROPERTIES)

This foundation stone for the Arthurs Quay shopping centre is inside the centre.

On first floor inside centre.

The next set of photos are of Patrick street as it is today and you can see many of the housed that were built by Patrick and his son Francis.

Built by Patrick Arthur

Buildings to left built by Patrick

The ones in the middle were built by Patrick and his son Francis.

This set are from Francis Street which was named for Francis Arthur the son of Patrick Arthur. None of the original buildings that were built by the Arthurs are visible in these three photos of Francis street.

These photos are from Ellen Street the third of the major streets built by the Arthur family in Limerick. The Ellen that it was named after was the first wife of Francis Arthur. The first two photos are of the modern Ellen Street but the third one does show some of the original Arthur buildings.

These photos are from Denmark Street. The Arthur family did not build Denmark Street but much of their business were bases in this street and it was from this base that they went on to build Arthurs Quay, Patrick Street, Francis Street and Ellen Street.

St. Mary's cathedral which is now the Church of Ireland Cathedral in Limerick was for many centuries the Catholic cathedral and a number of members of the Arthur family were priests and bishops there as well as many of the Arthur family being buried there. The first photo is of an old gravestone the second is a map of Limerick from 1650 on the wall of the Cathedral. The third is the back door of St Marys and the fourth is a full view of St. Mary's.

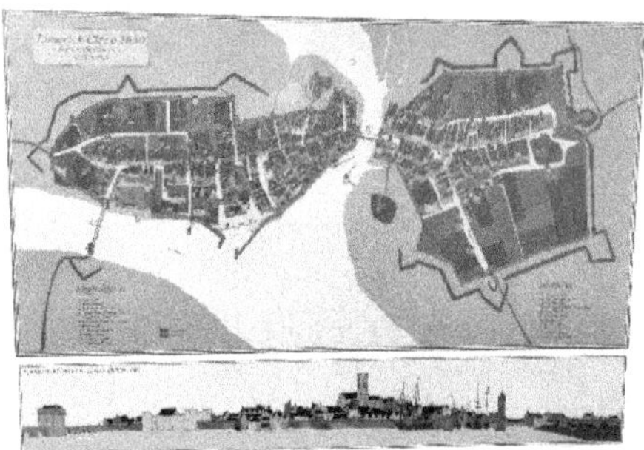

This last set is of St. Michaels Cathedral which is now the Catholic Cathedral in Limerick. This Cathedral was built on land donated by Patrick Arthur and some of the family are buried there.

Michaels Church, Robert St end, Denmark St, right side, Facing Patrick Street

St Michaels Church, Denmark St, right side, Facing Patrick Street

Model of St. Michaels that is inside the Cathedral.

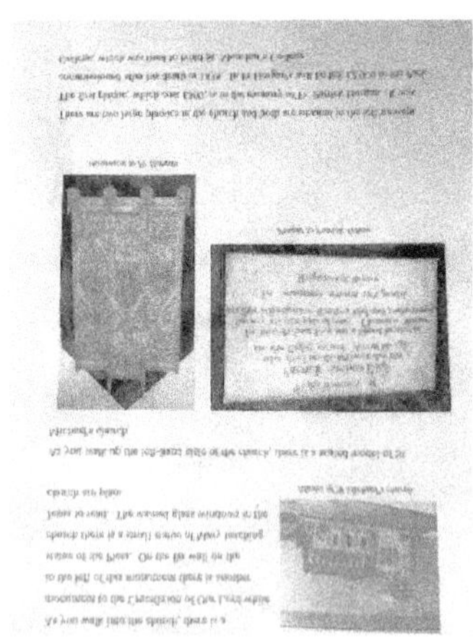

Info Sheets, beside Model of St Michael's Church, from left to right & Top to Bottom of the board.

Centre isle, St Michael's Church, from Main Altar end

Water fonts outside Denmark St side of St Michael's Church

Stained glass window St. Michael's

St. Michael's outside.

# *This is not the end of the story.*

This story will never end because the family will go on.

There is so much more that yet needs to be discovered about the Arthur family of Limerick things like where they were as well as where they are now.

Are you a missing member of the family and do you have a story to tell.

www.ingramcontent.com/pod-product-compliance
Lightning Source LLC
Chambersburg PA
CBHW030936150426
42812CB00064B/2931/J

* 9 7 8 1 9 1 6 2 0 8 6 1 2 *